# CONTRACT LAW

2025-26 edition

Michael Pugh

Series editors: Amy Sixsmith and David Sixsmith

First published in 2022 by Fink Publishing Ltd
2025–26 edition published in 2025

Apart from any fair dealing for the purposes of research, private study, or criticism or review, as permitted under the Copyright, Designs and Patents Act, 1988, this publication may not be reproduced, stored or transmitted in any form, or by any means, without the prior permission in writing of the publisher, or in the case of reprographic reproduction, in accordance with the terms of licences issued by the Copyright Licensing Agency. Enquiries concerning reproduction outside those terms should be sent to the publisher.

Crown Copyright material is published with the permission of the controller of the Stationery Office.

© 2025 Michael Pugh

Impression number 10 9 8 7 6 5 4 3 2 1

*British Library Cataloguing in Publication Data*
A catalogue record for this book is available from the British Library
ISBN: 9781917183321

This book is also available in various ebook formats.
Ebook ISBN: 9781917183338

The right of Michael Pugh to be identified as the author of this work has been asserted by him in accordance with sections 77 and 78 of the Copyright, Designs and Patents Act 1988.

Production and typesetting by Westchester Publishing Services (UK)
Cover and text design by BMLD (bmld.uk)
Multiple-choice questions advisor: Mark Thomas
Indexing by Terence Halliday

**Fink Publishing Ltd**
**E-mail: hello@revise4law.co.uk**
**www.revise4law.co.uk**

## Notes from the publisher

1. This book reflects the SQE1 assessment specification (updated April 2025) applicable for assessments from 1 September 2025.

2. While Fink Publishing has made every attempt to ensure that advice on the qualification and its assessment is accurate, the official specification and associated assessment guidance materials are the only authoritative source of information and should always be referred to for definitive guidance. See the SRA website at https://sqe.sra.org.uk. Note that the SRA may amend their assessment guidance (including the contents of the assessment specifications) at any point.

3. Fink Publishing has robust editorial processes to ensure the accuracy of the content in this publication, and every effort is made to ensure this publication is free of errors. We are, however, only human, and occasionally errors do occur. Fink Publishing is not liable for any misunderstandings that arise as a result of errors in this publication, but it is our priority to ensure that the content is accurate. If you spot an error, please do contact us at revise4law.co.uk so we can make sure it is corrected.

# Contents

*Dedication* iv
*Contributors* iv
*Introduction to Revise SQE* v

1 Offer and acceptance 1

2 Consideration 26

3 The intention to create legal relations, certainty and capacity 45

4 Privity of contract and rights of third parties 64

5 Contents of a contract 1: Sources and interpretation 83

6 Contents of a contract 2: Exemption clauses and unfair terms 101

7 Misrepresentation 122

8 Mistake, duress, undue influence and illegality 145

9 The discharge of contracts 167

10 Remedies 190

Index 211

# Dedication

To my late father, David Byrne Pugh, teacher and friend.

# Contributors

### THE AUTHOR
Michael Pugh is a senior lecturer teaching contract law, business law, company law and international commercial arbitration at St Mary's University (St Mary's). He is also an advisor to start-ups in the tech industry and acts as an expert on finance matters in international arbitrations. Before joining St Mary's, Michael was a senior lecturer at London South Bank University and a partner at Hogan Lovells. Michael has worked in London and Moscow on financings and refinancings involving parties ranging from Turkmenistan to Bolivia.

### SERIES EDITORS
Amy Sixsmith is an associate professor in law at the University of Sunderland and a senior fellow of Advance HE (previously the Higher Education Academy).

David Sixsmith is assistant professor in law at Northumbria Law School and a senior fellow of Advance HE (previously the Higher Education Academy).

# Introduction to Revise SQE

Welcome to *Revise SQE*, a series of revision guides designed to help you in your preparation for, and achievement in, the Solicitors Qualifying Examination 1 (SQE1) assessment. SQE1 is designed to assess what the Solicitors Regulation Authority (SRA) refer to as 'functioning legal knowledge' (FLK); this is the legal knowledge and competencies required of a newly qualified solicitor in England and Wales. The SRA has chosen single best answer multiple-choice questions (MCQs) to test this knowledge, and *Revise SQE* is here to help.

## PREPARING YOURSELF FOR SQE

The SQE is the relatively new route to qualification for aspiring solicitors, introduced in September 2021 as one of the final stages towards qualification as a solicitor. The SQE consists of two parts:

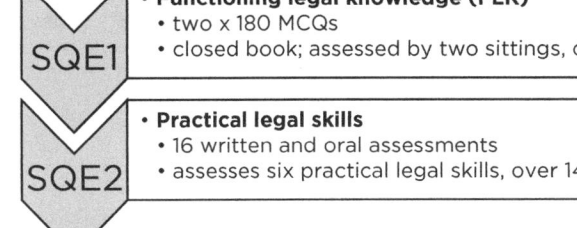

In addition to the above, any candidate will have to undertake two years' qualifying work experience. More information on the SQE assessments can be found on the SRA's dedicated SQE website; this revision guide series will focus on FLK and preparation for SQE1.

It is important to note that the SQE can be perceived to be a 'harder' set of assessments than the Legal Practice Course (LPC). The reason for this, explained by the SRA, is that the LPC is designed to prepare candidates for 'day one' of their training contract; the SQE, on the other hand, is designed to prepare candidates for 'day one' of being a newly qualified solicitor. Indeed, the SRA has chosen the SQE1 assessment to be 'closed book' (ie without permitting use of any materials) on the basis that a newly qualified solicitor would know all of the information tested, without having to refer to books or other sources.

With that in mind, and a different style of assessments in place, it is understandable that many readers may feel nervous or wary of the SQE. This is especially so given that this style of assessment is likely to be different from what readers will have experienced before. In this *Introduction* and revision guide series, we hope to alleviate some of those concerns with guidance on preparing for the SQE assessment, tips on how to approach single best answer MCQs and expertly written guides to aid in your revision.

## What does SQE1 entail?

SQE1 consists of two assessments, containing 180 single best answer MCQs each (360 MCQs in total). The table below breaks down what is featured in each of these assessments.

| Assessment | Contents of assessment ('functioning legal knowledge') |
| --- | --- |
| FLK assessment 1 | • Business law and practice<br>• Dispute resolution<br>• Contract<br>• Tort<br>• The legal system (the legal system of England and Wales and sources of law, constitutional and administrative law and European Union law and legal services) |
| FLK assessment 2 | • Property practice<br>• Wills and the administration of estates<br>• Solicitors, accounts<br>• Land law<br>• Trusts<br>• Criminal law and practice |

Please be aware that in addition to the above, ethics and professional conduct will be examined pervasively across the two assessments (ie it could crop up anywhere).

Each substantive topic is allocated a percentage of the assessment paper (eg 'legal services' will form 12–16% of the FLK1 assessment) and is broken down further into 'core principles'. Candidates are advised to read the SQE1 Assessment Specification in full (available on the SQE website). We have also provided a *Revise SQE checklist* to help you in your preparation and revision for SQE1 (see below).

## HOW DO I PREPARE FOR SQE1?

Given the vastly different nature of SQE1 compared to anything you may have done previously, it can be quite daunting to consider how you could possibly prepare for 360 single best answer MCQs, spanning 11 different substantive topics (especially given that it is 'closed book'). The *Revise SQE FAQ* below, however, will set you off on the right path to success.

*Revise SQE FAQ*

| Question | Answer |
| --- | --- |
| 1. Where do I start? | We would advise that you begin by reviewing the assessment specification for SQE1. You need to identify what subject matter can be assessed under each substantive topic. For each topic, you should honestly ask yourself whether you would be prepared to answer an MCQ on that topic in SQE1. |
| | We have helped you in this process by providing a *Revise SQE checklist* on our website (revise4law.co.uk) that allows you to read the subject matter of each topic and identify where you consider your knowledge to be at any given time. We have also helpfully cross-referenced each topic to a chapter and page of our *Revise SQE* revision guides. |
| 2. Do I need to know legal authorities, such as case law? | In the majority of circumstances, candidates are not required to know or use legal authorities. This includes statutory provisions, case law or procedural rules. Of course, candidates will need to be aware of legal principles deriving from common law and statute. |
| | There may be occasions, however, where the assessment specification does identify a legal authority (such as *Rylands v Fletcher* in tort law). In this case, candidates will be required to know the name of that case, the principles of that case and how to apply that case to the facts of an MCQ. These circumstances are clearly highlighted in the assessment specification and candidates are advised to ensure they engage with those legal authorities in full. In each of our texts in the *Revise SQE* series, we detail clearly which authorities are required for that subject. Any authorities provided in addition are designed to assist in your revision by acting as an aide-mémoire. |

*Revise SQE FAQ (continued)*

| Question | Answer |
|---|---|
| 3. Do I need to know the history behind a certain area of law? | While understanding the history and development of a certain area of law is beneficial, there is no requirement for you to know or prepare for any questions relating to the development of the law (eg in criminal law, candidates will not need to be aware of the development from objective to subjective recklessness). SQE1 will be testing a candidate's knowledge of the law as it stands four calendar months prior to the date of the first assessment in an assessment window. The SRA on the SQE website has helpfully provided the exact cut off date for each assessment in the cycle; it is worth checking this when you are preparing for your assessment. |
| 4. Do I need to be aware of academic opinion or proposed reforms to the law? | Candidates preparing for SQE1 do not need to focus on critical evaluation of the law, or proposed reforms to the law either. |
| 5. How do I prepare for single best answer MCQs? | See our separate *Revise SQE* guide on preparing for single best answer MCQs below. |

## Where does *Revise SQE* come into it?

The *Revise SQE* series of revision guides is designed to aid your revision and consolidate your understanding; the series is not designed to replace your substantive learning of the SQE1 topics. We hope that this series will provide clarity as to assessment focus, useful tips for sitting SQE1 and act as a general revision aid.

There are also materials on our website to help you prepare and revise for the SQE1, such as a *Revise SQE checklist*. This *checklist* is designed to help you identify which substantive topics you feel confident about heading into the exam – see below for an example.

*Revise SQE checklist*

Contract Law

| SQE content | Corresponding chapter | *Revise SQE checklist* | | |
|---|---|---|---|---|
| Formation<br>• Offer and acceptance | Chapter 1, pages 1–25 | I do not know this subject and I am not ready for SQE1 ☐ | I partially know this subject, but I am not ready for SQE1 ☐ | I know this subject and I am ready for SQE1 ☐ |

*Contract Law (continued)*

| SQE content | Corresponding chapter | *Revise SQE checklist* | | |
|---|---|---|---|---|
| Formation<br>• Consideration | Chapter 2, pages 26–44 | I do not know this subject and I am not ready for SQE1 ☐ | I partially know this subject, but I am not ready for SQE1 ☐ | I know this subject and I am ready for SQE1 ☐ |
| Formation<br>• The intention to create legal relations | Chapter 3, pages 45–52 | I do not know this subject and I am not ready for SQE1 ☐ | I partially know this subject, but I am not ready for SQE1 ☐ | I know this subject and I am ready for SQE1 ☐ |

## PREPARING FOR SINGLE BEST ANSWER MCQs

As discussed above, SQE1 will be a challenging assessment for all candidates. This is partly due to the quantity of information a candidate must be aware of in two separate sittings. In addition, however, an extra complexity is added due to the nature of the assessment itself: MCQs.

The SRA has identified that MCQs are the most appropriate way to test a candidate's knowledge and understanding of fundamental legal principles. While this may be the case, it is likely that many candidates have little, if any, experience of MCQs as part of their previous study. Even if a candidate does have experience of MCQs, SQE1 will feature a special form of MCQs known as 'single best answer' questions.

## What are single best answer MCQs and what do they look like?

Single best answer MCQs are a specialised form of question, used extensively in other fields such as in training medical professionals. The idea behind single best answer MCQs is that the multitude of options available to a candidate may each bear merit, sharing commonalities and correct statements of law or principle, but only one option is absolutely correct (in the sense that it is the 'best' answer). In this regard, single best answer MCQs are different from traditional MCQs.

A traditional MCQ will feature answers that are implausible in the sense that the distractors are 'obviously wrong'. Indeed, distractors in a traditional MCQ are often very dissimilar, resulting in a candidate being able to spot answers that are clearly wrong with greater ease.

In a well-constructed single best answer MCQ, on the other hand, each option should look equally attractive given their similarities and subtle differences. The skill of the candidate will be identifying which, out of the options provided, is the single best answer. This requires a much greater level of engagement with the question than a traditional MCQ would require; candidates must take the time to read the questions carefully in the exam.

## How are single best answer MCQs structured?

For SQE1, single best answer MCQs will be structured as follows:

| | |
|---|---|
| A woman is charged with battery, having thrown a rock towards another person intending to scare them. The rock hits the person in the head, causing no injury. The woman claims that she never intended that the rock hit the person, but the prosecution allege that the woman was reckless as to whether the rock would hit the other person. | **The factual scenario.** First, the candidate will be provided with a factual scenario that sets the scene for the question to be asked (known as the 'lead in'). |
| **Which of the following is the most accurate statement regarding the test for recklessness in relation to a battery?** | **The question.** Next, the candidate will be provided with the question (known as the 'stem') that they must find the single best answer to. |
| A. There must have been a risk that force would be applied by the rock, and that the reasonable person would have foreseen that risk and unjustifiably taken it.<br>B. There must have been a risk that force would be applied by the rock, and that the woman should have foreseen that risk and unjustifiably taken it.<br>C. There must have been a risk that force would be applied by the rock, and that the woman must have foreseen that risk and unjustifiably taken it.<br>D. There must have been a risk that force would be applied by the rock, and that both the woman and the reasonable person should have foreseen that risk and unjustifiably taken it.<br>E. There must have been a risk that force would be applied by the rock, but there is no requirement that the risk be foreseen. | **The possible answers.** Finally, the candidate will be provided with **five** possible answers. There is only one single best answer that must be chosen. The other answers, known as 'distractors', are not the 'best' answer available. |

It will be beneficial to guide you through each aspect of the MCQ to further your understanding of the writing process.

## The lead in

The lead in (ie scenario) will differ according to each MCQ and what it is seeking to test. If the MCQ is seeking simply to test a candidate's basic knowledge of the law, without application, then the lead in is likely to be short. Where, however, the MCQ is seeking to have a candidate analyse a factual pattern, and apply it to the options available, the lead in will be significantly longer.

In general, however, a lead in should be a concise and clear introduction to the issue at hand. A well written lead in should contain all material facts relevant to answering the question about to be asked (new facts should not be introduced in the stem or the distractors). The lead in should not be ambiguous or open to interpretation.

## The stem

The stem will be a short question and can be phrased in a variety of ways. The stem should provide the candidate with everything they need to answer the question. There should be no ambiguity or double meanings.

The length and nature of the stem will vary dependent on the type of question being asked. These categories of MCQ are detailed in the table below.

| Categories of MCQs | Explanation and example |
| --- | --- |
| 'Knows' MCQs | To *recall* a specific answer (eg the author of X is Y) |
| 'Shows How' MCQs | To *analyse* a fact pattern and *apply* (eg the application of X in this case is Y) |
| 'Knows How' MCQs | To *know* the answer, and *show* the reason *why* (eg the purpose of X is Y because ...) |

Most commonly, a stem may be phrased as:
- Which of the following statements best describes ...?
- Which of the following statements best summarises ...?
- Which of the following best explains ...?

A stem will not, however, be phrased as:
- Which of the following is true?
- What is the rule for X?
- Which one of the following is not correct?

## The options

You will be provided with five possible answers and only one is correct (whether that be outright correct, or the single best).

The options will not ask a candidate to identify multiple options as being correct (eg 'A, C and D are correct; B and E are wrong'). Nor will the options feature an 'all of the above' option.

A well written MCQ will avoid vague language in the options. Words such as 'rarely', 'usually' etc should be avoided as they present too much ambiguity. On the other hand, absolute words such as 'only', 'always' and 'never' should equally be avoided because they are often obvious distractors (there rarely being a circumstance in English and Welsh law where the legal position is absolute without exception).

If written well, each option should be plausible (meaning that some candidates would choose it). Plausibility can come from drawing on faulty reasoning and common misconceptions. It may be the case that some options share identical wording save for one word (eg a change from 'may' to 'must'). You therefore need to pay close attention to the wording of the options.

To achieve that, all options will be of a fairly equal length to ensure that they are consistent with one another. It is often said that the correct answer is likely to be the longest; so the writers of the MCQs will have that in mind.

In addition, to ensure plausibility, each option is either likely to be a variation of the other, or each option will be entirely different to the others. MCQ drafters will often rely on the rule of 'Three and Two'. The idea behind this rule is that three options will be fairly similar to each other (eg starting with 'Yes'), whilst the remaining two answers will be equally similar to each other (eg starting with 'No'). If you know the answer is definitely 'Yes', that therefore removes the 'No' options immediately. If the MCQ has not adopted the rule of Three and Two, it is likely that you will be able to pick out the 'obvious' distractor.

Now that you know what the MCQs will look like on SQE1, let us talk about how you may go about tackling an MCQ.

## How do I tackle single best answer MCQs?

No exact art exists in terms of answering single best answer MCQs; your success depends on your subject knowledge and understanding of how that subject knowledge can be applied. Despite this, there are tips and tricks that may be helpful for you to consider when confronted with a single best answer MCQ.

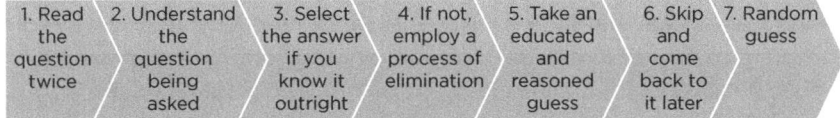

These tips and tricks are essential for preparing you to sit the SQE1 assessment. Each session will involve 90 MCQs, to be answered over 2 hours, 33 minutes. Answering 90 MCQs in that timescale allows *1 minute, 42 seconds per question*, under exam conditions. Of course, some questions will take more or less time to answer than others.

Please take a moment to think about that: on average, within 1 minute and 42 seconds you will have to:
- read the MCQ, including the various answers
- distil from that MCQ what the question is assessing
- work out which of the five possible answers is the correct (or 'single best') answer.

This will be an intensive assessment. You must ensure that you are properly prepared for it, in terms of your subject knowledge and also your mental resilience and time management. Your ability to navigate MCQs will also assist greatly.

## *1. Read the entire question at least twice*

This sounds obvious but is so often overlooked. You are advised to read the entire question once, taking in all relevant pieces of information, understanding what the question is asking you and being aware of the options available. Once you have done that, read the entire question again and this time pay careful attention to the wording that is used.
- **In the factual scenario:** Does it use any words that stand out? Do any words used have legal bearing? What are you told and what are you not told?
- **In the stem:** What are you being asked? Are there certain words to look out for (eg 'should', 'must', 'will', 'shall')?
- **In the answers:** What are the differences between each option? Are they substantial differences or subtle differences? Do any differences turn on a word or a phrase?

You should be prepared to give each question at least two viewings to mitigate any misunderstandings or oversights.

## 2. Understand the question being asked

It is important first that you understand what the question is asking of you. The SRA has identified that the FLK assessments may consist of single best answer MCQs that, for example:
- require the candidate to simply identify a correct legal principle or rule
- require the candidate to not only identify the correct legal principle or rule, but also apply that principle or rule to the factual scenario
- provide the candidate with the correct legal principle or rule, but require the candidate to identify how it should be properly applied and/or the outcome of that proper application.

By first identifying what the question is asking you to do, you can then understand what the creators of that question are seeking to test and how to approach the answers available. Many candidates actually find it beneficial to start with the 'stem', before reading the scenario. This gives them the opportunity to understand what the scenario will likely entail. You need to decide what works best for you, so take the opportunity to try both ways.

## 3. Select the answer if you know it outright

You may feel as though a particular answer 'jumps out' at you, and that you are certain it is correct. It is very likely that the answer is correct. While you should be confident in your answers, do not allow your confidence (and perhaps overconfidence) to rush you into making a decision. Review all of your options one final time before you move on to the next question.

## 4. If you do not know the answer outright, employ a process of elimination

There may be situations in which the answer is not obvious from the outset. This may be due to the close similarities between different answers. Remember, it is the 'single best answer' that you are looking for. If you keep this in your mind, it will thereafter be easier to employ a process of elimination. Identify which answers you are sure are not correct (or not the 'best') and whittle down your options. Get rid of the distractors. Once you have only two options remaining, carefully scrutinise the wording used in both answers and look back to the question being asked. Identify what you consider to be the best answer, in light of that question. Review your answer and move on to the next question.

## 5. Take an educated and reasoned guess

There may be circumstances, quite commonly, in which you do not know the answer to the question. In this circumstance, you should try as hard as possible to eliminate any distractors that you are positive are incorrect and then take an educated and reasoned guess based on the options available. 'Always select C' will not work in this assessment; the correct answers will be randomly distributed amongst the MCQs as options A–E.

## 6. Skip and come back to it later

If time permits, you may think it appropriate to skip a question that you are unsure of and return to it before the end of the assessment. The assessment portal will highlight any questions that have not been answered, and you are also able to 'flag' questions for your review later on in the assessment (time permitting). If you do so, we would advise that you:
- make a note of what question you have skipped or click 'Flag for Review' on your screen, and
- ensure you leave sufficient time for you to go back to that question before the end of the assessment.

The same advice is applicable to any question that you have answered but for which you remain unsure.

## 7. Random guess

As a matter of absolute last resort, being unable even to take an educated and reasoned guess, you should simply choose an answer. There is no negative marking in the SQE1 assessments, so it is better for you to select an answer with the possibility, by sheer luck, of answering it correctly than it is to leave the answer blank and have no chance of scoring a point. The advice is simple: answer all of the questions, even if you have to guess at the end.

We hope that this brief guide will assist you in your preparation towards, and engagement with, single best answer MCQs.

## **GUIDED TOUR**

Each chapter contains a number of features to help you revise, apply and test your knowledge.

**Make sure you know**   Each chapter begins with an overview of the main topics covered and why you need to understand them for the purpose of the SQE1 assessments.

**SQE assessment advice**   This identifies what you need to pay particular attention to in your revision as you work through the chapter.

**What do you know already?** These questions help you to assess which topics you feel confident with and which topics you may need to spend more time on (and where to find them in the chapter).

**Key term** Key terms are highlighted in bold where they first appear and defined in a separate box.

**Exam warning** This feature offers advice on where it is possible to go wrong in the assessments.

**Revision tip** Throughout the chapters are ideas to help you revise effectively and be best prepared for the assessment.

**Summary** This handy box brings together key information in an easy to revise and remember form.

**Practice example** These examples take a similar format to SQE-type questions and provide an opportunity to see how content might be applied to a scenario.

**Procedural link** Where relevant, this element shows how a concept might apply to another procedural topic in the series.

**Key point checklist** At the end of each chapter there is a bullet-point summary of its most important content.

**Key terms and concepts** These are listed at the end of each chapter to help ensure you know, or can revise, terms and concepts you will need to be familiar with for the assessments.

**SQE-style questions** Five SQE-style questions on the chapter topic give you an opportunity to test your knowledge.

**Answers to questions** Check how you did with answers to both the quick knowledge test from the start of the chapter and the SQE-style questions at the end of the chapter.

**Key cases, rules, statutes and instruments** These list the key sources candidates need to be familiar with for the SQE assessment.

## SQE1 LEGAL AUTHORITIES

The SQE1 Assessment Specification advises that on occasion in legal practice a case name or statutory provision is used to describe a legal principle or procedural step (for example 'the St Martins Property exception' (Chapter 4, page 74)). In such circumstances, you are required to know and be able to use such case names or statutory provisions etc. In all other circumstances candidates are not required to recall specific case names or cite statutory authorities.

## TABLE OF CASES

Arnold v Britton [2015] UKSC 36... 95
Attwood v Small 7 ER 684... 132

B&S Contracts & Design Ltd v Victor Green Publications Ltd [1984] ICR 419... 153
Bannerman v White 142 ER 685... 88
Bettini v Gye (1876) QBD 183... 174
Bisset v Wilkinson [1927] AC 177 PC (NZ)... 129
Brogden v Metropolitan Railway Co. (1876-1877) LR 2 App Cas 666 HL... 11

Carlill v Carbolic Smoke Ball Company [1893] 1 QB 256 CA... 10
Cehave NV v Bremer Handelsgesellschaft MBH [1976] QB 44... 175
Chapelton v Barry Urban District Council [1940] 1 KB 532... 108
CIBC Mortgages plc v Pitt [1994] 1 AC 200... 155
Cundy v Lindsay (1877-78) LR 2 App Cas 459... 152
Curtis v Chemical Cleaning & Dyeing Co [1951] 1 KB 805... 104

Davis Contractors v Fareham UDC [1956] AC 696... 180
Dimmock v Hallett (1866-67) LR 2 Ch App 21... 128
Dunlop Pneumatic Tyre Co Ltd v Selfridge & Co Ltd [1915] AC 847 HL... 66

Edgington v Fitzmaurice (1885) LR 29 Ch D 459 CA... 130

Gardner v Coutts & Co [1968] WLR 173... 91
Gordon v Selico (1986) 17 HLR 219... 127

Hoenig v Isaacs [1952] 2 All ER 176... 178
Houghton v Trafalgar Insurance Co Ltd [1954] 1 QB 247... 110
Hyde v Wrench 49 ER 132... 18, 23

J. Lauritzen A/S v Wijsmuller BV, The Super Servant Two [1990] 1 Lloyd's Rep 1... 182-3
Jackson v Horizon Holidays Ltd [1975] 1 WLR 1468... 74

Kleinwort Benson Ltd v Malaysia Corporation Bhd [1989] 1 WLR 379... 51
Krell v Henry [1903] 2 KB 740 CA... 182

L. Schuler AG v Wickman Machine Tools Sales Ltd [1974] AC 235... 172
Lambert v Lewis [1982] AC 225... 196
Liverpool City Council v Irwin [1977] AC 239... 90
Lloyds Bank Ltd v Bundy [1975] QB 326... 158

McCutcheon v David MacBrayne Ltd [1964] 1 WLR 125... 108
The Moorcock (1889) 14 PD 64... 92

Nash v Inman [1908] 2 KB 1 CA... 56

Olley v Marlborough Court Ltd [1949] 1 KB 532... 106

ParkingEye Ltd v Beavis [2015] UKSC 67... 114, 200
Philips v Brooks [1919] 2 KB 243 KBD... 151
Proactive Sports Management Ltd v Rooney [2011] EWCA Civ 1444... 160

Raffles v Wichelhaus and Another 159 ER 375... 148
Robinson v Davison (1870-71) LR 6 Ex 269... 181
Ruxley Electronics & Construction Ltd v Forsyth [1996] AC 344... 195
Rylands v Fletcher [1868] LR 3 HL 330 (HL)... vii

Saunders v Anglia Building Society [1971] AC 1004... 105
Scriven Bros and Co. v Hindley [1913] 3 KB 564 KBD... 147
Shanklin Pier Ltd v Detel Products Ltd [1951] 2 KB 854... 71
Sky Petroleum Ltd v VIP Petroleum Ltd [1974] 1 WLR 576... 202
Smith v Hughes (1871) LR 6 QB 597... 149-50
Smith v Land & House Property Corporation (1884) LR 28 Ch D 7 CA... 129
Storer v Manchester City Council [1974] 1 WLR 1403... 7
Sumpter v Hedges [1898] 1 QB 673 CA... 177

Tamplin v James (1880) LR 15 Ch D 215... 148-9
Taylor v Caldwell (1863) 122 ER 309... 180

Victoria Laundry (Windsor) Ltd v Newman Industries Ltd [1949] 2 KB 528... 197

White v John Warwick & Co Ltd [1953] 1 WLR 1285... 112
William Sindall plc v Cambridgeshire County Council [1994] 1 WLR 1016... 138
Williams v Bayley [1866] LR 1 HL 200 HL... 154
With v O'Flanagan [1936] Ch 575 CA... 126

## TABLE OF STATUTES

Carriage of Goods by Sea Act 1992 ... 67
Companies Act 2006 ... 158
Consumer Rights Act 2015 (CRA 2015) ... 88, 95, 100, 111, 113-15, 121, 124, 173
   s 9-11... 93, 113, 115

s 12... 113, 115
s 13–15... 93, 113, 115
s 16... 94, 115
ss 19–24... 173
s 49... 94, 113
s 50... 124
s 52... 94
s 62... 113
s 62(4)... 112, 114
s 65... 111
Sch 2, Pt 1... 114
Contracts (Rights of Third Parties) Act 1999 (CRTPA 1999) ... 65, 67–8, 72, 75, 80–2

Digital Markets, Competition and Consumers Act 2024 ... 124

Law Reform (Frustrated Contracts) Act 1943 (LRFCA 1943) ... 179, 183

Married Women's Property Act 1882 ... 67
Mental Capacity Act (MCA) 2005 ... 55
Minors' Contracts Act 1987 ... 55
Misrepresentation Act 1967 ... 134, 135–7
    s 2(2)... 137

Road Traffic Act 1988 ... 67

Sale of Goods Act 1979 (SGA 1979) ... 84, 95, 112–13, 115, 120, 172–3
    s 12(1)... 93
    s 13... 113, 115
    s 13(1)... 93, 172
    s 14... 113, 115
    s 14(2)... 93, 172
    s 15... 113, 115
    s 15(2)... 93, 172
    s 15A... 172, 173
Supply of Goods and Services Act 1982 (SGSA 1982) ... 92–3, 95
    s 13... 93

Third Parties (Rights against Insurers) Act 2010 ... 67

Unfair Contract Terms Act 1977 (UCTA 1977) ... 111, 112–13, 120
    s 2(2)... 112
    s 6... 113
    s 11... 113
    Sch 2... 113

# 1

# Offer and acceptance

## ■ MAKE SURE YOU KNOW

This chapter covers the core principles relating to offer and acceptance that you need to know and understand for the SQE1 assessment.

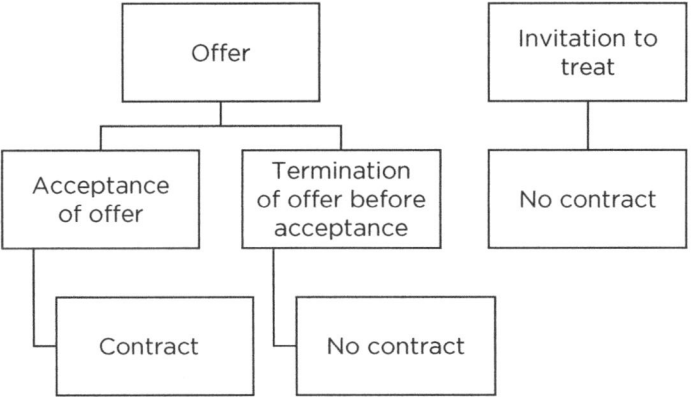

2    Offer and acceptance

## ■ SQE ASSESSMENT ADVICE

For the SQE1 assessment, you will need to be able to apply the legal principles discussed in this chapter to determine whether a contract has been formed. As you work through this chapter, remember to pay particular attention in your revision to:
- The distinction between an offer and an invitation to treat.
- The difference between bilateral offers and unilateral offers, and the different rules that determine how these different types of offers are accepted.
- The various methods of communication for offers and acceptance.
- The effect of counter-offers and requests for further information on offers.
- The termination of offers.

## ■ WHAT DO YOU KNOW ALREADY?

Have a go at these questions before reading this chapter. If you find some difficult or cannot remember the answers, make a note to look more closely at that area during your revision.

1) What is the difference between an offer and an invitation to treat?

   **[Distinguishing between an offer and an invitation to treat, page 4]**

2) True or false? The person who makes the offer is the *offeror*, and the person to whom the offer is made is the *offeree*.

   **[Introduction to offer and acceptance, page 3]**

3) What is the difference between a bilateral offer and a unilateral offer?

   **[Bilateral offers and unilateral offers, page 9]**

4) In respect of which type of offer is the offeree *not* required to communicate their acceptance of the offer?

   **[Forms of acceptance for unilateral offers, page 16]**

5) What is the mirror-image rule in the context of offer and acceptance?

   **[Acceptance, page 10]**

6) In which of the following examples has an offer been destroyed?
   a) John offers Wahid a ton of apples for £100. Wahid asks John whether he will take £50 a month over two months for the apples.
   b) John offers Henriki a ton of apples for £100. Henriki offers John £90 for the ton of apples.

   **[Acceptance, page 10 and The termination of an offer – counter-offers, page 18]**

## INTRODUCTION TO OFFER AND ACCEPTANCE

Offer and acceptance are two of the four elements required to form a legally binding contract. The other elements are consideration and the intention to create legal relations, and are considered later in this book (see **Chapter 2** and **Chapter 3**). In order to form a binding contract, the **offeror** must make an *offer*, which is *accepted* by the **offeree**.

> **Key term: offeror**
>
> The person who makes the offer is the offeror.

> **Key term: offeree**
>
> The person to whom the offer is made is the offeree.

> **Exam warning**
>
> Although there are usually four elements required to form a legally binding contract, be sure that when a question is asking you to focus on offer and acceptance that you focus on these elements, rather than the intention to create legal relations and consideration.

### The objective test

The courts generally use an **objective test** to determine the existence of a binding agreement between the parties. This means that the courts consider how the interaction between the parties looks to a reasonable person.

> **Key term: the objective test**
>
> The objective test is the test used by the courts to determine whether an agreement has been formed. The courts analyse the interaction between the parties from the point of view of a reasonable person.

### The subjective test

In some specified circumstances, the courts apply a subjective test instead of an objective test to determine the existence of an agreement. The subjective test is applied where the offeree knew, or ought to have known, that the offeror has made a mistake. For example, where the offeree knows that the offeror does not intend the terms of the offer to be those that the natural meaning of the words would suggest. It is important to remember this exception to the general rule because if it can be shown that the offeree knew, or ought to have known, that the offeror is mistaken, the offeror is not bound by the terms of the contract. Note that this exception *only* applies if the mistake relates to a term of the contract (such as the price) rather than a collateral matter (such as the colour of an item). Take a look at **Practice example 1.1** to see this in action.

> **Practice example 1.1**
>
> Rusty sells crabs. He has been in correspondence with Delphine previously and has offered to sell her a consignment of crabs at £10 per crab. Two weeks later, he mistakenly offers to sell her the entire consignment of crabs for £10. Delphine accepts the offer, but when Rusty realises he has made a mistake, he refuses to sell her the consignment of crabs for £10.
>
> Can Delphine force Rusty to sell her the consignment of crabs for £10?
>
> The answer is no *if* Rusty can provide the court with evidence to show that Delphine knew, or must have known, that his offer was a mistake, and that Delphine could not have reasonably concluded that the offer reflected Rusty's real intention. In scenarios like this, if the evidence shows that:
> - the market practice for selling crabs is to sell them at a price per crab, and
> - there is a substantial difference between the price per crab and the price per consignment, and
> - there is previous correspondence from Rusty to sell at a price per crab,
>
> the courts will rule that Delphine knew, or should have known, that Rusty was mistaken and Rusty will not be bound to sell Delphine the entire consignment of crabs for £10.

## DISTINGUISHING BETWEEN AN OFFER AND AN INVITATION TO TREAT

For the SQE1 assessment, you must be able to determine whether a communication from a person is an **offer** or an **invitation to treat**. *Only* an offer can be accepted to form a legally binding contract.

> **Key term: offer**
>
> An offer is a communication from a person in which that person agrees to be legally bound to contract with another party (the offeree) on specified terms if the offeree accepts.

Distinguishing between an offer and an invitation to treat

> **Key term: invitation to treat**
>
> An invitation to treat is a communication that a person would like to negotiate or discuss the terms on which goods may be sold, or services may be provided, that will lead to a contract at a later date.

## Identifying an invitation to treat

Specific words used in communications help us to determine whether a communication is an offer or an invitation to treat. For example, the words 'may be prepared to sell' are unlikely to be viewed as an offer. This is because the phrase 'may be prepared to sell' is conditional, and does not oblige the statement-maker to sell if the other party replies 'yes'. In other words, it is not a firm commitment from the statement-maker. This conditional nature is a key element of an invitation to treat.

**Table 1.1** shows specific situations that the law classifies as invitations to treat. You must be able to apply the general rules, and the exceptions to these general rules, in your SQE1 assessment.

*Table 1.1: Examples of invitations to treat*

| Specific situation | General rule | Explanation |
| --- | --- | --- |
| Advertisements | Invitation to treat | The general rule is that advertisements are invitations to treat. The person who reads the advertisement should make an offer that the advertiser can accept or reject. |
| | | The logic for this approach is that if an advertisement is treated as an offer, a person could accept it to form a legally binding contract. This would oblige the advertiser to supply the advertised goods to whoever accepted the offer, or face a claim for breach of contract. Classifying advertisements as invitations to treat reflects business common sense by allowing the supplier to decide whether to make a legally binding contract with the person who wishes to buy the goods in the advertisement. The same principle applies to wine lists and other lists of goods from which a customer can make an order. |

6    Offer and acceptance

*Examples of invitations to treat (continued)*

| Specific situation | General rule | Explanation |
|---|---|---|
|  |  | Note the exception to the general rule that applies to certain advertisements that are unilateral offers. See **Identifying an offer, page 7**. |
| Display of goods | Invitation to treat | Goods on display in a shop are an invitation to treat, not an offer. The offer is made by the customer who wishes to buy them, and the shopkeeper can accept or reject this offer. |
| Websites | Invitation to treat | Generally, a website through which goods can be bought is an invitation to treat. It is the order made by the person wishing to buy through the website that is the offer. |
| Auction sales | Invitation to treat | An auctioneer's request for bids at an auction is an invitation to treat, even when it refers to lots being 'offered for sale'. The same rule applies to an advertisement that an auction is being held. A bidder's offer is accepted by the auctioneer when the auctioneer taps the hammer down. But note the exception in respect of auctions 'without reserve'. See **Identifying an offer, page 7**. |
| Tenders (requests for quotes, and bids) | Invitation to treat | The person making the requests for quotes (typically this is the person who organises the tender) can decide whether to accept the bids (offers) that they receive. |
|  |  | But note the exception to the general rule in respect of tenders that promise to accept the most competitive bid amounts; and promise to consider bids that conform to the tender conditions. Such tenders are unilateral offers. See **Identifying an offer, page 7**. |

> **Exam warning**
>
> When you identify a clue in the question, for example an advertisement, and the general rule is that an advertisement is an invitation to treat, make sure that you stress-test your initial conclusion and check whether an exception to the general rule applies, which could change your answer.

## Identifying an offer

Words, and the *intention* of the person who makes the communication, help the courts (and us!) to identify whether a communication is an offer or an invitation to treat. Which criteria do the courts use to identify an offer?

- The first key requirement of an offer is that the communication must be precise enough, with no further details to be agreed, so that the person to whom it is addressed can answer 'Yes' to form a binding contract.
- The second requirement is that the person making the communication must have the *intention* to be bound. The courts decide whether such intention exists through an objective analysis of the words used in the communication.

The case of *Storer v Manchester City Council* [1974] 1 WLR 1403 is a good example of an offer. Manchester City Council sent Storer an agreement for sale and asked him to sign the agreement and return it to the council if he accepted the offer to buy. The court held that this language was certain, and showed a clear intention to be bound if the offeree signed the agreement and returned it, so it was an offer. **Table 1.2** provides further examples of offers.

*Table 1.2: Examples of offers*

| Specific situation | General rule | Explanation |
| --- | --- | --- |
| Unilateral advertisements | Offer | Unilateral advertisements are an exception to the general rule that advertisements are invitations to treat. An example of a unilateral advertisement is where an offeror makes a promise in exchange for the offeree performing an act, for example, a promise of a reward for the person who finds a lost cat. The offeree is not obliged to perform the act, but if the offeree performs the act and finds the lost cat, they will have accepted the offer and will be entitled to the reward that was offered. Another example of a unilateral advertisement |

*Examples of offers (continued)*

| Specific situation | General rule | Explanation |
|---|---|---|
|  |  | would be The Best Insurance Company advertising free holiday insurance to a person who books a holiday with a company in its network. Such an advertisement would be a unilateral offer of free holiday insurance that can be accepted by any person who performs the specified act (in this case, booking the holiday with a network company of The Best Insurance Company). |
| Auctions 'without reserve' | Offer | Auctions 'without reserve' are categorised as unilateral offers. In other words, they are a promise to sell the goods being auctioned to the highest bidder in the auction. |
| Tenders to accept the most competitive bid, and to consider tenders that conform to the bid conditions | Offer | Tenders to accept the most competitive bid are treated as unilateral offers that are accepted by the party who submits the most competitive bid to form a legally binding contract. In addition, a tender that promises to consider bids that conform to the tender conditions is a unilateral offer that is accepted by any person who submits a bid that confirms to the tender conditions to form a legally binding contract. |
| Automatic vending machines | Offer | Goods displayed or offered by vending machines are offers. A person who puts money in the vending machine, or pays by card, accepts the offer being made to form a legally binding contract. |

Attempt **Practice example 1.2** to test your ability to distinguish between offers and invitations to treat.

### Practice example 1.2

Marco bumps into Maria at a coffee shop. Marco mentions that he may be selling his laptop. Maria tells Marco that she would like to buy it.

Has Marco made an offer to sell his laptop to Maria?

The answer is no. Marco's communication is an invitation to treat. The key clues are:
- the use of the word 'may'
- the absence of any certainty in Marco's communication
- the lack of evidence to indicate that Marco has an intention to sell to Maria. (Marco does not include any details about the laptop, such as the model, age or price, and he does not use any direct words, such as 'Would you like to buy my laptop for £300?')

Maria cannot respond *yes* to Marco's communication and so Marco's communication cannot be an offer.

### Revision tip
When analysing scenarios such as the one in **Practice example 1.2**, try putting yourself in the shoes of Marco. If you were to tell someone that you may be selling your dog, would you expect someone who responded with the words *yes I will buy it* to have formed a legally binding contract that obliges you to sell your dog to them? The answer is no.

## Bilateral offers and unilateral offers

It is critical that you are able to identify the difference between **bilateral offers** and **unilateral offers**. In a bilateral offer scenario, an offer (or promise) is exchanged for an offer (or promise). For example, Olga promises to pay £10 for a book in exchange for Bogdan agreeing to sell Olga the book for £10. By contrast, in a unilateral offer scenario, Bogdan may offer to sell the book to the first person who brings him £10. Olga is not obliged to bring Bogdan £10, but if she chooses to bring Bogdan £10 and is the first person to do so, Bogdan will be bound to sell the book to Olga. Make sure you understand these important terms.

### Key term: bilateral offer
A bilateral offer is an offer or promise in exchange for an offer or promise.

### Key term: unilateral offer
A unilateral offer is an offer in exchange for a specified act, made either to a specific person, or to a wider group of persons, including to the public.

Now put your knowledge to the test and attempt **Practice example 1.3**.

### Practice example 1.3

A medical company advertises a medical product. The advertisement states that the company will pay £100 to anyone who catches flu after using their product in a specified way for a specified period of time. Veronika sees the advertisement and buys the medical product. She uses the medical product in the prescribed way for the prescribed time, but catches flu.

Has Veronika formed a legally binding contract with the medical company?

The answer is yes. This scenario is based on the facts of *Carlill v Carbolic Smoke Ball Company* [1893] 1 QB 256 CA. The Court of Appeal held that the claimant was entitled to the £100 on the grounds that the advertisement was a unilateral offer that the claimant had accepted by the act of buying the medical product and using it in the prescribed way to form a legally binding contract.

*An offer must be communicated to be effective*
In order to be effective, an offer must be communicated to the offeree (a person cannot accept an offer if they do not know about it). So a person who finds a lost cat and returns it to its owner will only be able to claim any reward offered for the lost cat *if* the person knew about the offer when they returned the lost cat.

## ACCEPTANCE

Once you have identified an offer, you must be able to determine whether there has been an **acceptance** of the offer. The **'mirror-image rule'** is a helpful principle to apply to work out whether an offer has been accepted. If the response from the offeree is not the mirror image of the offer, for example, because the offeree has introduced a new term, then it is not a valid acceptance.

### Key term: acceptance

An acceptance is the complete agreement to the terms of the offer.

### Key term: mirror-image rule

The mirror-image rule means that an acceptance must be exactly the same as the offer to which it relates.

Note that acceptance can be made through words or by conduct (what the offeree does). Conduct is a key issue because it means that where a person who receives an offer does not communicate a response in writing or orally but nonetheless starts to perform their obligations in accordance with the terms of the offer, this performance will amount to acceptance of the offer by conduct. Now try to answer **Practice example 1.4**.

### Practice example 1.4

Ali sends a draft contract to Benazir. Benazir fills in the name of the arbitrator who will resolve any disputes that arise, marks the draft as *approved* and sends it back to Ali. Ali receives the draft and puts it in a file. Both Ali and Benazir start to perform their respective obligations under the terms of the draft contract.

Has a contract been concluded between Ali and Benazir?

The answer is yes. This example is based on the scenario in *Brogden v Metropolitan Railway Co.* (1876-1877) LR 2 App Cas 666 HL. The House of Lords held that Party B (Benazir in our scenario) made a counter-offer to Party A (Ali in our scenario) by filling in the name of the arbitrator and sending him the contract. The fact that Party A started to perform his obligations after receiving the contract was held to mean that Party A had accepted Party B's offer by conduct to form a legally binding contract.

## Counter-offers and requests for flexibility in payment terms

An attempt by the offeree to introduce new terms when responding to an offer is a **counter-offer**. A counter-offer terminates an offer so that the offeree can no longer accept it . But the new counter-offer can be accepted by the person to whom it is addressed to form a binding contract. See also **The termination of an offer, page 16**.

### Key term: counter-offer

A counter-offer is a response to an offer that introduces new terms to what is offered. A counter-offer is not an acceptance, and destroys the original offer, which can no longer be accepted by the person who makes the counter-offer.

Now put your knowledge to the test and attempt **Practice example 1.5**.

## 12 Offer and acceptance

> **Practice example 1.5**
>
> Maria offers a car for sale to Pavol for £1,000. In response, Pavol says to Maria, 'The car is not worth £1,000, but I will give you £800 for it'. The next day, Pavol changes his mind and tells Maria that he accepts her offer and will buy the car for £1,000.
>
> Has a legally binding contract been formed between Maria and Pavol?
>
> **The answer is no. Pavol's response to Maria that he would give her £800 for the car is a counter-offer that destroyed Maria's offer so that it is no longer open for Pavol to accept.**

It is important to distinguish between a counter-offer, and a **request for flexibility in payment terms**. An example of a request for flexibility in payment terms is where the offeree asks whether they could pay for the goods or services offered over a period of time or in instalments. Such communications are not counter-offers, so they do not terminate the offer. SQE1 assessment questions may test a candidate's ability to distinguish between the effects of counter-offers and requests for flexibility in payment terms.

> **Key term: request for flexibility in payment terms**
>
> A request for flexibility of payment terms is a response to an offer that enquires whether the amount required for the offered goods can be paid in instalments or later than set out in the offer, and leaves the original offer open for acceptance.

Now put your knowledge to the test and attempt **Practice example 1.6**.

> **Practice example 1.6**
>
> John offers to sell gold to Gregor for £1,000 an ounce. Gregor asks John if he will accept payment in instalments over 2 months. John tells Gregor that he will accept payments in instalments over 2 months. Gregor tells John that he accepts his offer.
>
> Has a legally binding contract been formed between John and Gregor?
>
> **The answer is yes. Gregor's question to John about paying in instalments was a request for information about flexibility in payment terms that left John's offer open for Gregor to accept, which he did.**

## Acceptance

### *The 'battle of the forms'*

When parties send each other their own standard terms of business with the aim of persuading the other party to use the first party's standard terms, this is often called the battle of the forms.

The general rule in respect of the battle of the forms is that 'the last shot' prevails. This means that the last set of terms of business sent by one party to the other party before the other party starts to perform their obligations will apply to the contract.

### The offeree's acceptance must be in respect of the offer

If the offeree performs an act that would normally qualify as an acceptance of the offer, the act will only constitute acceptance of the offer if the offeree knows about the offer. Provided the offeree knows about the offer, their motive in performing the act that constitutes acceptance is irrelevant. For example, where an offer is made to give a £100 reward to any person who provides specified information about a crime, a person who provides such information about the crime will be entitled to the reward, *provided they know about it*, even if their motive in providing the information is not to receive the reward, but something different, like clearing their conscience.

### Forms of acceptance for bilateral offers

In this section, we look at the impact of the offeror's requirements as to how acceptance should be communicated. The legal position in respect of bilateral offers is different from the position for unilateral offers (see **Forms of acceptance for unilateral offers, page 16**).

The general rule is that an acceptance of a bilateral offer *must* be communicated to the offeror to create a legally binding contract (the **receipt rule**).

> **Key term: receipt rule**
> 
> The rule that an offeror must actually *receive* an acceptance for the acceptance to be valid.

The requirement for communication of acceptance underpins the rule that silence cannot amount to acceptance. So if an offeror tells an offeree that they will assume that their offer has been accepted if they do not hear from them, this has no legal effect. In other words, if the offeree does not respond to such a communication from the offeror, it will *not* form a legally binding contract.

There are two main issues to consider as regards the form of acceptance:
- If the offeror has specified or implied that acceptance must be in a specific form, for example, *in person*, then the acceptance must be communicated as specified.
- If the offeror has not made it very clear that acceptance must only be made in a specified form, then the offeree can use another form for acceptance, provided it is no slower. For example, if the offeror has required acceptance to be made by a telephone, acceptance by a personal visit would be a sufficient alternative, provided it was not significantly slower.

The postal acceptance rule (considered below) is an important exception to the rule that an acceptance of a bilateral contract must be communicated to be effective.

### The postal acceptance rule

If the interaction between the offeror and the offeree makes it clear that the post might be used by the offeree to communicate acceptance, the postal acceptance rule will apply. The postal acceptance rule provides that the offeree's acceptance is effective to form a legally binding contract *as soon as the acceptance is posted*. So even if the offeror never receives the acceptance, they are still bound by the contract that was formed when the acceptance was posted.

For such a powerful rule to apply, certain requirements need to be satisfied, including the requirement that the letter of acceptance be properly addressed, and posted through a post office or a Royal Mail postbox. The postal acceptance rule does not apply to letters that are handed to the postperson or sent through a courier company. The parties are free to exclude the postal acceptance rule, for example, by the offeror stating that an acceptance must not be sent by post, and by specifying an alternative means of communication.

When the postal acceptance rule does not apply, the position on communication of acceptance is as set out in **Table 1.3** below.

*Table 1.3: Communicating acceptance outside the postal acceptance rule*

| Means of communication | General position |
| --- | --- |
| Instantaneous media, including the telephone, fax and telex. | The general position is that the receipt rule applies, which means that the offeror must receive an acceptance for it to be communicated. |

*Communicating acceptance outside the postal acceptance rule (continued)*

| Means of communication | General position |
|---|---|
| | As a general rule, the offeree is responsible for ensuring that the offeror has received the acceptance. In respect of acceptances by telephone, the offeror and the offeree are treated as if they were interacting face to face. So if the offeror does not hear or understand the acceptance, it will not have been communicated. In respect of fax, if the offeror is aware that the acceptance is being sent but does not receive it or it is unreadable when it is received, the offeror must ask the offeree to re-send the acceptance. |
| Instantaneous media sent during office hours | If the acceptance is communicated to a business during office hours, acceptance is held to be communicated at the time when the acceptance is actually received by the fax. |
| Instantaneous media sent outside office hours | If the acceptance is sent outside 'ordinary business hours', it will be deemed to be received at the start of the following working day. |
| Acceptance by email | The general position is that the receipt rule applies. |
| Acceptance through a website | Unless the parties are businesses and agree otherwise, the order and acknowledgement of receipt of order will be deemed to be received when the parties to whom they are addressed are able to access them. |

> **Revision tip**
>
> Ensure you understand the two main rules in respect of the acceptance of bilateral offers.
> - Firstly, communications of acceptance are deemed received by the offeror when they are actually received. But note how the rule is varied when acceptances are sent out of office hours.
> - Secondly, the postal acceptance rule provides that the acceptance is effective to create a legally binding contract when it is properly posted.

**Practice example 1.7** explores the difference between receipt rule and the postal acceptance rule.

## Practice example 1.7

BigBank sends an offer of a loan to Oneyema by post. BigBank tells Oneyema that if she wishes to accept the loan, the bank must receive her acceptance in writing by 5 PM on Friday. Oneyema decides to send her response in a letter to BigBank that she posts in a Royal Mail postbox before 5 PM on Friday

Has Oneyema's response formed a legally binding contract with BigBank?

No, Oneyema has not formed a legally binding contract with BigBank. The words in the offer state that the bank must receive her acceptance in writing by 5 PM. This displaces the postal acceptance rule. This means that BigBank must actually receive Oneyema's acceptance by 5 PM on Friday for it to form a legally binding contract.

## Forms of acceptance for unilateral offers

The rules for the acceptance of unilateral offers are different from the rules of acceptance of bilateral offers. The key difference is that the offeree *accepts* a unilateral offer *by conduct* and this acceptance does not need to be communicated to the offeror in order to form a legally binding contract.

## Exam warning

Make sure that you clearly identify whether a question on acceptance relates to a bilateral offer or a unilateral offer because the rules for acceptance of bilateral and unilateral offers are different. In addition, make sure that you identify whether it aims to test your knowledge of the receipt rule or the postal acceptance rule, and remember the limitations to the postal acceptance rule in respect of letters that are not properly addressed/not properly posted, or where the offeror has specified that they require actual notice of acceptance.

## THE TERMINATION OF AN OFFER

The last topic that we consider in this chapter is the termination of an offer.

Once an offer has been terminated, it cannot be accepted. An offeror may wish to terminate an offer because of a change in circumstances. Or an offeree may wish to ask questions about the offer without terminating the offer, for example, by making a counter-offer (see **Counter-offers, page 18**).

For your SQE1 assessment, you must be able to determine whether an offer has been terminated. In the sections below we consider the different ways offers can be terminated.

## The offeror can revoke the offer

An offeror is free to revoke an offer before it is accepted. However, if the offeror has agreed with the offeree to keep an offer open for a specific time, the offeror is bound to do so.

### *Revocation must be communicated*

As regards bilateral offers, the revocation must be communicated to the offeree to be effective. It makes no difference whether it is the offeror or a third party who communicates the revocation to the offeree. The postal acceptance rule does not apply to the revocation of offers. Different rules apply to the revocation of unilateral offers (see below).

## The revocation of unilateral offers

Different rules apply to the revocation of unilateral offers. This is because there can be a lack of proximity between the offeror of a unilateral offer and the offeree. For example, where the offer is made in a newspaper, the offeror may not know who has accepted their offer until such person makes themselves known to them.

As a general rule, an offeror who makes a unilateral offer cannot revoke it once the offeree has started to perform the act specified in the offer. The offeror must let the offeree finish performing the specified act.

### *Communicating the revocation of unilateral offers*

In contrast to the position in respect of bilateral offers, the offeror can effectively revoke a unilateral offer without such revocation actually being communicated to the offeree. All that is required is that the offeror must use the same means to revoke the offer as they used to make the offer in the first place. For example, if Leroy offers his laptop through a unilateral advertisement in *The Evening Standard*, and then decides to revoke his offer, he would need to advertise his revocation in the same publication, or in one that had the same readership. If Leroy were to try and revoke his offer by publication of an announcement in *Hello*

*Magazine*, which has different readership from *The Evening Standard*, the revocation would not be effective.

## Counter-offers

As we have noted above, a counter-offer does not amount to an acceptance and it terminates an offer. Now put your knowledge to the test and attempt **Practice example 1.8**.

> **Practice example 1.8**
>
> Anne offered to sell land for £1,000. Paul offered £950 in response. When Anne refused to accept Paul's £950, Paul said that he accepted Anne's offer to buy the land for £1,000.
>
> Was Anne bound by Paul's acceptance of her offer to sell the land for £1,000?
>
> The answer is no. This scenario is based on the facts of *Hyde v Wrench* 49 ER 132. The court held that the offeree's offer of £950 was a counter-offer that destroyed the offeror's original offer. So there was no offer to be accepted by the offeree when he tried to accept the original offer to sell for £1,000.

## The termination of an offer through lapse of time

An offer may be stated to be open for a specific period of time so that it will terminate on a set date. In other cases where no time frame is mentioned, if the offeree takes longer than reasonable to respond to the offer, the courts may hold that there was no offer open to accept because it had expired. There is no absolute rule as to what will constitute a reasonable time frame, it depends upon the subject matter of the contract.

## The termination of an offer by the offeror making a new offer

Let us imagine that Nelson wants to sell his camera. First, he offers the camera to Bronwen for £100. But later the same day, Nelson finds out that his camera is worth £200. When Nelson sees Bronwen later that day, he tells her that his camera is worth more than £100 and he offers Bronwen his camera for £200. Nelson's second offer will terminate his first offer.

## ■ KEY POINT CHECKLIST

This chapter has covered the following key knowledge points. You can use these to structure your revision around, making sure to recall the key details for each point, as covered in this chapter.
- As a general rule, the courts adopt an objective approach to determine whether a contract has been formed.
- A bilateral offer is an offer or promise in exchange for an offer or promise.
- A unilateral offer is an offer in exchange for a specified act.
- An invitation to treat is a communication that a person might like to negotiate or discuss the terms of a contract.
- Acceptance of a bilateral offer must be communicated to be effective, except where the postal acceptance rule applies.
- The postal acceptance rule provides that acceptance is effective from the moment the letter is properly posted.
- Acceptance of a unilateral offer does not need to be communicated; the performance of the specified act is acceptance even if the offeree is not aware of this.
- A bilateral offer can be terminated through communication to the offeree, a counter-offer, lapse of time and the making of a new offer.
- A unilateral offer can be terminated by using the same method of communication that was used for the original offer.

## ■ KEY TERMS AND CONCEPTS
- offeror (**page 3**)
- offeree (**page 3**)
- the objective test (**page 3**)
- offer (**page 4**)
- invitation to treat (**page 5**)
- bilateral offer (**page 9**)
- unilateral offer (**page 9**)
- acceptance (**page 10**)
- mirror-image rule (**page 10**)
- counter-offer (**page 11**)
- request for flexibility in payment terms (**page 12**)
- receipt rule (**page 13**)

## ■ SQE1-STYLE QUESTIONS

**QUESTION 1**

A goat escapes from the zoo. The zookeeper offers a reward of £100 in the local paper to the first person to return the goat to the zoo. A man does not see the notice, but finds the goat on his morning walk and takes the goat to the zoo. The zookeeper tells the man that he is the first person to return the goat to the zoo and the zookeeper thanks the man with a chocolate bar. Later that day, the man's colleague tells him about the notice for a reward in the newspaper.

**Which one of the following statements most accurately describes the legal position of the parties?**

A. The zookeeper is not obliged to pay the man the £100 reward because the man did not claim the reward when he returned the goat to the zoo.

B. The zookeeper is obliged to pay the man the £100 reward because the man accepted the zookeeper's offer by exactly performing the specified actions.

C. The man can only claim the reward of £100 if he was aware of the advertisement when he brought the goat to the zoo.

D. By accepting the chocolate bar, the man accepted alternative performance by the zookeeper of the reward and is estopped from claiming the £100.

E. The man's act of returning the goat amounts to acceptance of a unilateral offer so it is irrelevant whether or not he knew of the advertisement when he performed the act.

**QUESTION 2**

A supplier is negotiating the sale of apples with a customer. The supplier writes an email to the customer on Friday morning to offer the customer 10 tons of apples for £2,000. The supplier says that she will start delivering apples as soon as the customer accepts the offer. The customer telephones the supplier to confirm that she accepts her offer. The telephone line is bad and the supplier cannot hear what the customer says and asks the customer to repeat her message. The customer repeats her message and then the telephone cuts out. The supplier did not hear the message the first time or the second time.

Which of the following statements best describes the legal position in the case?

A. The customer's acceptance has created a binding contract so the supplier must start delivering apples to the customer in accordance with the terms of their agreement.
B. The supplier is responsible for calling the customer back and checking what she said.
C. It is the customer's responsibility to ensure that the supplier hears her acceptance.
D. Given that the customer has tried two times to tell the supplier that she accepts her offer, the supplier will be in breach of contract if she does not deliver the apples to the customer as soon as possible.
E. It was the supplier's fault that she did not hear the customer's acceptance of her offer so she must take the consequences of this.

## QUESTION 3

A man sends a letter by Royal Mail to a colleague in which he offers to sell her his bicycle for £500 provided he hears back from her in two days. The colleague writes back saying that she will buy the bicycle for £400 and she posts her letter by Royal Mail within two days.

Which one of the following statements is the most accurate reflection of the legal position?

A. Provided the colleague put the correct address on the letter, the contract is formed when she posts it with Royal Mail.
B. The colleague's letter amounts to a counter-offer that destroys the man's offer.
C. The colleague's letter is a unilateral offer that the man can accept by conduct.
D. Pursuant to the postal acceptance rule a contract between the colleague and the man is formed at the moment that the colleague posts the letter back to the man.
E. The colleague's communication was an enquiry as to flexibility in payment terms so the man's offer remains open for the colleague to accept.

## QUESTION 4

A lawyer is walking through the town centre when she meets her friend, a shopkeeper. The shopkeeper tells the lawyer that she rents her shop from an insurance company and that she is worried because the insurance company recently demanded 50% more rent each year. In a panic, the shopkeeper sent a letter by post to the insurance company offering to pay 45% more per year, but after checking her finances, the shopkeeper has discovered that she cannot afford to pay 45% more per year.

Which of the following most accurately describes the legal position?

A. The lawyer (on behalf of the shopkeeper) should immediately telephone the insurance company to tell them that the shopkeeper has revoked her offer to pay a 45% increase. This will prevent the insurance company from accepting the shopkeeper's offer to form a binding contract.

B. The shopkeeper should revoke her offer to the insurance company immediately by sending a letter by courier to the insurance company to ensure that it does not accept the shopkeeper's offer of a 45% increase to form a binding contract.

C. The shopkeeper was bound by her offer to the insurance company from the moment she posted her letter.

D. The shopkeeper should revoke her offer to the insurance company by post because the postal acceptance rule provides that a message in a letter is effective from the moment it is posted in a Royal Mail postbox, regardless of whether or not the addressee receives it.

E. The shopkeeper should send a letter to the insurance company to investigate whether the insurance company would be prepared to accept a smaller increase in annual rent.

## QUESTION 5

On Monday, a man advertises his computer for sale in a trade magazine with the following words 'LENOVO IdeaPad Flex 5 13.3' for £200. I will sell to the first person who brings £200 to my office at 1 Oxford Street by 1 PM this Friday'. On Tuesday, the man changes his mind and decides to revoke his advertisement. The man cannot find the telephone number for the magazine so he places a notice in a national newspaper and the notice is published on Wednesday morning.

To which one of the following persons is the man obliged to sell his computer?

A. On Friday, a woman, having seen the advert on Monday, brings £200 to the man's office at 11:00 AM.
B. On Friday, a student, having seen the advert on Monday, arrives at the man's office at 10:15 AM and offers him £190 for the computer.
C. On Friday, a programmer, having seen the advert on Monday, arrives at the man's office at 1:05 PM and asks whether he will accept £200 for the computer payable in four monthly instalments of £50.
D. On Friday, an accountant, having seen the advert on Monday, arrives at the man's office at 11:30 AM with £200.
E. The man is not obliged to sell the computer to any person.

## ■ ANSWERS TO QUESTIONS

### Answers to 'What do you know already?' questions at the start of the chapter

1) An offer can be accepted to form a legally binding contract. No further negotiation is required. By contrast, an invitation to treat is an expression of willingness on the part of one person to enter into negotiations, which it is hoped will lead to the conclusion of a contract at a later date.
2) True.
3) A bilateral offer is an offer by one person in exchange for an offer or promise by another person. By contrast, a unilateral offer is a promise by one person in exchange for an act by another person.
4) A unilateral offer.
5) The mirror-image rule requires that an acceptance of an offer must be unconditional and it must correspond to the exact terms of the offer.
6) The correct answer was (b). Henriki's offer to John is a counter-offer. A counter-offer destroys an offer. The authority for this rule is *Hyde v Wrench*.

## Answers to end-of-chapter SQE1-style questions

Question 1:
The correct answer was C. It is a key requirement of an acceptance that the person purporting to accept the offer is aware of the offer. This means that Option E is incorrect. Option A is incorrect because if the party who performs the unilateral act is aware of the offer, they will be entitled to claim the reward, even if they do not claim it immediately. Option B is also incorrect because the person who purports to accept an offer must be aware of it. Option D is incorrect because the man is not aware of the offer so is not entitled to the reward of £100. If the man had been aware of the offer, he would still be able to claim the reward of £100, despite having been given a chocolate bar.

Question 2:
The correct answer was C. This is because in this bilateral offer scenario, an offeree (the customer) must communicate acceptance for it to be effective. Since the offeree's (the customer's) communication is by telephone, it is the offeree's responsibility to ensure that the offeror (the supplier) hears the acceptance. This means that Option A is incorrect. A binding contract has not been formed because the customer has not communicated acceptance to the supplier.
Option B is also incorrect because it is the offeree's responsibility to communicate acceptance. Option D is incorrect because no contract has been formed. Option E is incorrect as there is nothing in the fact pattern to indicate that it is the supplier's fault that the line is bad, and in any event, it is the offeree's (the customer's) responsibility to communicate acceptance, and she has not done this.

Question 3:
The correct answer was B. This is because the colleague's response to the man clearly shows that she wishes to buy the bicycle for £400, rather than for the £500 in the offer. This is a counter-offer, which destroys the original offer so that it can no longer be accepted. This lack of symmetry between the offer and the purported acceptance means that there is no agreement between the offeror (the man) and the offeree (the colleague) so there can be no binding contract. This also means that Options A and D are incorrect. Option C is incorrect because the colleague's counter-offer is a bilateral offer, not a unilateral offer. Option E is incorrect because the colleague's communication is an offer to buy the bicycle at a different price from the one originally offered (a counter-offer), rather than an enquiry as to whether payment of the £500 could be paid in instalments, which would be an example of an enquiry as to flexibility in payment terms.

Question 4:
   The correct answer was A. This is because the shopkeeper's communication to the insurance company was an offer, and an offer can be revoked before it is accepted. A communication of revocation to the offeree is effective regardless of whether it is made by the offeror or by a third party. The third party in this case is the lawyer. Watch out for the postal acceptance rule because it only applies to acceptances, and it is clear that the shopkeeper's offer to the insurance company to pay a 45% increase is an offer. Option B is incorrect because the shopkeeper's revocation will only be effective when it is received by the insurance company. Since delivery by courier is not immediate, it presents the risk that the insurance company can still accept the shopkeeper's offer before the courier delivers the revocation. Option C is incorrect because an offer can be revoked before it is accepted. Option D is incorrect because the postal acceptance rule only applies to acceptances, and not to revocations. Option E is incorrect because the shopkeeper wishes to withdraw her offer before the insurance company accepts it.

Question 5:
   The correct answer was A. This is because the man made a unilateral offer and the woman accepted through her conduct. Although the man tried to revoke his unilateral offer, he did not do so effectively because the revocation of a unilateral offer needs to be given the same 'notoriety' as its advertisement. On the basis that the man's initial advertisement was in a trade magazine, and his attempt at revocation was published in a national newspaper, it is clear that his revocation was not given the same notoriety as the initial advertisement. The readership of the magazine and the national newspaper will not be the same. This means that Option E is incorrect. Option B is not correct because the student makes a counter-offer to the man that destroys the man's offer so that a contract is not formed. Option C is not correct because the programmer arrives after the deadline to accept the offer and he has not brought £200, so the programmer has not performed the act required to accept the unilateral offer. Option D is incorrect because the accountant is not the first person to arrive at the man's office within the specified time frame. The first person arrived at 11 AM and accepted the offer. So there was no offer open to accept when the accountant arrived at 11:30 AM.

## ■ KEY CASES, RULES, STATUTES AND INSTRUMENTS

The SQE1 Assessment Specification does not require you to know any case names, or statutory materials, for this topic.

# 2

# Consideration

## ■ MAKE SURE YOU KNOW

This chapter explores the topic of consideration. Consideration is a promise, an act or an omission in exchange for a promise, an act or an omission and is one of the four ingredients required to form a legally binding contract. Consideration is required for all contracts, except for those made by deed. We have already looked at the first two requirements to form a legally binding contract (offer and acceptance in **Chapter 1**) and we will look at the final key requirement (the intention to create legal relations) in **Chapter 3**.

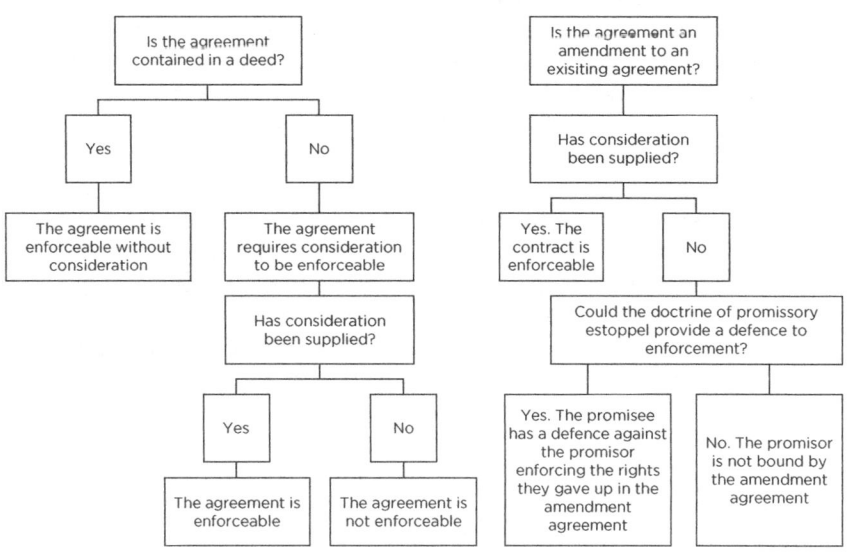

For the SQE1 assessments you are required to know the key aspects of consideration, and be able to apply the legal principles and rules of consideration to scenarios so that you can identify whether the parties have formed a legally binding agreement.

## ■ SQE ASSESSMENT ADVICE

As you work through this chapter, remember to pay particular attention in your revision to:
- The rule that consideration must be sufficient, but does not need to be adequate and cannot be past.
- Exchange as a key aspect of consideration.
- The general approach that performing an existing contractual or legal duty is not consideration.
- The different rules that apply to consideration in respect of promises to pay more and promises to pay less.
- The defence of promissory estoppel in scenarios where there is no consideration.

## ■ WHAT DO YOU KNOW ALREADY?

Have a go at these questions before reading this chapter. If you find some difficult or cannot remember the answers, make a note to look more closely at that area during your revision.

1) What does consideration mean in the context of English law?
   [Introduction to consideration, page 28]
2) Why is consideration important in the context of English law?
   [Introduction to consideration, page 28]
3) True or false? An act followed by a promise is consideration.
   [Consideration must not be past, page 30]
4) Does consideration need to reflect the economic value of the goods or services for which it is given?
   [Consideration must be sufficient but does not need to be adequate, page 28]
5) True or false? Promissory estoppel provides a defence to a party who has relied on an amendment to an agreement that lacks consideration.
   [Promissory estoppel, page 36]

## INTRODUCTION TO CONSIDERATION

For the SQE1 assessment, you will be required to demonstrate that you understand the importance of **consideration** as one of the four requirements to make a contract legally binding.

> **Key term: consideration**
>
> Consideration is an act, or promise, of value *in exchange* for an act, or promise, of value.

In this chapter, we will talk about the person who makes a promise (the **promisor**), and the person to whom the promise is made (the **promisee**). In most contracts each party is both the promisor and the promisee. For example, if Andrew agrees to buy John's gooseberries for £2 per kilo, Andrew is the promisor because he has promised to pay John £2 per kilo. Andrew is also the promisee because he is the person to whom John has promised to deliver the gooseberries in exchange for £2 per kilo. Similarly, John is both the promisor (in respect of his promise to deliver gooseberries) and the promisee (in respect of Andrew's promise to pay him £2 per kilo). When you seek to identify consideration, be careful to analyse whether each party is getting consideration *in exchange* for their promise. It is this consideration that makes the promise binding. Another key point to bear in mind is that the law classifies a promise as consideration even though neither the gooseberries nor the money have been exchanged. This is because *the exchange of promises makes each party liable to the other to deliver what has been promised*.

> **Key term: promisor**
>
> The party to a contract who makes a promise to the other party.

> **Key term: promisee**
>
> The party to a contract to whom a promise is made (by the promisor).

We will now explore the key features of consideration, including the rule that consideration must be **sufficient**, but it does not need to be **adequate**; and the requirement that consideration must not be past.

## Consideration must be sufficient but does not need to be adequate

Many of us will have heard the expression peppercorn rent. This reflects the position under English law that consideration does not need to be adequate. This means that the economic or monetary value of consideration provided under a contract does not need to match the value of what the other party promises to do or deliver in return. So, literally, a landlord can agree to rent a flat to a person in exchange for the tenant giving them a peppercorn. This peppercorn is consideration, *provided* it is what the landlord asked for in exchange for the flat. In other words, provided the landlord asked for a peppercorn in exchange for the flat, the consideration will be sufficient.

### Key term: adequate

Consideration does not need to be adequate. This means that there is no requirement for consideration to reflect the economic or monetary value of what is provided in exchange.

### Key term: sufficient

Consideration is sufficient provided it is what the promisor requested in exchange for this promise.

Now put your knowledge to the test and attempt **Practice example 2.1**.

### Practice example 2.1

Corinne sells her diamond ring to a pawnbroker in exchange for £5. The next day, Corinne changes her mind and asks the pawnbroker to return the diamond ring. Corinne explains that because the ring is worth much more than £5, the consideration that the pawnbroker paid does not count, and therefore the agreement is not legally binding.

Can Corinne force the pawnbroker to return the ring on the grounds that her contract with the pawnbroker is not legally binding because it lacks consideration?

**The answer is no. This is because English contract law is not concerned with whether the consideration is adequate. English law is concerned with whether the consideration is sufficient. The general position is that if what is provided is what the promisee asked for (or agreed to accept), then it is sufficient, and is therefore consideration to make the promise binding.**

> **Exam warning**
>
> When the price paid for something is less than its economic value, remember to check whether the price paid is what the other party requested. In general, so long as what is given is what the other party requested, it will be consideration because it will be sufficient.

## Consideration must not be past

In cases where an act is followed by a promise, the law considers that nothing is given *in exchange* for the promise; so the act is not consideration. This is known as **past consideration**.

> **Key term: past consideration**
>
> If an act is carried out before a promise is made, this is not consideration and does not make a promise binding.

> **Revision tip**
>
> When you answer SQE1 assessments on consideration, remember the importance of *exchange* as a feature of consideration. In particular, watch out for scenarios where one person performs an act (finding a dog, for example), and then another person promises something in return (a reward, for example). Past consideration is *not* effective to make the promise legally binding.

Test your ability to apply this principle in **Practice example 2.2**.

> **Practice example 2.2**
>
> Daniel finds an escaped cow in the village and takes it to Lynn, who owns the local farm. Lynn is very happy that Daniel has returned his lost cow and tells Daniel that she'll pay him £20 as a thank you. A few weeks pass and Lynn has still not paid Daniel his reward.
>
> Is Daniel able to sue Lynn for the £20 on the grounds of a legally binding contract?
>
> **The answer is no. The English law position is that Daniel has not provided any act in exchange for Lynn's promise. Daniel performed the act *before* Lynn made a promise to pay him £20. This lack of exchange between the parties means that the agreement is void for lack of consideration.**

## *The past consideration rule does not apply when the previous request device applies*

The past consideration rule does not apply when there is an understanding between the parties that the actions of one party will be paid for, and the exact amount will be fixed at a later date. This exception is called the 'previous request' device. It applies when a person performs an act at the request of another person and it is understood that the performance of the act is in exchange for payment or benefit. When these criteria are satisfied, provided the promise would have been enforceable if it had been made before or at the time of the request, then the act performed before the promise is consideration. See **Practice example 2.3** for an illustration of this.

---

**Practice example 2.3**

In 2018 Areeba asked John, who owned a marketing consultancy, to help her to market a vegan drink (Water Milk). John worked on marketing Water Milk for two years so that the brand became valuable. In 2020, Areeba signed an agreement with John in which she gave John 30% ownership of the Water Milk brand. Areeba died shortly afterwards and Areeba's husband failed to honour the agreement on the basis that John's consideration was past consideration so the agreement was not legally binding.

Is John's contract legally binding?

**The answer is yes because the criteria for the previous request device are satisfied. John performed the act at Areeba's request. In addition, John and Areeba were interacting in a commercial context where it is usual to be paid for such activity. These factors strongly suggest that both parties understood that John would be paid for his work.**

---

We will now consider situations in which a person does what they are already bound to do by contract or law.

# THE PERFORMANCE OF EXISTING DUTIES AND CONSIDERATION

If a person does what they are *already* bound to do by contract or law, this is *not* consideration because there is no element of exchange.

## The performance of a duty imposed by law is not consideration

As a general rule, if a person does what they are required to do by law, then this is not consideration. So, for example, if Laila promises Nelson that she will give evidence at a trial in exchange for £1,000 when Laila is already required by law to give evidence at the trial, then Laila's act of giving evidence at the trial is not consideration for Nelson's promise to pay her £1,000. But if a person does more than they are required to do by law, then the promise, act or omission that exceeds the legal requirement can be consideration. So, if the police, at the request of a business owner, provided additional security, at a level greater than they are legally required to provide, this additional security is consideration for a business owner's promise to pay them.

## The performance of an existing contractual duty owed to a third party is consideration

Assume that you are contractually bound to repay a loan to a bank (Big Bank). Another bank (Finance Bank) agrees to make a loan to you provided you repay your loan to Big Bank. In terms of your relations with Finance Bank, Big Bank is a third party. Although you are already contractually bound to repay the loan to Big Bank, English law recognises the repayment of the loan to Big Bank as consideration for Finance Bank's promise to make a loan to you *because* Big Bank is a third party to your relationship with Finance Bank.

## The performance of an existing contractual duty is not consideration as a general rule

The starting point is that when a contract is amended, new consideration *must* be provided to make the promisor's agreement legally binding, unless the contract is a deed and consideration is not required. For your SQE1 assessment and as a practicing lawyer, it is critical that you understand what promises, acts or omissions can be consideration for a contractual amendment.

### *A promise to pay more for the performance of an existing contractual duty owed to a promisor*

The general approach is that if the parties to a contract agree that one party will pay more than was agreed under the original contract, the promise to pay more is not binding *unless* the promisee makes an *additional* promise, act or omission as consideration. Without this, the element of exchange is missing because the promisee is doing nothing more than they were contractually bound to do under the original contract.

The performance of existing duties and consideration    33

Practice example 2.4 provides an illustration of this principle.

> **Practice example 2.4**
>
> Sinbad is a crew member on a sea voyage from Southampton to Jamaica. When the boat reaches Jamaica, two of the other crew members resign their positions, but the remaining crew is experienced and the work that the crew must carry out on the return journey to Southampton is the same as it was before the two crew members resigned. Sinbad tells the ship's captain that he will only make the journey back to Southampton if the captain pays him a 50% bonus and the captain agrees. When they reach Southampton, Sinbad asks the captain to pay him the 50% bonus, but the captain refuses.
>
> Can Sinbad sue the captain for his bonus on the basis that by working the return journey to Southampton, Sinbad provided consideration to make the captain's promise binding?
>
> **The answer is no. Sinbad has only done what he was contractually obliged to do under the original contract. So English law considers that he has not provided any consideration to make the captain's promise of a bonus binding.**

*An amendment to a contract in which a promisor promises additional money for something additional is consideration*
Remember that if the promisor under an existing contract promises to pay the promisee an additional amount *in exchange for an additional* promise, act or omission, then this *additional* promise, act or omission *is* consideration. This is because a key element of consideration is exchange, and this additional promise, act or omission *in exchange for* additional money will satisfy this requirement. In **Practice example 2.4**, Sinbad did not provide any additional consideration. However, if a significantly larger number of crew members had resigned and this had resulted in Sinbad and the remaining crew having to work significantly harder on the return journey then their additional work *would* constitute consideration and the captain's promise to pay the 50% bonus would be legally binding.

*A promise to pay more under an existing contract and practical benefit*
When analysing scenarios based on amendments to contracts to pay more, there is an additional test that you must apply. Does the promisor obtain a **practical benefit** as a result of making the promise to pay more? If they do, this practical benefit is consideration and makes the promise

legally binding. Note carefully that if the promisor agrees to pay more only as a result of pressure or threats from the promisee that gives them no choice, this will amount to duress and the promise will not be binding.

### Key term: practical benefit

Practical benefit describes any factual benefit that the promisor receives as a result of promising to pay more under an amendment agreement than was agreed under the original agreement.

Practice example 2.5 illustrates how this might arise in practice.

### Practice example 2.5

Joanna runs a property refurbishment company and has won a contract to refurbish a block of flats owned by Nicola. The contract between Joanna and Nicola contains a damages clause stating that Joanna must pay damages to Nicola if the refurbishment runs behind schedule. Joanna engages Ruth as a sub-contractor to do the carpentry part of the refurbishment. Ruth runs into difficulties that threaten to delay the completion of her part of the refurbishment, and Joanna is worried that this will delay her completion of the overall project. So Joanna offers to pay Ruth more to finish the job on time. Ruth accepts the offer and as a result of the promise of extra money she focuses on her carpentry job and finishes her work on time. This allows Joanna to complete the overall project on time and so she avoids having to pay damages to Nicola.

Is Joanna bound by her agreement to pay Ruth more?

**The answer is yes. The fact that Joanna avoided paying the penalty to Nicola as a result of making the promise is a practical benefit for Joanna. English law regards this practical benefit as consideration in respect of promises to pay more. So Joanna's promise to pay Ruth more than was agreed in the original contract is legally binding.**

### Revision tip

Remember that the starting point for agreement amendments to pay more than was initially agreed is that they are not enforceable due to lack of consideration *unless*:
- the promisee provides consideration by doing more than was initially agreed; or
- the promisor obtains a practical benefit as a result of making the promise.

## A promise to pay less under an existing contract

English law treats promises to pay less than is owed under an existing contract differently from promises to pay more. If a creditor agrees to accept less than they are owed under an existing contract, the payment by a debtor of this lesser amount is not consideration. This is always the rule *even if* the creditor obtains a practical benefit as a result of the debtor paying this lesser amount. See **Practice example 2.6**.

> **Practice example 2.6**
>
> Amir is an electrician and does some electrical work for Shakira at a cost of £100. Shakira is having cash flow problems and so she asks if Amir will accept £80 instead of £100. Amir agrees to accept £80 instead of £100, but then finds that he has cash flow problems too.
>
> Can Amir go back on this promise and sue Shakira for the balance of £20?
>
> **The answer is yes. By paying less than she owes Amir, Shakira has not provided any consideration to make her agreement legally binding. This is true even if Amir (as promisor) obtains a practical benefit, such as not needing to sue Shakira for the money she owes him.**

Note that there are some exceptions to this general rule. For instance, if Amir had asked Shakira to pay the £80 to satisfy the debt of £100 *before* it was due, or *in a different place* than was initially agreed (for example, directly into Amir's bank account), the position is different. Payment before it is due or in a different place from what was originally agreed *is* consideration, *provided* it is made at the creditor's request. In addition, if Amir accepted Shakira's handbag instead of the money debt, this would be consideration.

There are two further exceptions to the rule. The first is if Shakira cannot afford to pay all her debts and agrees with *all* of her creditors to pay a percentage (for example, 80%) of the debt she owes them, then Shakira's payment of 80% of her debts to all of her creditors is consideration. The second exception is if the payment of £80 is made to Amir by a third party, for example, by Shakira's sister. In both cases, Amir's agreement to accept these amounts would bind him and he would not be able to claim the shortfall.

> **Exam warning**
>
> In the SQE1 assessments, if a scenario concerns an agreement to amend the payment amount under an existing agreement, make sure that you carefully identify whether the amendment is concerned with paying *more* than was initially agreed or *less* than was initially agreed. Different rules apply depending on whether the amendment is to pay more or less, and you need to make sure that you apply the correct rules.

As we have seen, a promise to pay less than is originally agreed is generally not consideration. However, it is important to note that even if an agreement is not legally binding due to lack of consideration, promissory estoppel may prevent the promisor from going back on their promise to accept a lower amount. This is explored below.

## PROMISSORY ESTOPPEL

For contract amendments where no consideration can be identified, a key issue to explore is whether **promissory estoppel** applies. Promissory estoppel provides a defence for a promisee against a claim from a promisor who has agreed to accept a lesser amount than was originally agreed. This is likely to be tested in the SQE1 assessments.

> **Key term: promissory estoppel**
>
> Promissory estoppel is a doctrine that provides a defence to a debtor to stop a creditor from going back on their promise to accept a smaller amount than is owed under the original agreement.

**Table 2.1** outlines the criteria that need to be satisfied in order for promissory estoppel to apply.

*Table 2.1: Criteria that must be satisfied for promissory estoppel to apply*

| Criterion | Example |
| --- | --- |
| There must be a clear and unambiguous promise from the promisor that they will not enforce their rights under the contract. | Fred tells Caroline that he will not charge her rent for her shop for the month of July 2022 because of the financial instability connected with COVID-19. |
| Promissory estoppel applies to amendments to contracts, not formation contracts. | If Caroline has been renting the shop since January 2022, then Fred's agreement with Caroline is an amendment to the agreement that was made in January 2022. |

*Criteria that must be satisfied for promissory estoppel to apply (continued)*

| Criterion | Example |
|---|---|
| The promisee must have relied on the promise. | As a result of Fred's statement Caroline decides to keep renting the shop and not to bother looking for a cheaper shop to rent. |
| It must be inequitable (unfair) for the promisor to go back on their promise. | On the basis that Caroline continues to rent the shop and incurs liability to pay for all months other than July 2022, it is inequitable (unfair) for Fred to go back on his word.<br><br>If Caroline had threatened Fred, saying that if he did not agree to let her off her rent for July 2022 she would spread negative publicity about his business, then English law classifies this threat as duress. The effect of duress is that Fred is not bound by his promise to Caroline because it would be equitable (fair) to allow Fred to go back on his agreement. |

The rights provided by promissory estoppel are more limited than under a fully legally binding contract. Promissory estoppel simply prevents the promisor from going back on their promise not to enforce their rights under the contract. This is the reason why promissory estoppel is often described as a shield (for defence) but not a sword (for attack).

Now put your knowledge to the test with **Practice example 2.7**.

### Practice example 2.7

Central Properties leases a block of flats in London to Woodland Properties in November 2019. Woodland Properties agrees to pay Central Properties £10,000 per flat per year. There are over 100 flats in the block and Woodland Properties plans to rent out all the flats to the public for profit. In March 2020, many people leave London because of the COVID-19 pandemic; this means that Woodland Properties is unable to find people to rent the flats. Woodland Properties explains the problem to Central Properties and Central Properties agrees to reduce the charge per flat to £5,000 per flat. By June 2021, people are returning to London and Woodland Properties has managed to find tenants to rent all the flats, so Central Properties and Woodland Properties agree that the annual rent per flat will return to £10,000 from June 2021. In addition, Central Properties demands that Woodland Properties pay the full rent of £10,000 per flat per year for the period from March 2020 until June 2021.

Is Woodland Properties bound to pay the amount to Central Properties for the period when the flats were empty?

The answer is no. Despite the lack of consideration to make Central Properties' promise to accept less rent legally binding, promissory estoppel will prevent Central Properties from going back on its agreement. This is because the promissory estoppel criteria are satisfied; there is a clear and unambiguous promise from Central Properties that it will not enforce its rights under the contract; the contract is an amendment to an existing contract; Woodland Properties relied on Central Properties' statement; and it appears to be inequitable (unfair) for Central Properties to go back on its word.

### Exam warning

Where a scenario concerns an amendment agreement that is not legally binding due to lack of consideration, always consider whether promissory estoppel can provide the promisee with a defence.
**Table 2.1** summarises the criteria for promissory estoppel.

## ■ KEY POINT CHECKLIST

This chapter has covered the following key knowledge points. You can use these to structure your revision around, making sure to recall the key details for each point, as covered in this chapter.

- Consideration is one of the four elements required to make a legally binding contract. It is required for all contracts, except for deeds.
- Consideration is generally a promise of an act or omission, or an act or omission in exchange for the same.
- Consideration must be sufficient, but it does not need to be adequate. It does not need to be the monetary or economic equivalent of what is given in exchange, but it *must* be what the party receiving it *requires*.
- Consideration must not be past: exchange is a key element of consideration. This means that an act that is followed by a promise lacks the vital element of exchange and is not consideration. This rule does not apply if the previous request device applies.
- The performance of a legal duty is not consideration: if a person does what they are already obliged to do by law, this act is not consideration.

- If a person performs a duty that they are already obliged to perform to a third party, this act is consideration for a separate contract.
- The general principle is that when a promisor agrees to pay a party more than was agreed in the original contract, the performance of the existing contractual duty by the promisee is not consideration. But note the exceptions to the general position.
- Paying less than was originally agreed is not consideration, but note the exceptions that apply when the terms are varied in other ways.
- In cases where there is no consideration, check carefully whether the criteria of promissory estoppel are satisfied. If promissory estoppel applies, it will provide a defence for the promisee against an attempt by the promisor to go back on their word.

## ■ KEY TERMS AND CONCEPTS

- consideration (**page 28**)
- promisor (**page 28**)
- promisee (**page 28**)
- adequate (**page 29**)
- sufficient (**page 29**)
- past consideration (**page 30**)
- practical benefit (**page 34**)
- promissory estoppel (**page 36**)

## ■ SQE1-STYLE QUESTIONS

### QUESTION 1

An artist agrees on Monday to sell a painting to a woman for a basket of apples, with delivery of the painting and payment in apples to be made on Friday. On Tuesday, the artist receives an offer of £200 for the same painting from a man. Later on Tuesday, the artist tells the women that he no longer wishes to sell the painting to her because he was mistaken about the value of the painting.

**Which of the following best describes the artist's situation?**

A. The artist is bound by his agreement to sell the painting to the woman because sufficient consideration has been promised.

B. The artist is not bound by his agreement to sell the painting to the woman because the consideration is not adequate.

C. The artist is not bound by his agreement to sell the painting to the woman because she has not provided any consideration to make the agreement legally binding.
D. The artist is bound by his agreement to sell the painting to the woman on the basis of promissory estoppel.
E. The artist is not bound by his promise to sell the painting to the woman because the consideration is not effective until the apples have been delivered.

## QUESTION 2

A woman offers to help a man with work in the garden centre. After the woman has worked all day in the garden centre, the man tells her that he will pay her £100 for her work. The man never pays the woman £100.

**Which of the following best describes the legal position in this case?**

A. The man is bound by his promise to the woman as she provided consideration by working in the garden centre.
B. The man is not bound by his promise to the woman because the woman's work in the garden centre is past consideration.
C. The man is not bound by his promise to the woman because £100 for a day's work in the garden centre is not adequate.
D. The man is bound by his promise to the woman, provided the woman can show that she relied on the man's promise.
E. The man is bound by his promise to the woman because the practical benefit that he gained as a result of the woman's work is consideration to make the promise binding.

## QUESTION 3

A woman commissions a man to refit the bathrooms in a hotel that she is refurbishing under a contract that pays the man £2,000 per bathroom refit. The woman is responsible for all other aspects of the refurbishment, but she will be liable to pay damages to the owner of the hotel if any aspect of the refurbishment (including the refit of the bathrooms) is not complete before the deadline. The man who is refitting the bathrooms is running behind schedule because he is concerned about his financial situation. As a result, the woman offers the man an additional £500 per bathroom refit. The man is able to focus on this work, refits the bathrooms on time, and the woman finishes her refurbishment of the hotel on time and avoids paying damages to the hotel owner.

Which of the following best describes the woman's position with regard to her promise to pay the man an additional £500 per bathroom refit?

A. The woman is not bound by her promise to pay the additional amount because the man's performance of his existing contractual duty is not consideration to make the amendment to the original contract binding.

B. The woman is not bound by her promise to pay the additional amount to the man because she only offered to pay the man an additional amount under duress, and duress renders the contract voidable.

C. The woman is bound by her promise to pay the additional amount to the man because she received a practical benefit as a result of the additional payment because the man finished his work on time, meaning the woman avoided paying damages to the hotel owner for the late completion of the hotel refurbishment.

D. The woman is bound by her promise to pay the additional amount on the basis of promissory estoppel.

E. The woman is bound by her promise to pay the additional amount because the man's performance of his existing contractual duty amounts to the performance of an existing contractual duty owed to a third party and English law treats this as consideration.

## QUESTION 4

A man owes a woman £10,000 and it is due for payment. The man tells the woman that it will be difficult for him to repay £10,000 and he asks the woman to accept £8,000 in full and final settlement of the £10,000 that he owes her. The woman tells the man that she agrees to accept £8,000 in full and final settlement of the £10,000 that the man owes her. The man pays the woman £8,000. The woman later regrets her decision and is considering suing the man for the deficit of £2,000.

**Is the woman able to sue the man for the £2,000 deficit?**

A. No, the woman has agreed to accept £8,000 in full and final settlement of the claim and the man's payment of £8,000 is consideration to make the woman's promise binding.

B. No, the woman has received a practical benefit as a result of the man voluntarily paying her the £8,000. Practical benefit is consideration and makes a promise binding.

C. Yes, the woman can sue the man for the £2,000 on the grounds that the man provided no consideration for the woman's agreement to accept less than the full amount.

D. Yes, the woman can sue the man for the £2,000 on the grounds that the man put the woman under duress to accept the lesser amount.
E. No, the woman cannot sue the man for the £2,000 on the grounds that she agreed to accept £8,000, and consideration does not need to be adequate, provided it is sufficient.

## QUESTION 5

A woman takes out a lease on a small hotel for £100,000 per year. But within two years, the woman faces financial difficulties because she has no guests as a result of lockdowns related to a global outbreak of bubonic plague. The owner of the hotel and the woman agree that she can reduce her annual rent for the hotel to £50,000. The woman continues to rent the hotel. Six months after the hotel owner and the woman agree on the reduced rent, the hotel owner is short of cash and wonders if he is bound by his agreement with the woman.

**Which of the following best describes the options available to the hotel owner?**

A. The hotel owner can sue the woman for the full amount of rent because the woman did not provide any consideration for the reduction in rent.
B. The hotel owner cannot sue the woman for the full amount of rent because the agreement is binding on the basis of the practical benefit that the hotel owner received as a result of the woman continuing to rent the hotel.
C. The hotel owner can sue the woman for the full amount of rent because a rental payment of £50,000 in place of £100,000 is not adequate.
D. The hotel owner cannot sue the woman for the full amount of rent because of the doctrine of promissory estoppel.
E. The hotel owner cannot sue the woman for the full amount of rent because the woman has provided consideration that is sufficient.

## ■ ANSWERS TO QUESTIONS

### Answers to 'What do you know already?' questions at the start of the chapter

1) A promise, an act or an omission *in exchange* for a promise, an act or an omission.

2) Consideration is an essential requirement to make a contract legally binding for all contracts other than deeds.
3) False. An act followed by a promise is past consideration, not consideration.
4) Consideration does not need to reflect the economic value of goods or services for which it is given.
5) True. Promissory estoppel applies to an amendment agreement if one party has promised not to exercise certain rights and then goes back on their word. Promissory estoppel is a defence to prevent the promisor from exercising the rights that they have promised not to exercise. Promissory estoppel only applies if the applicable criteria are satisfied.

## Answers to end-of-chapter SQE1-style questions

Question 1:
   The correct answer was A. This is because sufficient consideration has been promised. Remember that even though the artist and the woman have only made promises to each other, an exchange of promises is consideration because each promisor makes themselves liable to be sued if they do not deliver what is promised. Option B is incorrect because consideration does not need to be adequate (the economic equivalent of what it is exchanged for). Option C is incorrect because the woman's promise to deliver a basket of apples *is* consideration because the woman can be sued for failing to deliver on her promise. Option D is incorrect because promissory estoppel only applies to amendment agreements to pay less, so it is not relevant here. Option E is incorrect because the artist and the woman have exchanged promises, which makes each party liable to deliver what is promised to the other.

Question 2:
   The correct answer was B. This is because an act followed by a promise is past consideration. Past consideration is not consideration and does not make a promise legally binding. Option A is incorrect because the woman did not provide consideration for the promise. As her act was performed before the promise, exchange as a key element of consideration is missing. Option C is incorrect because consideration does not need to be adequate. Option D is incorrect because reliance is not relevant to the existence of consideration, reliance is a key aspect of promissory estoppel, which is not relevant to this scenario. Option E is incorrect because practical benefit as

consideration applies to amendment promises to pay more, which is not relevant to this scenario.

Question 3:
The correct answer was C. This is because practical benefit is consideration in respect of amendments to existing contracts to pay more. It is also for this reason that option A cannot be correct. Option B is incorrect because there is no evidence of duress to force the woman to offer the man more money. Option D is incorrect because promissory estoppel only applies to amendment promises not to enforce rights, so it is not relevant in this scenario. Option E does not apply because the contract is between the man and the woman. The man does not owe a duty to a third party.

Question 4:
The correct answer was C. This is because the payment of a lesser amount than is owed under an original contract is not consideration. Option A is incorrect for the same reason. Option B is incorrect because English law does not recognise practical benefit as consideration for promises to pay less. Option D is incorrect because there is no evidence of a threat or pressure, which is a key element of duress. Option E is incorrect because the acceptance of less than is owed under a contract does not constitute consideration.

Question 5:
The correct answer was D. Promissory estoppel is a defence in respect of amendment agreements against a promisor who agrees to accept less than they are owed and then tries to go back on their word.
The applicable criteria are satisfied by the clear and unambiguous promise from the hotel owner that he will not enforce his rights under the contract, by the reliance of the woman in continuing to rent the hotel, and by the fact that it would be inequitable (unfair) for the promisor to go back on his word. Option A is incorrect: although it is correct to recognise that there is no consideration, a lack of consideration is precisely the scenario in which promissory estoppel applies as a defence. Option B is incorrect because practical benefit as consideration only applies in respect of promises to pay more, rather than promises to pay less. Option C is incorrect because consideration does not need to be adequate. Option E is incorrect: paying less than originally agreed is not consideration.

## ■ KEY CASES, RULES, STATUTES AND INSTRUMENTS

The SQE1 Assessment Specification does not require you to know any case names, or statutory materials, for this topic.

# 3

# The intention to create legal relations, certainty and capacity

## ■ MAKE SURE YOU KNOW

This chapter explores the topics of the intention to create legal relations, certainty and capacity.

The intention to create legal relations is one of the four key requirements to make a contract legally binding and it is required for all contracts. We have already considered the first three requirements (offer and acceptance in **Chapter 1**, and consideration in **Chapter 2**). For the SQE1 assessments, you are required to know the law in relation to the intention to create relations, as well as the principles required to determine whether an agreement is certain enough to be legally enforceable. You also need to know the rules concerning legal capacity so that you can determine whether a person is legally bound by an agreement.

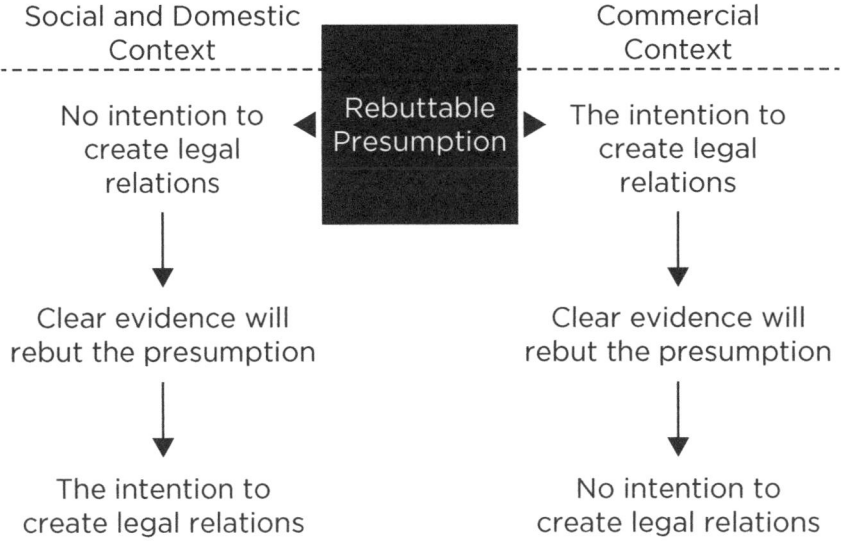

## ■ SQE ASSESSMENT ADVICE

As you work through this chapter, remember to pay particular attention in your revision to:
- The social and domestic context, and the commercial context, and the respective rebuttable presumptions that apply in respect of the intention to create legal relations.
- The factors that rebut the respective rebuttable presumptions.
- The certainty of the agreement.
- The capacity of the parties.

## ■ WHAT DO YOU KNOW ALREADY?

Have a go at these questions before reading this chapter. If you find some difficult or cannot remember the answers, make a note to look more closely at that area during your revision.

1) True or false? The rebuttable presumption in the social and domestic context is that there is an intention to create legal relations.
   [The rebuttable presumption in the social and domestic context, page 47]
2) True or false? The rebuttable presumption in the commercial context is that there is no intention to create legal relations.
   [The rebuttable presumption in the commercial context, page 50]
3) What is the effect of uncertainty on the enforceability of a contract?
   [Certainty, page 52]
4) What does 'capacity' mean in respect of a party to a contract?
   [Capacity, page 54]
5) What is a 'minor' and why is it relevant when we are asked to analyse whether a party is bound by a contract?
   [Contracts with minors, page 55]

## INTRODUCTION TO THE INTENTION TO CREATE LEGAL RELATIONS

**The intention to create legal relations** is a key requirement for a legally binding agreement. It means that the parties to a contract have the intention to be *legally* bound by the agreement.

Introduction to the intention to create legal relations 47

In everyday life people make agreements. For example, to meet a friend for a coffee, or to go to the cinema. But generally, the people who make such agreements only intend to be *morally* bound, rather than *legally* bound (they do not intend to be liable if they fail to keep their agreement). By contrast, where a businesswoman agrees to deliver 10,000 suits of protective equipment to a hospital for £10,000, the general expectation is that both parties have the intention to create legal relations so that either party can sue the other for failure to perform the relevant obligations.

> **Key term: the intention to create legal relations**
> This is the intention to be *legally* bound by the agreement.

The existence of the intention to create legal relations is determined *objectively* by applying the relevant **rebuttable presumption**.

> **Key term: rebuttable presumption**
> A rebuttable presumption is the default position under English law as to whether or not the parties to an agreement had the intention to create legal relations.

There are two different rebuttable presumptions:
- In the social and domestic context, there is a rebuttable presumption that parties to an agreement do not have the intention to create legal relations.
- In the commercial context, there is a rebuttable presumption that parties to an agreement have the intention to create legal relations.

Each presumption can be overturned (*rebutted*) by clear evidence.

## The rebuttable presumption in the social and domestic context

The social and domestic context describes interactions between a husband and wife, other close family members, relatives and friends. It can also apply to friends or flatmates in a close social setting. The applicable rebuttable presumption in the social and domestic context is that the parties *do not* have the intention to create legal relations.

However, the presumption can be rebutted by clear evidence drawn from the factors below:
- the terms of the agreement are certain
- the parties are not on friendly terms when they make the agreement
- the agreement is serious
- one party has relied on the agreement to their detriment.

Each factor is explained in more detail in **Table 3.1**.

*Table 3.1: Important factors to rebut the presumption of no intention to create legal relations in the social and domestic context*

| Factors | Explanation | Example |
|---|---|---|
| Certainty of agreement | A key issue to consider is whether an agreement is certain (for example, are each person's obligations clear?). The courts interpret lack of certainty as evidence that the parties did not intend to create legal relations. Where an agreement is uncertain, it is unlikely to rebut the presumption. | A father agrees to pay his son £15 per week for as long as he can. In this scenario, the obligation to pay for 'as long as he can' is uncertain. The law interprets this lack of certainty as evidence that the father and son lacked the intention to create legal relations, so the agreement would not be legally binding. |
| The parties are not on friendly terms when the agreement is made | Generally, the law presumes that family members and close friends do not intend to create legal relations when they make agreements. However, this presumption may be rebutted if the parties are not on friendly terms when the agreement was made. | A married couple are separating. Spouse A agrees to pay spouse B £2,000 a month. They agree that the mortgage payments must be paid from the £2,000 and, when the mortgage is paid off, the property will be transferred to spouse B. The fact that the agreement was made when the parties were separating illustrates that the couple did not have friendly relations when the agreement was made. This would be likely to rebut the presumption. |

*Important factors to rebut the presumption of no intention to create legal relations in the social and domestic context (continued)*

| Factors | Explanation | Example |
|---|---|---|
| The agreement is serious | The presumption of no intention to create legal relations when spouses or partners are living together on friendly terms is not absolute. If the agreement in question is sufficiently serious, this can rebut the presumption. | A couple are engaged to be married. Before they marry, they decide to make a prenuptial agreement that sets out how their assets will be divided should their relationship come to an end. Even though the couple are in a close relationship, living together and on friendly terms, the seriousness of the agreement rebuts the presumption. |
| One party has relied on the agreement to their detriment | If a party acts in reliance on the agreement to their detriment, this factor is evidence that the parties intended the agreement to be legally binding. | An elderly couple make an agreement with their niece. The agreement states that if the niece sells her home, moves in with the elderly couple and shares the household expenses (written in a detailed list), the elderly couple will leave a share of their property to the niece (the couple change their wills to provide for this). Once the niece moves in, she falls out with the couple and is forced to move out. The fact that the niece relied on the agreement to her detriment is a key factor to rebut the presumption. In addition, the fact that the agreement is certain and involves serious actions would also help to rebut the presumption. |

### Exam warning

In any SQE1 assessment on this topic, remember that you need to weigh up *all* of the factors *objectively* to decide whether they provide enough evidence to rebut the presumption. In addition, if an agreement lacks sufficient certainty, that can completely undermine the evidence of the other factors.

## The rebuttable presumption in the commercial context
- The rebuttable presumption in the commercial context is that the parties have the intention to create legal relations. References to the commercial context generally describe the world of business where people and companies seek to make money from the contracts that they make. The rebuttable presumption in this context means that parties who make agreements are bound by them, *unless* they can rebut the presumption.

The presumption can be rebutted with clear evidence of:
- clear words that the agreement shall not have legal effect
- uncertainty in the agreement terms.

See **Table 3.2** for more detail.

*Table 3.2: Evidence to rebut the presumption in the commercial context*

| Evidence to rebut the presumption | Explanation |
| --- | --- |
| Clear words that the agreement shall not have legal effect | If an agreement between parties contains a statement making it clear that the parties do not intend the agreement to have contractual effect, but only rely on each other's honour (for example, 'Binding in honour only'), this will rebut the presumption. Other examples of such words include 'Subject to contract' or 'This document is not and shall not be construed as a legally binding agreement'. |
| Uncertainty in the agreement terms | If the terms of an agreement are so uncertain that it is not clear how the parties should perform their respective obligations under the contract, the courts interpret this as evidence to rebut the presumption of the intention to create legal relations. |

## The names of documents in the commercial context
When analysing certain agreements or communications in the commercial context, you may be tempted to draw a conclusion based on the name of the agreement or communication. Be careful to test your initial conclusion by analysing any specific wording to determine whether or not it has legal effect. Two key examples of agreements and communications whose names are not conclusive as to whether they have legal effect are:
- comfort letters
- advertisements.

## Comfort letters

Comfort letters are used in the commercial context for various reasons and may or may not be legally binding. You need to look beyond the name of the document to determine its legal effect. In some cases, a comfort letter is provided to make a person feel more comfortable about a transaction, but it may be no more than a description of a party's current policy, rather than a promise or guarantee of what they will do in the future. A letter that is just a description of current policy will not be legally binding, whereas a comfort letter provided by an accountancy firm to confirm that the figures in an annual report are accurate will be. Take a look at **Practice example 3.1** for an illustration of this principle.

> **Practice example 3.1**
>
> Babyco is negotiating a loan with Nicebank. Nicebank asks Babyco's parent company (Mamaco) for a guarantee to support its loan to Babyco. Mamaco refuses to provide a guarantee, but agrees to write a comfort letter to Nicebank stating that its policy is that the business of its subsidiary Babyco is at all times in the position to meet its liabilities to Nicebank under the loan. Babyco's business collapses and it is unable to repay the loan.
>
> Can Nicebank claim against Mamaco on the grounds that it breached a promise to ensure that Babyco was at all times in a position to meet its liabilities to Nicebank?
>
> The answer is no. This scenario is based on the facts of *Kleinwort Benson Ltd v Malaysia Mining Corporation Bhd* [1989] 1 WLR 379. The Court of Appeal held that the statement in the letter was simply a statement of the parent company's policy at the time it signed the letter, not a promise as to its future conduct. So the court interpreted the wording as effective to rebut the presumption of the intention to create legal relations. The court also took into consideration the fact that the parent company refused to provide a guarantee.

## Advertisements

Advertisements are generally made in the commercial context. However, an advertisement that is obviously a gimmick or advertising puff, such as an aftershave that makes anyone who meets you fall madly in love with you, will not serve as evidence of the intention to be legally bound. However, evidence from the advertiser of an *intention* to perform the promise, such as providing holiday insurance, or depositing money into an account to serve as a reward, will serve as evidence of the intention to be legally bound to the person who acts in response to the advertisement.

> **Exam warning**
>
> In the SQE1 assessments, make sure that after you identify the context and the rebuttable presumption that applies, you check the scenario carefully to identify evidence that can rebut the applicable rebuttable presumption.

## CERTAINTY

It will be clear to you from the section above that if an agreement is too uncertain, it is not legally binding. The main reasons for an agreement being held as too uncertain are because:
- it is too vague
- it is not complete
- one or both of the parties to the agreement is mistaken (the topic of mistake will be dealt with separately in **Chapter 8, page 147**).

It is essential to note for the SQE1 assessment that the courts will not refuse to enforce every agreement that is vague or uncertain. The agreement needs to be *too* vague or *too* uncertain. This is because English law allows quite a high degree of contractual freedom; so if the contract is still certain enough to be performed, it will *not* be **void** for lack of certainty. You may be required to determine if an agreement is too uncertain to be legally binding on the grounds that it is too vague, or too incomplete.

> **Key term: void**
>
> The term 'void' means that an agreement has no legal effect.

### Agreements that are too vague

Let us image that Bernard agrees to sell textiles to Masha *in quantities and at prices that are in all the circumstances reasonable*. If neither Bernard nor Masha can supply evidence to support what the reasonable quantities and prices of the textiles are '*in all the circumstances*', then the agreement will be too vague to perform; and it will be void for lack of certainty.

However, in some situations a lack of certainty in respect of one term may not be too vague to perform. An example of this is an agreement that provides that any lack of clarity will be decided by an arbitrator. The effect of such a mechanism is that the parties to the agreement are obliged to ask an arbitrator to decide on the meaning of any term that is alleged to be too vague to perform. Only if the arbitrator fails to clarify the meaning of this vague term can a party to such an agreement successfully claim that the term is too vague to be performed. Alternatively, if, for example, an agreement is a framework for more than one transaction, and one or more transactions have been performed under the agreement, the courts will look at the terms of the transactions that have already been performed to see if they provide any evidence to clarify the meaning of the term that is unclear. Let us take a look at how this might work in **Practice example 3.2**.

> ### Practice example 3.2
>
> Jackie concludes an agreement with Attila to give Attila the option to buy 10,000 baskets of apples of *good quality* in 2018, and 80,000 baskets in 2019. In 2018 Attila exercises the first option and Jackie delivers Attila 10,000 baskets of apples. In 2019, Attila exercises the second option, but Jackie refuses to deliver the baskets of apples. Jackie argues that the term *baskets* for the 2019 option to buy 80,000 baskets is too vague to be enforceable.
>
> Can Attila sue Jackie to make her perform the 2019 option?
>
> **The answer is yes. It would be reasonable to imply the term of** *apples of good quality* **after the word** *basket* **so that the 2019 option is one to buy 80,000 baskets of apples of good quality.**

## Agreements where an essential term is missing

An agreement that is missing an essential term may be void due to lack of certainty. A key example of such an agreement is one where the price, quantity and other key matters have not been agreed by the parties. These agreements are often referred to as agreements to agree.

But note again the importance of performance. If the parties have already partially performed their obligations under the agreement (such as providing one delivery of oil under a framework agreement), then the terms of the transaction that have already been performed (such as one delivery of oil) may be applied to the transaction in respect of which a key term is missing. Further, the agreement is also unlikely to be held void for lack of certainty if it provides that the price (or other key term) will be determined by each party appointing a third party (such as a valuer or arbitrator).

> **Exam warning**
>
> When considering SQE1 scenarios that feature an agreement that seems to be too vague to be certain, check carefully if the scenario refers to any evidence that could be used to make the agreement certain enough to be enforceable. Examples of such evidence include previous transactions under the same agreement, objective evidence to clarify what an uncertain term means, and the option to appoint an independent third party to clarify any terms that are unclear.

## CAPACITY

In the SQE1 assessments, you may be required to determine whether a person has **capacity** to enter into a legally binding agreement. This is important because if a person lacks capacity, they may not be legally bound by the agreement.

> **Key term: capacity**
>
> The term 'capacity' describes a person's ability to enter into and be bound by an agreement.

We will consider the following issues in respect of capacity:
- mental incapacity
- intoxication
- the capacity of minors
- the capacity of companies.

### Mental incapacity

Two tests must be satisfied for a person to escape being bound by a legally binding agreement on the grounds of mental incapacity:
- the first is that a person must prove that they did not have mental capacity at the time they entered into the agreement; *and*
- the second is that a person must prove that the other party to the contract knew, or should have known, that this was the case.

If both tests are satisfied, it means the contract is **voidable**.

> **Key term: voidable**
>
> The term 'voidable' in respect of an agreement means that it is valid and binding, but can be set aside at the request of the party that has a remedy.

> **Revision tip**
>
> It is important to understand the difference between a contract that is void and a contract that is voidable. A contract that is void has no legal effect, whereas a contract that is voidable has legal effect until the party/parties choose to set it aside.

This area of law is governed by the Mental Capacity Act (MCA) 2005. Section 2(1) states that '*[a] person lacks capacity in relation to a matter if at the material time he is unable to make a decision for himself*'. Section 3(1) of the MCA 2005 clarifies that a person is unable to make a decision if they are unable to:
- understand the information relevant to the decision
- retain that information
- use or weigh that information as part of the process of making the decision, or
- communicate their decision (whether by talking, using sign language or any other means).

A person with mental incapacity may exercise the remedy to set the contract aside, which means that they will not be bound by the contract. But note the exception to this rule, which provides at s 7(2) that a person with mental incapacity must pay a reasonable price for goods and services that a person requires at the time they enter the agreement – the legal term for this is *necessaries*. The courts interpret *necessaries* as covering more than just the bare necessities. Check the full definition of necessaries, but note that if the person in question already has a good supply of the goods in question, they are unlikely to fall within the definition of necessaries.

### Intoxication or other mental incapacity

An agreement may also be voidable for a person who does not fall within the definition of the MCA 2005 but is nonetheless unable to understand the nature of their actions, or was intoxicated. For a person to set aside a contract as voidable, they will need to prove that the other party to the contract knew or ought to have known that they were intoxicated or otherwise unable to understand the nature of their actions at the relevant time. Note that the rule in respect of necessaries also applies.

### Contracts with minors

A minor is a person less than 18 years old. This area of law is governed by the Minors' Contracts Act 1987. An agreement with a minor is voidable but note that minors must pay a reasonable amount for necessaries (see also **Practice example 3.3**). A minor is, however, bound by agreements of employment, education and training, *unless* they lose more under the contract than they gain. In addition, the court may order the minor to return the goods they acquired under the contract to the other party if it is just and equitable to do so. If a person who has capacity (for example, a parent) guarantees the obligations of a minor, then the guarantor is bound by such agreement.

### Practice example 3.3

Joe is a minor. Vladimir, a shopkeeper, knows this. Joe enters a shop and buys 11 fancy waistcoats from Vladimir. Joe already has plenty of suitable clothes.

Is Joe legally bound to pay Vladimir for the fancy waistcoats on the basis that they are necessaries?

The answer is no. This example is based on the case of *Nash v Inman* [1908] 2 KB 1 CA. In this case, the evidence showed that the person with the incapacity already had plenty of suitable clothes so there was no evidence to show that the person required these clothes at the time.

### Exam warning

Remember that when analysing issues of capacity in respect of physical persons there are *two* tests that you must apply to determine whether a person with mental incapacity or who is intoxicated is bound. The first is the person must have mental incapacity or be intoxicated, and the second is that the other party to the contract must be aware of this mental incapacity or intoxication. In addition, remember that if the contract is voidable, the person who has the incapacity will still be bound to pay a reasonable amount for necessaries.

## Corporate capacity

Corporate organisations, such as companies, have the capacity to enter into, and be legally bound by, contracts. The constitutional documents of companies may contain provisions designed to limit the activities that a company carries out. But, if a party enters into an agreement with a company *in good faith*, the company will be bound by the agreement, even if the activity conflicts with a restriction in its constitutional documents.

## ■ KEY POINT CHECKLIST

This chapter has covered the following key knowledge points. You can use these to structure your revision, making sure to recall the key details for each point, as covered in this chapter.

- The intention to create legal relations is one of the four elements required to make a legally binding contract. It is required for all contracts.
- The social and domestic context describes interactions between spouses, partners, relatives and friends. There is a rebuttable presumption that there is no intention to create legal relations.
- The presumption in the social and domestic context can be rebutted if the parties are not on friendly terms when the agreement is made; if the agreement is serious; if the agreement is certain; and if one party has relied on the presumption to their detriment. Remember that the courts assess the collective weight of these factors.
- There is a rebuttable presumption in the commercial context that there is the intention to create legal relations.
- The presumption in the commercial context can be rebutted by clear words stating the agreement will not have legal effect; if the terms are so uncertain that it is not clear how the parties should perform their obligations; in specific documents such as comfort letters, especially if the letter states a present intention, rather than a promise; and in advertisements that are a gimmick. A high burden of proof is required to rebut the presumption.
- An agreement that is too uncertain to perform will be void. The lack of certainty can be due to vague or missing terms. Evidence of partial performance or mechanisms in the agreement, such as arbitration, to resolve the lack of certainty can *rescue* an agreement from lack of certainty.
- An agreement entered into by a person who lacks capacity is voidable. This remedy can be exercised by the person who lacked capacity, subject to the requirement to pay a reasonable price for necessaries. Additionally, a minor must return the goods acquired under the contract if it is just and equitable to do so.
- A company or limited liability partnership will generally be bound by an agreement with a third party acting in good faith, regardless of their capacity.

# ■ KEY TERMS AND CONCEPTS

- the intention to create legal relations (**page 47**)
- rebuttable presumption (**page 47**)
- void (**page 52**)
- capacity (**page 54**)
- voidable (**page 54**)

# ■ SQE1-STYLE QUESTIONS

### QUESTION 1

A man is about to marry a very wealthy woman. The man and the woman sign a prenuptial agreement that provides that the woman's assets shall remain the woman's assets after the man and the woman get married. The man and the woman get married, but a year later they have separated and file for divorce.

**Which of the following best describes the man's legal position towards the woman's assets under the prenuptial agreement?**

A. The man will be able to claim the assets covered by the prenuptial agreement. The prenuptial agreement is not legally binding because it was made in the social and domestic context.

B. The man will be able to claim the assets covered by the prenuptial agreement. The prenuptial agreement is not legally binding because it was made in the social and domestic context, and the fact that the woman and man were friendly at the time they made the agreement means that the presumption of no intention to create legal relations cannot be rebutted.

C. The man will not be able claim the woman's assets covered by the prenuptual agreement because prenuptual agreements are sufficiently serious to rebut the presumption of no intention to create legal relations.

D. The man will be able to claim the woman's assets because the subject matter of the prenuptial agreement is not sufficiently serious to rebut the presumption of no intention to create legal relations.

E. The man will not be able to claim the woman's assets because the rebuttable presumption in the social and domestic context only applies to a man and a woman who are married, and not to a man and a woman who are planning to get married.

## QUESTION 2

A mother is on friendly terms with her daughter and wants to motivate her to study law, so she promises that if her daughter gives up her job in New York and studies law in London she will pay her fees, give her an allowance and provide a house for her to live in. The daughter gives up her job in New York and moves to London and starts studying law. The mother pays her daughter's law school fees, buys a house for her daughter to live in, and pays her an allowance. After five years, the daughter is still studying and the mother seeks to reclaim possession of the house.

**Which one of the following statements best describes the legal position of the parties?**

A. The mother is bound by her agreement to let the daughter live in the house for as long as it takes the daughter to complete her legal studies.
B. The mother is not bound by her agreement to let the daughter live in the house.
C. The mother is bound by her agreement to let her daughter live in the house for a reasonable period of time.
D. The agreement between mother and daughter is voidable due to lack of certainty.
E. The mother is not bound by her agreement to let the daughter live in the house because she was on friendly terms with her daughter when they made the agreement. An agreement made between a mother and daughter on friendly terms will never rebut the presumption in the social and domestic context.

## QUESTION 3

An insurance company advertises a new insurance product in the offices of a large network of holiday companies. The advertisement states that any person booking a holiday with any member of the network of holiday companies will be covered for all claims by holiday insurance. A man sees this notice and books a holiday through a member of the network of holiday companies. The man's holiday is cancelled due to a national pandemic making all travel impossible.

## 60 The intention to create legal relations, certainty and capacity

Which of the following best describes the man's rights against the insurance company?

A. The man cannot claim against the insurance company because advertisements are an exception to rebuttable presumption in the commercial context and there is never an intention to create legal relations.
B. The man can claim against the insurance company because the advertisement of this kind is a promise of protection to anyone who books a holiday with a member of the network.
C. The man cannot claim against the insurance company because he booked his holiday with the holiday company, rather than with the insurance company.
D. The man can claim against the insurance company because the rebuttable presumption of the intention to create legal relations is practically impossible to rebut.
E. The man cannot claim against the insurance company as this is clearly a gimmick to drum up business and is not intended to create legal relations.

### QUESTION 4

A businesswoman agrees to sell her private zoo to a businessman. The price is agreed and the sale agreement is drawn up. But just before the parties sign the agreement, the businesswoman decides that she would like to be able to visit the animals in the zoo from time to time, so she asks if she can change the sale agreement. The businessman refuses this as he does not want to start amending an agreement that is in agreed form. As a result, the businessman and the businesswoman sign a separate document that provides for the businesswoman to be able to visit the animals in the zoo 'at times and subject to conditions to be agreed' by the businessman and the businesswoman.

Which of the following best describes the rights acquired by the woman under the separate document?

A. Given the lack of certainty in the letter, the woman has only the right to visit the animals in the zoo at reasonable times on weekdays.
B. The businesswoman has acquired the right to force the businessman to set out a schedule of visiting times and conditions for her.
C. The separate letter needs to be considered as a condition to the sale of the zoo so that if times and conditions for the businesswoman to

visit are not agreed, then the businesswoman can elect to set the whole transaction aside and sell the zoo to another party.
D. The businesswoman has acquired no rights under the separate document at all.
E. The businesswoman has acquired the right to force the businessman to negotiate with her in good faith.

## QUESTION 5

A 16-year-old schoolgirl goes on a shopping trip to a jewellery shop and buys a diamond tiara and a pearl necklace. The schoolgirl explains to the shop owner that she has left her credit cards at home but she promises to transfer funds to pay for the tiara and the necklace later that day. The schoolgirl fails to transfer the promised funds because she does not have them.

**Which of the following best describes the position of the shop owner?**

A. The shop owner can force the schoolgirl to pay a reasonable amount for the tiara and necklace on the grounds that they are necessaries.
B. The shop owner has no recourse against the schoolgirl because she is a minor.
C. The shop owner can petition the court to order the schoolgirl to return the tiara and necklace to him on the basis that it would be just and equitable to do so.
D. The shop owner can reclaim the goods from the schoolgirl on the basis that contracts with minors are void.
E. The shop owner is entitled to the return of the goods because the evidence indicates that the schoolgirl was acting in bad faith.

## ■ ANSWERS TO QUESTIONS

### Answers to 'What do you know already?' questions at the start of the chapter

1) False. The rebuttable presumption in the social and domestic context is that the parties have no intention to create legal relations.
2) False. The rebuttable presumption in the commercial context is that the parties have the intention to create legal relations.
3) A contract that is too uncertain to perform is void.
4) Capacity means the ability of a party to be legally bound by a contract.

5) A minor is a person under 18 years of age. It is a relevant question when we analyse whether a party is bound by a contract because a contract with a minor is voidable. This means that a minor can choose not to be bound by a contract, although they must pay a reasonable price for necessaries. In addition, a court may order a minor to return any goods received under the agreement if it is just and equitable to do so.

## Answers to end-of-chapter SQE1-style questions

Question 1:
  The correct answer was C. This is because prenuptual agreements are enforceable under English law despite being made in the social and domestic context. The scenario tells us that the woman is wealthy and this adds the factor of seriousness to the context, which also helps to rebut the presumption in the social and domestic context. Options A and B are incorrect because they ignore the factors that rebut the presumption in the social and domestic context mentioned above. It is important to note that friendly relations between the agreement parties do not prevent the presumption in the social and domestic context from being rebutted provided the subject matter is sufficiently serious. Option D is incorrect because English law recognises a prenuptial agreement as sufficiently serious to rebut the presumption. Option E is incorrect because the presumption can apply to a man and a woman who are planning to get married.

Question 2:
  The correct answer was B. This is because the agreement was made while the mother and daughter were on friendly terms, which, combined with the lack of certainty as to how long the arrangement was to continue for, means that the presumption is not rebutted. Option A is incorrect because although the detrimental reliance of the daughter and the seriousness of the promise are factors that can rebut the presumption, the lack of certainty as to how long the agreement should last will undermine the effect of these rebutting factors. Option C is incorrect: the agreement is unenforceable as the presumption has not been rebutted. But even if it were enforceable, there is no mention of a reasonable period of time in the mother's agreement with her daughter, and in any event, given the number of years that the daughter has taken for her legal studies, it is at least arguable that a reasonable time frame has already expired. Option D is incorrect: lack of certainty makes an agreement void, not voidable. But in any event, there is insufficient evidence to rebut the presumption of no intention to create legal relations. Option E is incorrect. A mother and daughter can make a legally binding agreement whilst on friendly terms, but there is insufficient evidence to rebut the presumption in this scenario.

Question 3:
   The correct answer was B. An advertisement such as this would be viewed by the courts as a binding offer to provide protection to a person who books a holiday with a member of the network. Option A is incorrect. Although it is true to say that some advertisements are gimmicks and do not evidence any intention to be legally bound, it is important to consider each advertisement individually. There is nothing in the scenario to suggest that the expectation of insurance cover is unrealistic or a gimmick. Option C is incorrect because the advertisement will be seen as an offer that the man accepted by booking the holiday, so the man has a claim under the agreement with the insurance company. Option D is incorrect. Although it is true to say that the man can claim against the insurance company, the rebuttable presumption in the commercial context can be rebutted with clear evidence. Option E is incorrect. Although the advertisement's clear aim is to drum up business, the question of whether an advertisement is a gimmick or not needs to be determined on a case by case basis.

Question 4:
   The correct answer was D. The separate document is an agreement to agree. Agreements to agree are not enforceable. Options A and B are incorrect as the businesswoman does not acquire any rights under the agreement. Option C is incorrect as the sale of the zoo is provided for under the sale agreement and nothing in the scenario tells you that the sale of the zoo is connected to the subject matter of the separate document. Option E is incorrect. In cases such as these where the separate document does not contain any essential terms, the document cannot be enforced at all.

Question 5:
   The correct answer was C. The court can exercise its discretion to require a minor to return property if it is just and equitable to do so, which would appear to be the case here. Option A is incorrect because there is no evidence to suggest that a diamond tiara and a pearl necklace fit the definition of necessaries for a 16-year-old schoolgirl. Option B is incorrect because it does not describe the situation fully because it fails to take account of the shop owner's recourse under Option C. Option D is incorrect on the basis that contracts with minors are voidable, not void. Option E is incorrect because bad faith is not a factor that provides for remedies against minors.

## ■ KEY CASES, RULES, STATUTES AND INSTRUMENTS

The SQE1 Assessment Specification does not require you to know any case names, or statutory materials, for this topic.

# Privity of contract and rights of third parties

### ■ MAKE SURE YOU KNOW

Generally speaking, a person cannot enforce rights under a contract unless they are a party to the contract. This is due to the doctrine of privity of contract. This chapter explores the doctrine of privity of contract, and its impact on third party rights. It also covers situations in which third parties can acquire rights under contracts.

For the SQE1 assessment, you are required to know these topics so that you can apply them and determine whether a third party has acquired rights under a contract to which they are not party.

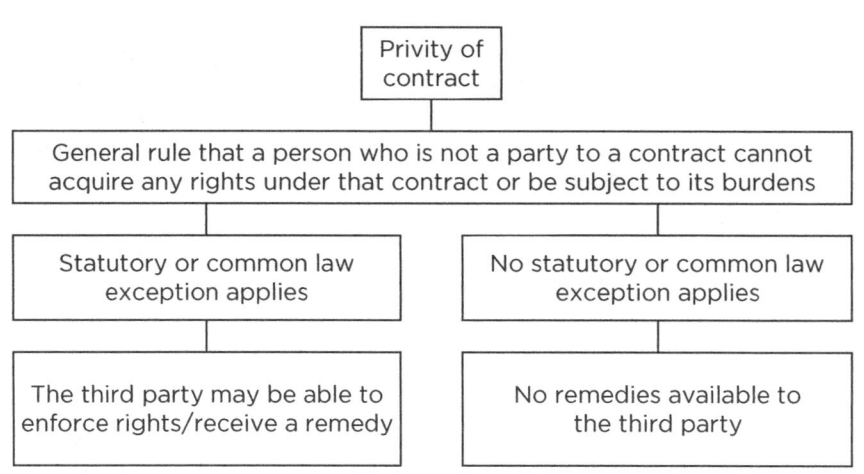

## ■ SQE ASSESSMENT ADVICE

As you work through this chapter, remember to pay particular attention in your revision to:
- Identifying the third party to a contract, and understanding the effect of the doctrine of privity of contract on the third party's rights.
- The requirement that a promisee must provide consideration for a promise and its impact on third party rights.
- The effect of the Contracts (Rights of Third Parties) Act 1999 on third party rights.
- The different ways in which third parties can acquire rights under contracts at common law.
- The different remedies that a party to a contract can exercise on behalf of a third party at common law.

## ■ WHAT DO YOU KNOW ALREADY?

Have a go at these questions before reading this chapter. If you find some difficult or cannot remember the answers, make a note to look more closely at that area during your revision.

1) What is the doctrine of privity of contract?
   [Introducing privity of contract, page 66]
2) True or false? The Contracts (Rights of Third Parties) Act 1999 applies to all contracts made since 2000.
   [The Contracts (Rights of Third Parties) Act 1999, page 67]
3) Which one of the following does NOT allow a third party to acquire rights in respect of a contract?
   a) Agency
   b) Assignment
   c) Collateral contracts
   d) Implied terms
   [Structures that give rights to third parties, page 68]
4) What is a collateral contract?
   [Collateral contracts, page 70]
5) True or false? A promisee can recover damages for the loss of third parties in respect of a contract of convenience.
   [What remedies can the promisee under a contract exercise for a third party?, page 72]

## INTRODUCTION TO PRIVITY OF CONTRACT

**Privity of contract** is an English law doctrine that establishes the general rule that a person who is not a party to a contract (a **third party**) cannot acquire any rights under that contract or be subject to its burdens.

> **Key term: privity of contract**
>
> The English law doctrine that a third party cannot acquire rights under a contract or be subject to its burdens.

> **Key term: third party**
>
> In relation to a contract, a third party is a person who is not a party to the contract.

Now let us look at **Practice example 4.1** to see how the doctrine of privity of contract might operate in practice.

> **Practice example 4.1**
>
> Dennis is a manufacturer of tyres and enters into a contract to sell tyres to David. Dennis is very keen to maintain the price of his tyres at a certain level so the contract contains a provision obliging David not to sell the tyres at less than a fixed price. In addition, under the contract David undertakes to require any other person to whom he sells tyres to agree not to sell them at less than the fixed price. David sells a quantity of tyres to Selina who agrees not to sell them at less than the fixed price. Selina sells the tyres at less than the fixed price.
>
> Can Dennis force Selina not to sell the tyres at less than the fixed price?
>
> **The answer is no.** This scenario is based on the facts of *Dunlop Pneumatic Tyre Co Ltd v Selfridge & Co Ltd* [1915] AC 847 HL. In this case, the House of Lords held that the original seller could not bring a claim against the party who sold the tyres at less than the fixed price. This was because the doctrine of privity of contract means that only a party to a contract can bring a claim under the contract.

The rule that only a party to a contract can bring a claim under the contract remains the general rule, *unless* a recognised exception applies. The exceptions are found under statute and at common law, and we shall explore them next.

# STATUTORY RIGHTS FOR THIRD PARTIES

Some statutes provide third parties with rights in respect of agreements to which they are not a party. Common examples include the Contracts (Rights of Third Parties) Act 1999, the Third Parties (Rights against Insurers) Act 2010, the Road Traffic Act 1988, the Married Women's Property Act 1882 and the Carriage of Goods by Sea Act 1992.

In preparation for your SQE1 assessment, we will focus on the Contracts (Rights of Third Parties) Act 1999 because it can apply to a very wide range of agreements and examiners often include references to it in assessments.

## The Contracts (Rights of Third Parties) Act 1999

The Contracts (Rights of Third Parties) Act (CRTPA) 1999 was enacted to allow a third party to acquire rights under a contract to which it is not party. These rights allow the third party to:
- enforce remedies for breach of contract; and
- rely on a clause that limits or excludes their liability.

A third party is not required to provide consideration to acquire rights under, or bring a claim under, a contract where the CRTPA 1999 applies.

The CRTPA 1999 requires the following criteria to be satisfied for the third party to acquire rights (and remedies):
- the contract must expressly state that the third party may enforce a term of the contract (either by referring to the third party by name, or as a class of person, such as a previous tenant); or
- a term in the contract must purport to confer a benefit on the third party, and no other provisions in the contract show that the parties to the contract did not intend for the term to be enforceable by the third party.

Test your ability to apply these criteria in **Practice example 4.2**.

> **Revision tip**
>
> Keep in mind the fact that *although* the CRTPA 1999 can override the doctrine of privity of contract to allow a third party to acquire rights and remedies under a contract to which they are not party, this only happens if the enforceability criteria set out above are satisfied. You will need to know these criteria so that you can apply them in your SQE1 assessments.

## Practice example 4.2

Graham is the tenant of a shop and his lease is with his landlord, PropertyCo. Graham no longer wishes to run the shop so assigns his lease to Margaret and he provides a guarantee to PropertyCo that the new tenant will pay the rent under the lease. Margaret enters into a separate agreement with PropertyCo that limits Margaret's liability under the lease to £5,000, and also limits the liability of 'any previous tenant' on a guarantee in respect of the lease to £5,000. Margaret fails to pay £10,000 rent under the lease.

Is PropertyCo entitled to claim the £10,000 from Graham under the guarantee?

No. PropertyCo's claim is limited to £5,000. Graham is entitled to rely on the clause in the agreement between Margaret and PropertyCo that limits his liability to £5,000 under the guarantee. This is because Graham clearly falls within the description of 'any previous tenant' and so the CRTPA 1999 is effective to override the doctrine of privity of contract.

### Excluding the CRTPA 1999

The parties to a contract may wish to exclude the CRTPA 1999 to prevent third parties from acquiring rights and remedies under the contract. Parties can exclude the CRTPA 1999 by clearly stating in the agreement that the CRTPA 1999 does not apply.

## STRUCTURES THAT GIVE RIGHTS TO THIRD PARTIES

The CRTPA 1999 is a relatively new statute and, as you have seen above, it does not apply in all scenarios. This means that for your SQE1 assessments, and in practice, you need to know the full range of structures that allow you to determine whether or not a third party has rights under a given agreement.

Let us explore the different ways *under common law* that a third party can acquire rights in respect of an agreement.

### Assignment

A person who has rights under an agreement may transfer (assign) their rights to a third party. To be effective, an assignment must be:

- permitted under the terms of the relevant agreement
- absolute (final)
- in writing.

In addition, notice of the assignment must be given to the person against whom the third party acquires rights as a result of the assignment.

## Agency

The law of agency allows an agreement to be made by one party on behalf of another. This means that where an agreement is made between Party A and Party B, but Party A is acting as Party C's agent, the legal position is that Party A has made an agreement between Party C and Party B. Party C, as a direct party to the agreement (and not a third party), is entitled to the rights and remedies under that agreement.

The rules of agency can allow parties who are not signatories to agreements to rely on the limitation clauses of such agreements.

The most common examples of the agency structure are where the agent has an agreement in its own right with the promisor, and the agent also makes an agreement for the third party and the promisor. This is typically done so that a third party can rely on a limitation clause in the agreement between the agent and the promisor. The following requirements must be satisfied for the agency structure to be effective:
- it must be clear in the main agreement between the agent and the promisor that the third party is intended to be protected by the limitation clause
- it must be clear in the main agreement that the party to the main contract is not just acting on their own account, but is also acting as the agent of the third party
- the party to the main contract must have authority from the third party to act as their agent
- the third party must provide consideration to the party to the main contract who promises to limit the third party's liability.

### Revision tip

You will be forgiven for thinking that these tests are quite technical. They are! So make sure that you memorise a checklist so that you know whether a third party can acquire rights through agency in your SQE1 assessments.

Let us look at how this works in **Practice example 4.3**.

> ### Practice example 4.3
> Tallships is a shipping company that enters into an agreement with Deliverit to transport a cargo. Deliverit separately enters into an agreement with Dockhand to unload the cargo when it arrives at the port. The agreement between Tallships and Deliverit contains the following provisions:
> - Tallships agrees to limit Deliverit's liability under the agreement to £1,000.
> - Tallships agrees that the limitation of liability also applies to Dockhand *in consideration for* Dockhand unloading the cargo.
> - Deliverit is acting as principal in respect of its obligations, and additionally as agent for Dockhand, with Dockhand's consent, in relation to Dockhand's agreement to unload the cargo.
>
> When Dockhand unloads the cargo at the port, it is damaged, but Dockhand has not been negligent. The cost of the damage is £20,000. Is Dockhand protected by the limitation clause?
>
> **The answer is yes. The agreement contains the requirements to be satisfied for agency to apply. Dockhand's consideration is Dockhand unloading the cargo in response to a unilateral offer from Tallships to limit Dockhand's liability.**

> ### Exam warning
> In the SQE1 assessments, look out for scenarios where a promisor has agreed to limit the liability of both the promisee, *and* the promisee's agents, servants, employees. It is likely that the promisee's agents, servants and employees will be third parties to the agreement between the promisee and the promisor. Check carefully if the requirements for an agency relationship have been satisfied. If so, the promisee, acting as agent for the third party, might have made a separate agreement between the third party and the promisor so that the third party can rely directly on the promisor's agreement to limit its liability.

## Collateral contracts

When faced with a situation where privity of contract suggests that a third party does not have any rights or remedies under a separate agreement between the promisee and the promisor, it may be possible to identify an additional contract (*a collateral contract*) between the third party and the promisor. A collateral contract avoids the doctrine of privity of contract by giving the person that is third party under the other contract direct contractual rights against the promisor under a separate contract.

Collateral contracts often involve situations where a producer makes an advertisement about the quality of a product, and a client instructs a contractor to buy that product. When the contractor buys the product, they conclude a contract with the producer. But, in addition, it may be shown that the client who instructs the contractor concludes a separate contract with the producer. This separate contract is seen as the client accepting the producer's offer of a quality product by instructing the contractor to buy the product and gives the client direct recourse against the producer under a separate (collateral) contract.

Practice example 4.4 illustrates how this might arise in practice.

### Practice example 4.4

Coastal owns a pier on the coast. Coastal hires Brushco to paint its pier. Coastal instructs Brushco to use Chemco's paint because it is advertised as guaranteed to last for ten years. Brushco buys Chemco's paint, uses it on the pier, but after one year, the paint has washed off.

Can Coastal claim against Chemco?

The answer is yes. This example is based on the facts of *Shanklin Pier Ltd v Detel Products Ltd* [1951] 2 KB 854. Although Coastal is a third party to the contract between Brushco and Chemco, Coastal can claim under a collateral contract with Brushco. The collateral contract is made by Coastal accepting Chemco's promise that its paint would last for ten years. Coastal's acceptance of (and consideration for) Chemco's promise is Coastal's instruction to Brushco to buy Chemco's paint.

### Exam warning

In the SQE1 assessments, watch out for scenarios in which a third party appears to be unable to claim for a product supplied to another party under a separate agreement. If the third party instructed the other party to buy the product, then check whether this instruction can amount to the third party's acceptance of an offer and consideration in respect of the promise from the supplier. If it does, then the third party may have acquired rights against the supplier under a collateral contract.

## Trusts created by contract

A party to a contract can give rights to a third party by declaring themselves to be a trustee for the third party beneficiary. Such an arrangement will not be effective unless the contract in question contains a declaration of trust and this reflects the requirement that the promisor must be aware of the trust relationship.

When third party rights are created through a declaration of trust, it allows the promisee (who is a party to the contract) to enforce the third party's rights, or the third party beneficiary can enforce the relevant rights against the promisor directly. Any rights created for a third party under a trust arrangement are in addition to any rights created under the CRTPA 1999 (if it applies).

Have a look at how this might be applied in **Practice example 4.5**.

> **Practice example 4.5**
>
> A broking company (BrokerCo) arranges a transaction pursuant to which the owner of a ship (ShipCo) agrees to allow a charterer (CharterCo) to use its ship. The contract states that ShipCo will pay BrokerCo a commission for arranging the agreement between ShipCo and CharterCo, and that CharterCo is the trustee of BrokerCo's right to recover the commission. ShipCo refuses to pay the commission to BrokerCo.
>
> Can CharterCo recover the commission from ShipCo as trustee for BrokerCo?
>
> **The answer is yes.** The contract between ShipCo and CharterCo contains a clear declaration of trust in favour of BrokerCo. CharterCo can enforce this right on behalf of BrokerCo in its capacity as trustee for BrokerCo.

## WHAT REMEDIES CAN THE PROMISEE UNDER A CONTRACT EXERCISE FOR A THIRD PARTY?

We have explored the grounds on which a third party may be able to bring a claim under statute or through the use of common law structures. But in some scenarios, you may conclude that a third party cannot bring a claim in its own name. Where does this leave the third party? The third party will have to rely on the promisee under the contract to bring

a claim in respect of the third party's loss. Let us explore this below in relation to:
- damages,
- specific performance, and
- injunctions.

## Damages

There is a general rule under English law that a party to a contract cannot sue and recover for the loss of a third party, but there are exceptions. We have already looked at how a trustee can recover for the beneficiary of a trust. We will now look at two exceptions that do not depend on a trust relationship:
- contracts of convenience, and
- the St Martins Property exception.

### Contracts of convenience

The law recognises that for reasons of convenience, one person may enter into a contract with another person, on their own behalf, but also on behalf of others. Key examples include:
- family holidays,
- ordering meals in restaurants for a party, and
- hiring a taxi for a group.

In this limited range of examples, the person who entered into the contract can recover for their own loss *and* for the loss of those persons on whose behalf they made the contract.

Practice example 4.6 illustrates how this exception might arise in practice.

### Practice example 4.6

James books a holiday for himself and his wife and two children. James described specifically to the holiday company ('HolidayCo') what he expected from the holiday in terms of accommodation, food and facilities at the hotel where he and his family would stay. The cost of the holiday was £1,400. Shortly after James booked the holiday, HolidayCo told him that the hotel was not ready but that another hotel was available and it would be as good as the hotel that James had initially booked. In fact, the accommodation, food, services, facilities and general standard of the hotel were so unsatisfactory that the whole family suffered discomfort, vexation, inconvenience and distress, and went home disappointed.

Can James claim for the distress and discomfort of his wife and children in addition to his own distress and discomfort?

The answer is yes. This scenario is based on the facts of *Jackson v Horizon Holidays Ltd* [1975] 1 WLR 1468. The Court of Appeal held that the father was entitled to recover damages for himself and his family members because he had contracted on behalf of himself, and also on behalf of his family. Later case law limited the application of recovery to contracts of convenience, such as family holidays, ordering meals in restaurants and booking taxis.

## *The St Martins Property exception*

The other exception to privity of contract exists in the commercial context. In such cases, the promisee (a party to the contract) does not need to show any loss in order to claim for the loss of a third party.

One of the classic examples of where this applies is where Party A engages Party B to do work on their property, and both Party A and Party B understand that Party A will transfer the property to another party (Party C). If, after Party C has acquired the property, it turns out that Party B's work for Party A was defective, Party A is allowed to sue Party B for Party C's loss, even though Party A has not suffered any loss.

Let us have a look at how this might work in **Practice example 4.7**.

### Practice example 4.7

LawCo is a tenant of a building in London and the building contains asbestos. LawCo hires SolutionsCo to remove the asbestos from the building. After SolutionsCo has finished its work, LawCo assigns its lease of the building to OtherCo. OtherCo finds asbestos in the building and will incur substantial costs to remove it.

Can LawCo sue SolutionsCo for the costs that OtherCo will incur due to SolutionsCo's failure to remove the asbestos?

**The answer is yes. OtherCo does not have a contract with SolutionsCo. But due to an exception to the privity rule, LawCo can sue SolutionsCo for OtherCo's loss, even if LawCo itself has not**

incurred any loss as a result of SolutionsCo's defective work. To do this, LawCo must prove that:
- it was in the contemplation of LawCo and SolutionsCo that the building would be transferred to another party, such as OtherCo, and
- it is the intention of the parties to the contract (LawCo and SolutionsCo) that LawCo is treated as entering into the contract for the benefit of those who may acquire an interest in the subject matter of the contract (in this case the building).

## Specific performance

This remedy is at the discretion of the court and is potentially available where damages would not be an adequate remedy. It can only be used if the promisee under the original contract is willing to enforce its rights under the contract. This means that it will only be appropriate if the promisor has not yet performed its obligations in full under the contract. Remedies are discussed in more detail in **Chapter 10**.

## Injunctions

A promisee may be able to obtain an injunction to prevent a promisor from doing something that they agreed not to do.

## ■ KEY POINT CHECKLIST

This chapter has covered the following key knowledge points. You can use these to structure your revision around, making sure to recall the key details for each point, as covered in this chapter.
- The doctrine of privity of contract provides the general rule that a person who is not a party to a contract cannot acquire any rights under that contract or be subject to its burdens.
- There are exceptions to the rule of privity of contract. These exceptions allow a third party to enforce a promise in the contract or obtain remedies under a contract to which they are not party.
- There are exceptions to the rule of privity of contract provided under statute. The key statutory exception is contained within the Contracts (Rights of Third Parties) Act 1999.
- There are also common law exceptions to the doctrine of privity. The structures and devices used under common law to avoid the rule of privity of contract include assignment, agency, collateral contracts and trusts.
- A promisee may enforce certain remedies for the benefit of a third party. The remedies available include: damages, specific performance and injunctions.

# Privity of contract and rights of third parties

## ■ KEY TERMS AND CONCEPTS
- privity of contract (**page 66**)
- third party (**page 66**)

## ■ SQE1-STYLE QUESTIONS

### QUESTION 1

A manufacturer agrees to sell chairs to a dealer at a discounted price on the condition that the dealer will not sell the chairs at less than the fixed price, and that the dealer will require any person to whom it sells the chairs not to sell them at less than the fixed price. The dealer sells the chairs to a discounter in a contract that requires the discounter not to sell at below a fixed price. But the discounter sells the chairs at below the fixed price.

**Which of the following best describes the manufacturer's rights against the discounter?**

A. The manufacturer can force the discounter not to sell at a lower price than the fixed price. This is because the manufacturer has a direct contract with the discounter that was made by the dealer, acting as the manufacturer's agent.

B. The manufacturer can force the discounter not to sell at a lower price than the fixed price. This is because the manufacturer has a direct collateral contract with the discounter.

C. The manufacturer can force the discounter not to sell at lower than the fixed price because English statute law gives third parties rights to enforce contract terms in their favour, unless such rights are excluded.

D. The manufacturer cannot force the discounter not to sell at a lower price than the fixed price. This is because although English statute law *can* give rights to third parties, provided it is not excluded, the required criteria for third party rights to apply have not been satisfied.

E. The manufacturer cannot force the discounter not to sell at lower than the fixed price. This is because English statute law requires a third party who seeks to rely on statutory third party rights to provide consideration, and the manufacturer has not provided any consideration.

## QUESTION 2

A man hired a woman to refurbish his bathroom. The woman's performance was defective and, as a result, the woman was liable to the man. However, the woman sold her business to a company on terms whereby the company agreed to 'complete outstanding orders taking into account any deposits paid by customers as at 31 March 2021 and to pay in the normal course of time any liabilities properly incurred by the woman as at 31 March 2021'.

**Which of the following best describes the man's rights against the company?**

A. The man can claim against the company under statute because his claim falls within the definition of 'liabilities' in the contract between the woman and the company.

B. The man can claim against the company under statute because there are no provisions in the agreement to show that the contract was not to be enforceable by a third party.

C. The man cannot claim against the company under statute because he is not expressly identified in the contract between the woman and the company.

D. The man cannot claim against the company under statute because he has not provided consideration to the company as consideration for being able to claim.

E. The man cannot claim against the company under statute because the contract between the woman and the company must expressly incorporate any statute that gives third parties rights in respect of contracts to which they are not parties.

## QUESTION 3

A developer owns an office building and hires a decorating company to paint the building. The developer has seen an advertisement from a paint manufacturer that promises that its paint is so good that it will last for ten years. So the developer instructs the decorating company to buy the paint manufacturer's paint and to use it on the office building. The decorating company buys the paint from the paint manufacturer in a contract that excludes the third party rights under English statute law. One week after the decorating company has painted the office building there is a rainstorm and the paint completely washes off the office building.

# 78  Privity of contract and rights of third parties

Which of the following best describes the property company's rights against the paint company?

A. There is no basis on which the developer can claim against the paint manufacturer because there is no contract between the developer and the paint manufacturer.

B. Although there is an exception to the doctrine of privity of contract that would allow the decorating company to claim for the developer's loss on the grounds that this is a contract of convenience, this exception only applies where the decorating company has suffered a loss and there is nothing in the scenario to show that the decorating company has suffered a loss.

C. The developer can claim against the paint manufacturer on the basis of a collateral contract between the developer and the paint manufacturer.

D. The developer can claim against the paint manufacturer on the grounds that the decorating company acted as the developer's agent so that there is a direct contract between the developer and the paint manufacturer.

E. The decorating company can claim against the paint manufacturer as trustee for the developer and the decorating company will be bound to hold any damages recovered from the paint manufacturer on trust for the developer.

## QUESTION 4

A mother books a meal in a restaurant for herself, her husband, and her six children to celebrate the mother's birthday. All eight of them went for the meal at the restaurant. The food at the restaurant was of such poor quality that none of the group could eat it. In addition, the service was poor, and all who attended were sick with food poisoning after the meal. The bill was £200.

Which of the following best describes the mother's right to claim for damages against the restaurant?

A. The mother can only claim for her loss because a claimant cannot recover more than the amount required to compensate his loss.

B. The mother can claim as trustee for the children and her husband.

C. The mother can only claim for her loss because the rule of privity of contract provides that a party to contract cannot sue and recover for the loss of a third party, and the husband and children are third parties in this scenario.

D. The mother can claim damages for herself, her husband and her children under an exception to the rule of privity of contract because this is a contract of convenience.

E. The mother can only claim for herself because she provided consideration, but her husband and the children did not.

## QUESTION 5

A developer is in the process of developing some land. The land is contaminated so she makes a contract with a cleaning company to decontaminate the land. The contract excludes the statutory third party rights. The developer tells the cleaning company that she plans to sell the land to another party as soon as the decontamination process is complete. The cleaning company performs the decontamination work. Next, the developer sells the land to a builder who subsequently finds that the land is contaminated because the cleaning company breached its agreement with the developer to effectively decontaminate the land.

**Which of the following best describes the builder's rights against the cleaning company?**

A. The builder can claim for its loss if the developer is prepared to bring a claim against the cleaning company for the builder's loss.

B. The builder can only claim for its loss through the developer if the developer has also suffered a loss, and there is no evidence in the scenario that the developer has suffered a loss.

C. Since the doctrine of privity of contract provides that a person who is not a party to a contract cannot acquire any rights under such a contract, the builder is unable to bring any claim directly or indirectly against the cleaning company.

D. The builder can claim directly against the cleaning company as a third party on the basis of statute.

E. The builder is entitled to ask the property developer to sue on its behalf in its capacity as trustee.

80 Privity of contract and rights of third parties

# ■ ANSWERS TO QUESTIONS

## Answers to 'What do you know already?' questions at the start of the chapter

1) The doctrine of privity of contract establishes the general rule that a person who is not a party to a contract cannot acquire any rights under that contract or be subject to its burdens.
2) False. The CRTPA 1999 only applies to contracts when it is not excluded and when the enforceability criteria are satisfied.
3) The correct answer was (d). Implied terms is the odd one out because implied terms do not allow third parties to acquire rights in respect of a contract.
4) A collateral contract is a separate contract (in addition to the main contract) that is identified between the promisor and the third party. It has the effect of making the third party a direct party to an agreement with the promisor so that it can enforce the agreement in its own right against the promisor.
5) True. Contracts of convenience are one of the exceptions to the doctrine of privity of contract that allow a promisee to recover damages for third parties in addition to their own damages.

## Answers to end-of-chapter SQE1-style questions

Question 1:
The correct answer was D. When you analyse whether or not a third party can rely on the Contracts (Rights of Third Parties) Act 1999, you must check whether the enforceability criteria have been satisfied. The criteria are set out at s 1 (1) of the Contracts (Rights of Third Parties) Act 1999 and they require that a third party may enforce a term if the contract expressly provides that they may, or if a term in the contract purports to confer a benefit on such person. There is nothing in the scenario to allow us to conclude that the enforceability criteria have been satisfied. Option C is incorrect for the same reasons. Option A is incorrect because there is no evidence in the scenario to suggest that the dealer is the manufacturer's agent, or that the discounter is aware of any agency relationship. Option B is incorrect because there is no evidence of a collateral contract. An example of a collateral contract would be the discounter promising not to sell the chairs at a price lower than a fixed amount, and the manufacturer accepting this promise by instructing the dealer to enter into a

contract with the discounter. Option E is incorrect as it misstates the requirements for a third party to rely on the Contracts (Rights of Third Parties) Act 1999. In fact, a third party may acquire rights under the act *without* providing any consideration to the promisor.

Question 2:
The correct answer was C. This is because the enforceability criteria must be satisfied in order for the man to bring a claim as a third party to the contract between the woman and the company. A key requirement of the enforceability criteria is that the man must be expressly identified by name or as a class of persons, such as a customer. The relevant term in the agreement is 'liabilities' and this would not satisfy the enforceability criteria as it only encompasses unidentified classes of third parties. It is for the reasons above that Option A is incorrect. Option B is incorrect because a third party must satisfy the enforceability criteria in order to bring a claim under applicable statute. Option D is incorrect because there is no requirement that a third party provide consideration to rely on the act. Option E is incorrect because the act applies, unless it is excluded.

Question 3:
The correct answer was C. This is because the paint manufacturer's advertisement about the quality of the paint is a unilateral offer that the developer accepts and for which it provides consideration by instructing the decorating company to buy the paint. This means that Option A is incorrect. Option B is incorrect because the scenario does not describe a contract of convenience, which only applies in very limited circumstances, such as family holidays, taxis or meals in a restaurant. Option D is incorrect because for an agency argument to succeed the scenario would need to refer to an agency relationship and the paint manufacturer would need to be aware that the decorating company was the developer's agent, and there is nothing in the scenario to suggest this. Option E is incorrect because there is nothing in the scenario to suggest a trust relationship, or that the paint manufacturer, as promisor, was aware of any declaration of trust.

Question 4:
The correct answer was D. The scenario is a classic example of a contract of convenience. Contracts of convenience are an exception to the general rule that a party to a contract can only claim for their own loss. The exception means that the mother can claim for her own loss, and also for those on whose behalf she made the contract with the restaurant. This means that Options A and C are incorrect. Option B is incorrect because the scenario does not mention a

declaration of trust or that the restaurant owner was aware of a trust relationship. Option E is incorrect because there is no requirement for those on whose behalf a contract is made to provide consideration when the contracts of convenience exception applies.

Question 5:
The correct answer was A. The scenario is covered by common law exception to the rule of privity of contract (the St Martins Property exception). This exception applies where party A engages party B to do work on their property and both parties know that party A will transfer the property to another party (party C). If, after party C acquires the property, it turns out that party B's work for party A was defective, party A can sue party B for party's C's loss, even if party A has not suffered any loss. Option B is incorrect because the developer is not required to suffer a loss in order to bring a claim for the builder's loss. Option C is incorrect because it does not take account of the exception to the doctrine of privity of contract provided by the St Martins Property exception. Option D is incorrect because the Contract (Rights of Third Parties) Act 1999 does not apply to a contract if it is excluded. Option E is incorrect because there is no evidence in the scenario of a declaration of trust being made in favour of the builder; and a declaration of trust is an essential requirement to establish a trust relationship.

## ■ KEY CASES, RULES, STATUTES AND INSTRUMENTS

The SQE1 Assessment Specification does not require you to know any case names, or statutory materials, for this topic.

# 5

# Contents of a contract 1: Sources and interpretation

## ■ MAKE SURE YOU KNOW

Parties often exchange verbal or written statements before the contact is concluded. For the SQE1 assessment, you need to be able to determine whether pre-contractual statements made by parties to a contract are classified as terms, representations or puff. A term agreed (orally or in writing) between the parties to a contract is an express term. You are also required to know which terms are implied into a contract by the courts, by custom and by statute. Such terms are called implied terms.

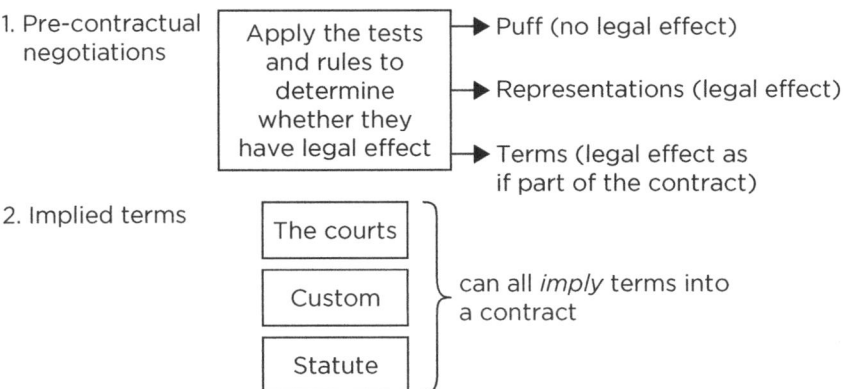

1. Pre-contractual negotiations → Apply the tests and rules to determine whether they have legal effect
   - → Puff (no legal effect)
   - → Representations (legal effect)
   - → Terms (legal effect as if part of the contract)

2. Implied terms — The courts, Custom, Statute can all *imply* terms into a contract

3. How do the courts *interpret* the words in a contract?

## ■ SQE ASSESSMENT ADVICE

As you work through this chapter, remember to pay particular attention in your revision to:
- The difference between representations, terms, and puff.
- The different common law tests used to determine whether a statement made before a contract is concluded is a representation or a term.
- The statutory rules that provide that certain statements are terms.
- The parol evidence rule.
- Terms implied into contracts by the courts, custom and statute.
- The difference between express terms and implied terms.
- The approach taken by the courts to interpret the words used in contracts.

## ■ WHAT DO YOU KNOW ALREADY?

Have a go at these questions before reading this chapter. If you find some difficult or cannot remember the answers, make a note to look more closely at that area during your revision.

1) What is the difference between a representation and a term?
   **[Introduction to terms, representations and puff, page 85]**
2) Which one of the following pointers is NOT used at common law to determine whether a pre-contractual statement is a term or a representation?
   a) The statement-maker's special knowledge or expertise
   b) The importance of the statement to the person to whom it was said
   c) Whether the person to whom it was said understood the statement
   d) Whether the statement-maker assumes responsibility
   **[The common law tests to determine whether a pre-contractual statement is a term or a representation, page 86]**
3) True or false? The parol evidence rule raises the presumption when a contract is in writing that the written contract contains all the terms of the contract.
   **[The parol evidence rule and pre-contractual statements, page 88]**
4) What term is implied by section 12 of the Sale of Goods Act 1979?
   **[Terms implied by statute in the B2B regime, page 92]**
5) True or false? When courts interpret contracts, if the parties have used clear language in the contract, the general approach is that the courts must apply it without considering the context within which it was made.
   **[The interpretation of contract terms, page 94]**

# INTRODUCTION TO TERMS, REPRESENTATIONS AND PUFF

Parties may exchange many oral or written statements before a contract is made. The law classifies these **pre-contractual statements** as **terms**, **representations** and **puff**. Remember that a term agreed (orally or in writing) by the parties to a contract is an express term, as opposed to an implied term.

### Key term: pre-contractual statement
A statement made by a party before a contract is made.

### Key term: term
A pre-contractual statement that contains a promise that something is true, which becomes part of the contract.

### Key term: representation
A pre-contractual statement that is not a promise that something is true, but induces the other party to enter into the contract.

### Key term: puff
An extravagant statement (often found in advertisements) that a reasonable person would recognise as not intended to have legal consequences. Puffs do not have legal consequences.

In practice and for the purpose of your SQE1 assessment, you need to know how the courts determine whether a pre-contractual statement is a term, representation or puff. This is important because the classification of a pre-contractual statement determines its legal effect, and this informs the remedies that are available to the **representee**.

### Key term: representee
The person to whom the pre-contractual statement is made.

## How can you tell whether a pre-contractual statement is puff?

In some cases, the **representor** will make extravagant (or flippant) comments that no reasonable person would take literally, or recognise as having the intention to have legal consequences.

## Key term: representor
The person who makes the pre-contractual statement.

Statements used in advertisements are often, *but not always*, puff. These statements tend to be extravagant or flippant to attract the attention of the target audience. Classic examples include a sign outside a funfair ride that reads 'Guaranteed to scare your socks off'. English law takes the view that a reasonable person would *not* take such statements literally, which means that these statements have no legal effect. In other words, a person could not successfully sue a funfair on the basis of the statement referred to above if the funfair ride did not scare their socks off.

In the section that follows, we will explore factors that make pre-contractual statements, including advertisements, legally binding as terms or representations.

## How can you tell whether a pre-contractual statement is a term or a representation?

In determining whether a pre-contractual statement is a term or a representation, the courts analyse all available evidence. The courts analyse the evidence *objectively* to determine whether the representor *intended* to make a contractually binding promise that the statement was true, and for that statement to be incorporated into the contract. If the courts decide that they did, then the statement will be a term. If they did not, but nonetheless intended the statement to *induce* the representee to enter into the contract, the statement will be a representation. If the contract is in writing, the courts assume that the parties included all the terms in the contract, and the longer the time between the statement being made and the contract being made, the greater the presumption that it was *not* intended to be a term. In addition, the courts use the following secondary tests to help them to determine the intention of the representor.

### The common law tests to determine whether a pre-contractual statement is a term or a representation

Figure 5.1 summarises the secondary tests applied to the interaction between the representor and the representee to determine whether the pre-contractual statement is a term or representation.

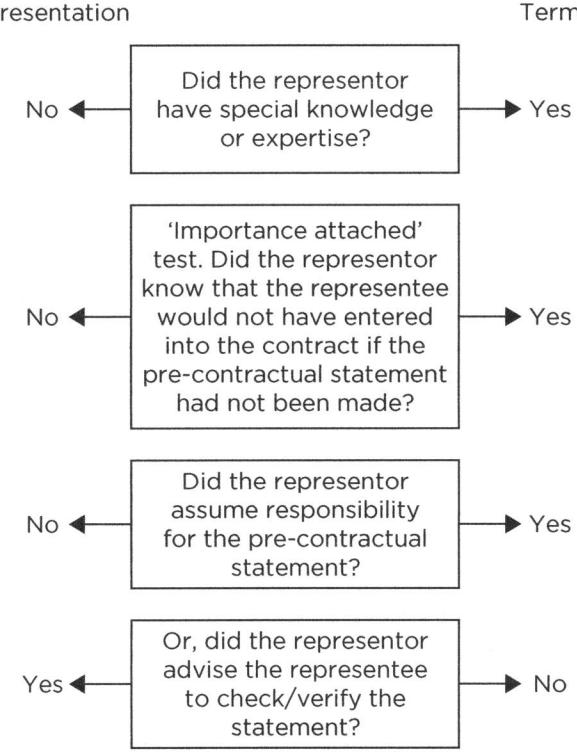

*Figure 5.1: Distinguishing between a term and a representation*

Now put your knowledge to the test and attempt **Practice example 5.1**.

> **Practice example 5.1**
>
> Bob, a trader, is interested in buying hops from Ellie, a farmer. Bob asks Ellie whether sulphur has been used on the hops, and adds that he would not even ask the price if sulphur has been used. Ellie responds to say that sulphur has not been used on the hops. So Bob buys the hops, but then finds out that they have been treated with sulphur.
>
> Is Ellie's statement that sulphur has not been used on the hops a term or a representation?

> Ellie's statement that sulphur has not been used on the hops is a term. These were the facts of *Bannerman v White* 142 ER 685. The court's decision was driven by the fact that the information was so important to the representee that he would not have bought the hops if the statement had not been made. This is an example of the 'importance attached' test.

*The parol evidence rule and pre-contractual statements*

The **parol evidence rule** presumes that when a contract is in writing it contains all the terms of a contract. Because this is a presumption, it can be rebutted in certain circumstances. In addition, it does not prevent the courts from implying terms into a contract (see **Implied terms, page 90**). In practice, parties often include an entire agreement clause in contracts, which makes it more difficult to rebut the presumption. An entire agreement clause provides that the written agreement contains all the terms agreed between the parties, and that no party has relied on any pre-contractual statements.

> **Key term: parol evidence rule**
> The presumption that if a contract is in writing, all of the terms are included in writing.

> **Exam warning**
> Remember that even where the parol evidence rule applies, terms can still be implied into a contract.

*Using statute to determine whether a pre-contractual statement is a term or a representation*

Certain statutes set out circumstances in which certain pre-contractual statements are treated as terms of a contract. For example, section 9 of the Consumer Rights Act (CRA) 2015 treats every contract to supply goods as including a term that the quality of goods is satisfactory.

Next, we shall consider the legal consequences of terms and representations.

### The legal consequences of pre-contractual statements that are terms and representations

Table 5.1 shows the different legal consequences that result from a pre-contractual statement being classified as a term or a representation.

Table 5.1: The different legal consequences of pre-contractual statements that are terms or representations

| Pre-contractual statement | Damages available to the representee for breach | Aim of damages | How are the damages calculated? | Other remedies |
|---|---|---|---|---|
| Term | Damages | To put the representee in the position they would have been in if the contract had been properly performed | All losses incurred by the representee that were within the reasonable contemplation of both parties to the contract at the time the contract was made | Terminate, or affirm, the contract |
| Representation | Damages (generally only available for a fraudulent or negligent misrepresentation) | To put the representee in the position they would have been in if the contract had not been made | All direct losses incurred by the representee. In contrast to damages for breach of term, these losses do not need to have been within the reasonable contemplation of the parties | Rescind the contract |

## IMPLIED TERMS

As noted above, terms that are agreed (orally or in writing) between parties to a contract are express terms. However, in some circumstances, English law *implies* a term into a contract. Terms may be implied into contracts in the following three ways:
- by the courts
- by custom
- by statute.

Where a term is implied into a contract, the implied term is part of the contract.

Let us explore in more detail the ways in which a term is implied into a contract.

### Terms implied by the courts

Terms are implied into contracts by the courts as a matter of policy. There are two main grounds on which the courts imply such terms:
- terms implied in law
- terms implied in fact.

*Terms implied in law*

Terms are implied in law to make the contract work as the courts believe is necessary (a 'necessary incident'). **Practice example 5.2** provides a useful example of a term implied in law.

> **Practice example 5.2**
>
> A council let properties in a tower block to tenants. The tower was in a very bad state of repair: the lifts frequently broke down, and the rubbish chutes were often blocked. Although the tenancy agreements between the council and the tenants imposed obligations upon the tenants, the agreements did not impose any obligations upon the council.
>
> Could a term be implied into the agreement that the council should keep the property in good working order?
>
> The answer is yes. These are the facts of *Liverpool City Council v Irwin* [1977] AC 239. The House of Lords implied a term (as a necessary incident) into the tenancy agreement that the council should take reasonable care to keep the common parts of the tower block in reasonable repair and usability.

In addition, there have also been cases where the courts have implied terms into specific categories of contract. For example, the courts implied a term into employment contracts that the employer must not act in a way that is likely to destroy or damage the relationship of confidence and trust between an employer and an employee.

## Terms implied in fact

Terms are implied in fact where the court considers that it is *necessary* to do so to make the contract work. The courts reach their conclusion by applying the following tests:
- the 'officious bystander' test
- the 'business efficacy' test.

These tests are explained in more detail in **Table 5.2**.

*Table 5.2: Tests for terms implied in fact*

| Test | Worked example |
| --- | --- |
| The 'officious bystander' test<br><br>This test refers to a term, which, if suggested by an 'officious bystander' who was observing the process, the parties in negotiation would agree with wholeheartedly. | Ambrose entered into an agreement with Kennedy in which he agreed to give Kennedy the right to buy Ambrose's land plot for £3,000 *if* Ambrose decided to sell it. Ambrose then gave the land plot to his sister.<br><br>Can Kennedy sue Ambrose for breach of the agreement?<br><br>The answer is yes. The facts in this scenario are similar to those in *Gardner v Coutts & Co* [1968] WLR 173. If an officious bystander had been present when Ambrose made the agreement with Kennedy, he would have implied a term that the agreement to give Kennedy the right to buy the land plot would also prevent him from giving the land plot to anyone else. |
| The 'business efficacy' test<br><br>This test refers to a term without which the contract could not function as the parties must have *objectively* intended. | Darren signed a contract with Burton River Ports so that he could moor his boat on its jetty at Burton docks. Both Darren and Burton River Ports knew that when the tide went out, the boat would rest on the riverbed. When the tide went out, Darren's boat was damaged because it rested on the hard surface of the riverbed. Darren checks his contract with Burton River Ports, but there is no term to say that the surface of the riverbed is suitable for boats to settle on. |

*Tests for terms implied in fact (continued)*

| Test | Worked example |
|---|---|
| | Can Darren rely on the courts to imply a term into his agreement with Burton River Ports that the riverbed was safe for his boat to rest on when the tide went out? |
| | The answer is yes. The facts in this scenario are analogous to those of *The Moorcock* (1889) 14 PD 64 where the Court of Appeal held that the parties must have intended to contract on the basis that the jetty owner had taken reasonable care to check that the riverbed was safe for the boat when the tide went out. The court implied a term into the contract that the jetty owner would take reasonable care to ensure that it was safe to moor boats at the jetty. |

**Exam warning**

You should note carefully that the law has set out quite precisely the circumstances in which a term is implied into a contract. Do not be tempted to conclude that a court will imply a term into a contract to make it fairer (as it seems to you). You should stick to the examples provided above.

## Terms implied by custom

Terms may be implied into a contract to reflect the established and well-known customs and practices of particular industries or markets, provided that such terms do not conflict with the express terms of a contract.

## Terms implied by statute

Certain statutes imply terms into contracts. Key examples of terms implied by statute include the sale and supply of goods, and the standard of performance of a service. The statutes are effective in two main regimes:
- business to business (B2B)
- business to consumer (B2C).

### Terms implied by statute in the B2B regime

The B2B regime is that of businesses dealing with businesses. We will focus on the Sale of Goods Act (SGA) 1979 and the Supply of Goods and

Services Act (SGSA) 1982. The key terms implied by these statutes are summarised in **Table 5.3**.

*Table 5.3: Key terms implied in the business-to-business context*

| Statute | Implied term |
| --- | --- |
| s 12(1) SGA 1979 | The seller has the right to sell the goods |
| s 13(1) SGA 1979 | If goods are sold by description, they will correspond with their description |
| s 14(2) SGA 1979 | The goods are of satisfactory quality, other than where defects are pointed out, or the defects are such that should have been revealed when the buyer examined the goods (if applicable) |
| s 15(2) SGA 1979 | If goods are sold by sample, the bulk will correspond with the sample |
| s 13 SGSA 1982 | Where the supplier is acting in the course of a business, there is an implied term that the supplier will carry out the service with reasonable care and skill |

*Terms included by statute in the B2C regime*
The CRA 2015 contains a number of key terms that are deemed to be included terms in contracts between a consumer and trader. These are summarised in **Table 5.4**.

*Table 5.4: Terms included by the Consumer Rights Act 2015*

| Section | Term |
| --- | --- |
| s 9 | The quality of the goods is satisfactory |
| s 10 | The goods are reasonably fit for any particular purpose that the consumer makes known to the trader before buying the goods |
| s 11 | The goods will match the description |
| s 13 | Where goods are sold by sample, the goods will match the sample |
| s 14 | Where a model is seen or examined before the goods are bought, the goods will match the model |
| s 15 | Correct installation is part of conformity of goods with the contract |

*Terms included by the Consumer Rights Act 2015 (continued)*

| Section | Term |
|---|---|
| s 16 | Items that include digital content must conform to the contract |
| s 49 | Services should be performed with reasonable care and skill |
| s 52 | Services should be performed within a reasonable time |

> **Exam warning**
>
> Be careful to distinguish between the two different regimes that apply to parties operating in the B2B context, and in the B2C context.

## THE INTERPRETATION OF CONTRACT TERMS

It is important for your SQE1 assessments, and in practice, to know what approach the courts will take when interpreting (sometimes referred to as *construing*) the terms of a contract.

If the words in the contract are clear, then the courts will interpret them through what they see as the viewpoint of a reasonable person without looking at the commercial context. This is sometimes referred to as the *four corners approach* because it only looks at what is written within the four corners of a page. If the words in the contract are ambiguous or unclear, then the courts may use commercial common sense to interpret the contract. An example of this would be where the wording has more than one meaning and the court could interpret the words in a way that better reflects what they see as the aim of the contract, and is consistent with business common sense.

Now work through **Practice example 5.3** to test your understanding.

> **Practice example 5.3**
>
> In the 1970s, Pat entered into a lease for a site for a static caravan with Jeff, the owner of the caravan park. The lease provided quite clearly that the service charge that Pat would pay would increase on a compound basis by 10% annually. In 2013, Pat challenges the service charge on the grounds that the 10% compound increase is too high. Pat argues that the prevailing interest rates in 2013 are much lower than 10% and therefore that it was not the intention of Jeff, the lessor, that the service charge would increase to such a large extent. Pat argues that the lease should be read so that she must pay a proportionate part of reasonable expenses, subject to a cap.
> Can Pat successfully challenge the lease on the grounds set out above?

The answer is no. This scenario is similar to *Arnold v Britton* [2015] UKSC 36. It was held that the language in the lease was clear and reflected the intention of the parties at the time the lease was made. Although the provision was commercially imprudent for Pat, as lessee, commercial imprudence was not a basis for the court to change its interpretation of the service charge clause. The wording is clear and Pat is bound by it.

## ■ KEY POINT CHECKLIST

This chapter has covered the following key knowledge points. You can use these to structure your revision around, making sure to recall the key details for each point, as covered in this chapter.

- Pre-contractual statements may be classified as terms, representations or puff.
- A term is a pre-contractual statement that contains a promise that something is true.
- A representation is a pre-contractual statement that is not a promise that something is true, but still induces the other party to enter into the contract.
- The courts assess the statement-maker's intention by applying an objective test, and various secondary tests.
- Terms agreed (orally or in writing) by the parties to a contract are express terms.
- Terms may be implied into contracts by the courts (implied terms).
- Terms are sometimes implied in fact, mainly, through the 'officious bystander' and the 'business efficacy' tests.
- Terms may be implied by custom to reflect well-known and established custom.
- Terms are implied by statute by the SGA 1979, SGSA 1982 (in the B2B regime) and by the CRA 2015 (in the B2C regime).
- Where the words in the contract are clear, the courts will generally interpret the contract based on what the words would mean to a reasonable person. Where the words are unclear or could have more than one meaning, then the court can examine the commercial context to identify the most suitable meaning for the words.

## ■ KEY TERMS AND CONCEPTS

- pre-contractual statement (**page 85**)

96   Contents of a contract 1: Sources and interpretation

- term (**page 85**)
  - express term (**page 83**)
  - implied term (**page 90**)
- representation (**page 85**)
- puff (**page 85**)
- representee (**page 85**)
- representor (**page 86**)
- parol evidence rule (**page 88**)

## ■ SQE1-STYLE QUESTIONS

### QUESTION 1

A man visits a car-dealer because he wants to buy a car. While the man is looking at a car, the car-dealer tells him that the car has done 30,000 miles. The next day, the man returns to the car-dealer and buys the car in an oral agreement. The man uses the car for a few months during which time the car's performance is problematic. Subsequently, the man finds out that the car had actually done 80,000 miles when he bought it.

**Which of the following statements best describes whether the man can claim against the car-dealer?**

A. The man cannot claim against the car-dealer because the statement about the car mileage was made at a different time from the sale agreement and it does not form part of the agreement of sale.

B. The man can rescind the agreement on the basis that the car-dealer's statement about the car's mileage was a representation.

C. The man can claim damages on the basis that the car-dealer's statement about the car's mileage was a term of the sale agreement.

D. The man cannot claim damages against the car-dealer because he continued to use the car without fixing the problems and this amounts to affirmation of the agreement.

E. The man cannot claim against the car-dealer because he was in as good a position as the car-dealer to discover the truth of this statement.

### QUESTION 2

A woman goes to a horse stud farm as she is planning to buy a horse. The woman sees a horse that she would like to buy and starts to examine it. The owner of the horse farm sees the woman and tells her 'There is no need to look for anything. The horse is perfectly sound. If there were anything wrong with the horse, I would tell you'. As a result, the woman stops examining the horse and buys it. Subsequently, the woman discovers that the horse has a damaged hoof and cannot walk for more than half an hour.

**Which of the following best describes whether the woman can claim against the owner of the horse?**

A. The woman cannot claim against the owner unless she can prove that she would have discovered that the horse had a damaged hoof if she had continued her inspection.
B. The woman cannot claim against the owner because it was her responsibility to undertake due diligence on the horse.
C. The woman cannot claim against the owner as his statement is puff.
D. The woman can claim against the owner for breach of representation.
E. The woman can claim against the owner for breach of term.

## QUESTION 3

A runner tells a sports shoe manufacturer that she needs heat-resistant running shoes for a well-known marathon race that she plans to run in a very hot desert. The sports shoe manufacturer produces the shoes for the runner to participate in the run. The runner wears the shoes for the marathon in the very hot desert, but they melt halfway through the race.

**Which one of the following statements best describes the runner's grounds to claim against the sports shoe manufacturer?**

A. The runner can make a claim based on the breach of an implied term that the goods be produced with reasonable care and skill.
B. The runner can make a claim based on the breach of an implied term that the goods be produced in accordance with industry practice.
C. The runner can make a claim based on the breach of an included term that the goods are reasonably fit for any particular purpose made known to the sports shoe manufacturer.
D. The runner can make a claim based on the breach of an implied term that the goods are reasonably fit for any particular purpose made known to the sports shoe manufacturer.
E. The runner can make a claim on the grounds of an implied term that the goods are of satisfactory quality.

## QUESTION 4

A man lives in a block of flats owned by the local council. The man is unhappy with the fact that the lift in the block does not work, the rubbish is not cleared regularly, and the communal areas of the block are dirty. The man reviews his lease agreement and notes that although, as lessee, he is subject to terms that he must comply with, the council, as lessor, is not subject to any terms.

**Which of the following best describes the legal position in this case?**

A. A term would be implied in law that both the man and the council should make reasonable efforts to agree a block maintenance plan.
B. No term would be implied because the language is clear and the courts are restricted to consider only what is written in the four corners of an agreement, in this case, the lease.
C. No term would be implied because it is the responsibility of the lessees to keep the block in reasonable repair and usability.
D. A term would be implied in law that the council should take reasonable care to keep the communal parts of the block in reasonable repair and usability.
E. Since the terms imposed upon the council are vague, the court will consider the commercial context to try to bring meaning to them.

## QUESTION 5

A man advertised a boat for sale. A woman visited the man's boatyard and asked to see the boat. The pair chatted for some time, and the man said, 'She is a sound boat, but are you not going to get her surveyed before buying her?'. The woman returned home, and came back the next day and bought the boat in a written agreement that contained an entire agreement clause.

**Which of the following best describes the effect of the man's statement to the woman about the boat?**

A. The statement is a term of the contract.
B. The parol evidence rule means that the statement does not form part of the written agreement.
C. The statement is a representation.
D. The parol evidence rule establishes the presumption that the statement does not form part of the written agreement.

E. The effect of the parol evidence rule, together with the entire agreement clause in the written contract, mean that the man's oral statement has no legal effect.

# ■ ANSWERS TO QUESTIONS

## Answers to 'What do you know already?' questions at the start of the chapter

1) A term is a promise that a pre-contractual statement is true and becomes part of the contract. A representation is not a promise that a pre-contractual statement is true, but is still an inducement for the other party to enter into the contract.
2) The correct answer was (c). Whether or not the person to whom it was said understood it is *not* a pointer used at common law to determine whether or not a pre-contractual statement is a term or a representation.
3) True. The parol evidence rule raises the presumption when a contract is in writing that the written contract contains all of the terms of the contract.
4) The seller has the right to sell the goods.
5) True. This is often called the four corners approach.

## Answers to end-of-chapter SQE1-style questions

Question 1:
   The correct answer was C. This is because the courts are most likely to interpret pre-contractual statements made by persons acting in a professional capacity, such as a car-dealer, to be terms. Option B is therefore incorrect; rescission is a remedy for breach of a representation, rather than a term. Option E is incorrect because the courts consider that a car-dealer's expertise puts it in a better position to know the true state of affairs than an ordinary man. Option A is incorrect because pre-contractual statements can be viewed as representations, or terms, of an agreement in certain cases. Option D is incorrect because although the innocent party may lose the right to rescind a contract if they affirm it after discovering the true state of affairs, there is no evidence to show that the man discovered the true state of affairs as to mileage while he continued to use the car.

Question 2:
   The correct answer was E. This is because the courts are most likely to interpret the statement from the owner as a promise of the truth of the statement, for which the owner intends to be responsible. This

means that Option D is incorrect. This also means that Options A and B are incorrect because whether or not the woman would have discovered the damage on inspection is irrelevant to the status of the pre-contractual statement. Option C is incorrect because the statement in the scenario does not fit the definition of puff, which is something incredible or unrealistic, like an advertising gimmick.

Question 3:

The correct answer was C. The trainers must be 'reasonably fit for any particular purpose that the consumer makes known to the trader before buying the goods' (s 10 of the CRA 2015). In the business to business regime terms are implied by statute. In the consumer regime terms are *included* by virtue of the CRA 2015. Options D and E are incorrect because they refer to terms being *implied* rather than *included*. Options A and B are incorrect as there are no such terms.

Question 4:

The correct answer was D. There is no such basis that leads to Option A. Option B is not correct. The reference to the four corners approach refers to the role of the courts in interpreting language in a contract. When the language is clear, the courts are reluctant to look outside the four corners of the contract. By contrast, the current scenario is focused on the question of whether, in the *absence of wording to cover the matter of concern*, a term should be implied into the contract/lease. This means that Option E is incorrect because the terms imposed upon the council are not vague, or unclear; it is rather the point that there are no terms binding upon the council. Option C is incorrect as there are no grounds to lead to this conclusion.

Question 5:

The correct answer was E. In this case, the agreement is in writing. As a result, the parol evidence rule applies that leads to the presumption that all written terms are included in the written agreement. This presumption is further reinforced by the entire agreement clause. This means that Options A and C are incorrect. Option B is incorrect because the parol evidence rule is a presumption rather than an absolute rule, and the statement is incomplete because it does not take account of the entire agreement clause. Option D is incorrect as it is incomplete by not taking account of the entire agreement clause.

## ■ KEY CASES, RULES, STATUTES AND INSTRUMENTS

The SQE1 Assessment Specification does not require you to know any case names, or statutory materials, for this topic.

# 6

# Contents of a contract 2: Exemption clauses and unfair terms

## ■ MAKE SURE YOU KNOW

Generally, the express terms of a contract are legally binding. However, *unfair* terms may be deemed to be unenforceable or may only be enforceable to the extent that they are reasonable. For the SQE1 assessment, you will need to know what exemption clauses and unfair terms are, and you will need to know and be able to apply the rules that govern such terms/clauses in both the business to business (B2B) and the business to consumer (B2C) contexts.

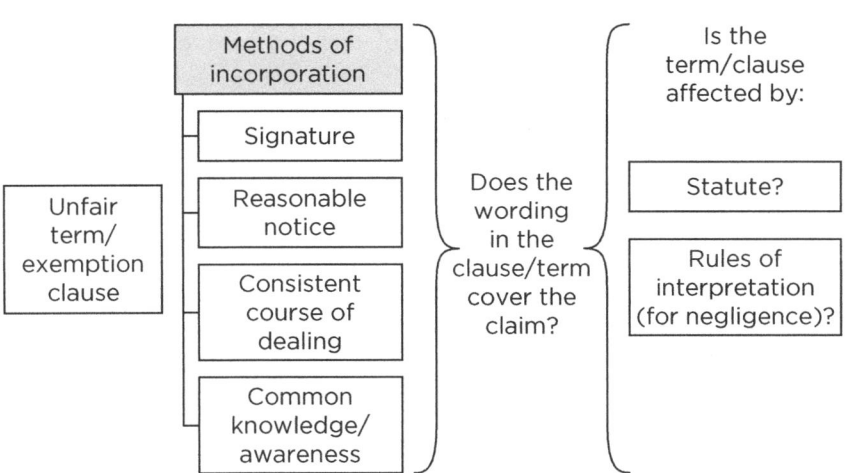

## ■ SQE ASSESSMENT ADVICE

As you work through this chapter, remember to pay particular attention in your revision to:
- The different ways in which unfair terms and exemption clauses can be incorporated into a contract.
- The rules that govern the interpretation of unfair terms and exemption clauses.
- The rules that govern exemption clauses relating to negligence.
- The different regimes of B2B, and B2C, that regulate the enforceability of unfair terms and exemption clauses.

## ■ WHAT DO YOU KNOW ALREADY?

Have a go at these questions before reading this chapter. If you find some difficult or cannot remember the answers, make a note to look more closely at that area during your revision.

1) What are the exceptions to the rule that a term is incorporated into a contract by signature?

   **[Incorporation by signature, page 104]**

2) True or false? An exemption clause that is brought to the attention of a hotel guest after they have checked in at a hotel reception is incorporated into the agreement between the guest and the hotel by reasonable notice.

   **[Timely notice, page 106]**

3) What is the *contra proferentem* rule?

   **[The *contra proferentem* rule, page 110]**

4) In the B2B context, to what extent can a person use an exemption clause to exclude their liability for negligence (other than for death or personal injury)?

   **[Negligence liability other than for death or personal injury, page 112]**

5) True or false? An unfair term is not binding on the consumer.

   **[The statutory control of unfair terms and exemption clauses in the B2C regime, page 113]**

## INTRODUCTION TO UNFAIR TERMS AND EXEMPTION CLAUSES

English law applies special rules to **unfair terms**. This is because unfair terms exclude or limit the remedies available to an injured party, or are otherwise unfair. English law seeks to correct this imbalance. This means that in some cases unfair terms are not enforceable at all, or are only enforceable to the extent that they are reasonable.

> **Key term: unfair term**
>
> The expression unfair term refers to any term of a contract that causes a significant imbalance in the parties' rights and obligations.

The largest category of unfair terms is that of **exemption clauses**.

> **Key term: exemption clause**
>
> An exemption clause is a term in a contract that excludes or limits a party's liability, for example, by limiting it to a specific amount, or by restricting liability to a certain time frame.

Unfair terms are only enforceable if:
- they have been incorporated into the contract,
- the wording in the clause covers the claim, and
- they are not rendered unenforceable by statute or common law.

Let us start by exploring the tests that allow you to determine whether a term has been incorporated into a contract.

## THE INCORPORATION OF UNFAIR TERMS

The same basic rules apply to the incorporation of *all* contract terms, but the rules concerning incorporation are included in this chapter because the common law rules are based mainly on unfair terms and exemption clauses.

Unfair terms can be incorporated into contracts by:
- signature
- reasonable notice
- consistent course of dealing
- common knowledge/awareness.

## Incorporation by signature

The general position is that if a person signs a document, they are bound by it *even* if they have not read it, and do not know what it says.

There are three exceptions to this rule:
- fraud/misrepresentation
- *non est factum*/it is not my deed
- the document is not contractual.

### A person signs a document as a result of fraud or misrepresentation

If a person signs a document containing an exemption clause as a result of fraud or misrepresentation, the person is not bound by the exemption clause.

Practice example 6.1 illustrates how this might arise in practice.

> **Practice example 6.1**
>
> Natasha takes her wedding dress to the dry cleaner to be cleaned. Oxana, who runs the dry cleaners, takes the dress and asks Natasha to sign a receipt that includes a term that the dry-cleaning company is not liable for any damage to the dress. Natasha asks Oxana about this, who tells her that the term only applies to beads and sequins. Natasha signs the receipt and when she returns to collect the dress, she finds that it has been damaged.
>
> Can Oxana rely on the term in the receipt that excludes all liability for damage to the dress?
>
> The answer is no. This example is based on the facts of *Curtis v Chemical Cleaning & Dyeing Co* [1951] 1 KB 805. The Court of Appeal held that the defendant could not rely on the term to exclude liability because the claimant had signed the receipt on the basis of a misrepresentation.

### Non est factum/it is not my deed

*Non est factum* provides a person with a defence against enforcement if the following conditions are satisfied:
- *through no fault of their own*, the person who signed the document did not understand the document they signed, and
- there was a radical or very substantial difference between what the person signed and what the person believed they were signing.

Now work through **Practice example 6.2** to test your understanding.

> **Practice example 6.2**
>
> Rose owns a house and wishes to help her nephew, Bob. Todd, a friend of Bob, asks Rose to sign a document, but Rose cannot read the document because her glasses are broken. Todd tells Rose that the document is a gift of her house to her nephew, so Rose signs the document. In reality, the document is a transfer of Rose's house to Todd for £3,000, which Todd does not pay. Todd takes out a mortgage on the house and defaults on the mortgage. The bank claims the house.
>
> Can Rose rely on the grounds of *non est factum* as a defence against enforcement by the bank?
>
> The answer is no. This example is based on the facts of *Saunders v Anglia Building Society* [1971] AC 1004. The House of Lords considered that the document that Rose signed was not substantially different from the document she thought she was signing; it was a transfer of her house to another person. This meant that a key condition required for the operation of *non est factum* had not been satisfied. In addition, the court felt that Rose was at fault for not checking which document she was signing.

> **Revision tip**
>
> The courts take a very restrictive approach to applying the defence of *non est factum*. When you are considering whether the tests for the operation of *non est factum* have been satisfied, make sure that you take a similarly restrictive approach.

### The document signed does not normally have contractual effect

A person is generally not bound by a term in a document that they sign if the document is one that would not normally have contractual effect. Key examples of such documents include timesheets, invoices and receipts.

### Incorporation by reasonable notice

Some documents form contracts between parties without being signed. A key example of such a document is a train ticket. The terms in such documents are incorporated into the contract, *provided reasonable notice is given to the other party*.

You can determine whether reasonable notice has been given by applying the following tests:
- notice must be timely,
- reasonable steps must be taken to bring the term to the notice of the other party, and
- the document must be one that normally has contractual effect.

> **Revision tip**
>
> When revising this topic, use the letters TRC to remind you of the three tests that need to be satisfied to evidence reasonable notice.
> T = Timely (notice must be ...)
> R = Reasonable (steps ...)
> C = Contractual (effect of the document)

*Timely notice*
To be timely, notice of the term must be communicated to the other party *before* or *at the time* the contract is made.

You can test your understanding of this requirement in **Practice example 6.3**.

> **Practice example 6.3**
>
> Andrew and Louise check into a hotel and pay for their week's holiday at the reception desk. When they enter their bedroom, there is a notice on the back of the door stating, 'The hotel is not responsible for any articles lost or stolen, unless they are delivered to the reception desk for safekeeping'. There was no mention of this when Andrew and Louise checked into the hotel at the reception desk. While Andrew and Louise are out for dinner, a thief sneaks into the hotel bedroom and steals Louise's diamond bracelet. Louise asks the hotel for reimbursement, but the hotel owner says that the hotel is not liable because of the notice on the back of the door.
>
> Was notice of the term on the back of the hotel door timely?
>
> **The answer is no.** This example is based on the facts of *Olley v Marlborough Court Ltd* [1949] 1 KB 532. Here, the Court of Appeal held that the contract between the hotel and the guests was concluded at the reception desk when the guests were not aware of this notice. The hotel guests only saw the notice *after* the contract was concluded. This means that the notice was not timely, so it has no contractual effect.

## Reasonable steps must be taken to bring the term to the notice of the other party

The second test is that reasonable steps must be taken to bring the notice to the attention of the other party.

If the term is *usual* in the given context, it will be incorporated if it, or a reference to it, is prominently displayed on the front of the relevant document. An example of this would be a notice on the front of a train ticket, or on a website. In the case of a reference to the terms, the terms themselves must be accessible. If a term is displayed on the back of a ticket, it is *not* likely to be incorporated *unless* there is wording on the front of the document that alerts the person to the wording on the back. Wording that is obscured by a stamp is not likely to be incorporated.

The approach is different for *onerous* or *unusual* terms. An example of an unusual term is one that imposes a higher cost or burden than is usual. If the term is unusual or onerous, additional measures must be used to bring it to the attention of the other party. This requirement to make additional efforts to bring the term to the attention of the other party is sometimes referred to as the 'red hand rule', although in practice the words are usually in bold, in large print or placed in boxes.

## The document must be one with contractual effect

If the term is in an agreement that is not generally understood to have contractual effect, it will not be incorporated.

**Practice example 6.4** illustrates how this might arise in practice.

### Practice example 6.4

Grace went to sunbathe in the park and spotted a sign that read 'Hire of chairs, £2 for three hours. Tickets can be obtained from the park attendant and should be retained for inspection'. Grace paid £2 to the park attendant and received a deckchair and a ticket in return. Grace glanced at the ticket before putting it in her pocket and then sat in the deckchair to sunbathe. Unfortunately, the deckchair snapped shut and trapped Grace in it. Grace contacted the park attendant who showed her the exemption clause on the back of the ticket: 'The park authority will not be liable for any accident or damage arising from the hire of the deckchair'.

Is the exemption clause incorporated into Grace's contract with the park authority?

The answer is no. This example is based on the facts of *Chapelton v Barry Urban District Council* [1940] 1 KB 532. The Court of Appeal held that the ticket given to the customer was a receipt for money paid, and not a contractual document.

## Incorporation by consistent course of dealing

If parties work together *consistently* on specific terms, a term may be incorporated into a specific contract, even if it was not brought to the attention of the other party in the specific contract to which a claim relates. You should note that the courts are more open to finding consistency in B2B dealings.

Consider the approach that a court takes in practice to arguments of a consistent course of dealing in **Practice example 6.5**.

### Practice example 6.5

Douglas paid a ferry company to ship a car to Scotland and was given a receipt by the ferry company. While the ferry company was taking the car to Scotland, it sank and the car was lost. Douglas brings a claim against the ferry company, which says that it is not liable because of an exemption clause in its standard terms and conditions. The ferry company argues that although Douglas did not sign a copy of a risk note containing its standard terms and conditions on the occasion when the ferry sank, he had done so in the past when he transacted with them. Based on the evidence, Douglas shows that sometimes he signed the risk note containing the standard terms and conditions and sometimes he did not.

Is the exemption clause in the ferry company's standard terms and conditions incorporated into the contract with Douglas as a result of a consistent course of dealing?

The answer is no. This example is based on the facts of *McCutcheon v David MacBrayne Ltd* [1964] 1 WLR 125. The person who took the car to the ferry company gave evidence to show that sometimes, *but not always*, he was asked to sign a risk note containing the terms and conditions. This lack of consistency undermined the ferry company's argument that the terms were incorporated through a consistent course of dealing.

### Exam warning

Incorporation by consistent course of dealing is dependent upon evidence of consistency. If the scenario shows that a term is not included *every single* time, this can undermine the argument of incorporation through consistent course of dealing, even if the parties have been dealing for a long period of time.

## Incorporation by common knowledge/awareness of industry practice

The final way in which a term may be incorporated into a contract is through evidence to show a common understanding of the parties that a term is included in the contract *based on industry practice*. In other words, evidence that both the parties knew that a particular term applied to their transaction because the term is in standard use in that industry or trade. An example of this is where two parties work together in the crane hire industry without agreeing all the terms of their cooperation in detail. If the evidence shows that parties in the crane hire industry *always* operate on the basis of specific terms, then the court will hold that such terms are incorporated into the contract between such parties on the basis of industry practice. It is not necessary to show that the parties had worked together previously.

### Exam warning

Be careful to look out for scenarios where parties operate in similar industries, but not the same ones. The courts apply these rules restrictively so they are unlikely to decide that a term is incorporated by common knowledge of industry practice unless the parties are in *exactly* the same industry.

## AS A MATTER OF INTERPRETATION, IS THE CLAIM COVERED BY THE WORDING IN THE EXEMPTION CLAUSE?

If you conclude that a term has been incorporated into a contract, the next step is to analyse whether the words used in the term cover the claim in question. Most commonly this means checking whether the claim that an injured party could bring is excluded or limited by the exemption clause.

The approach is the same as that discussed in **Chapter 5**, which is that if the wording is clear, you must analyse the ordinary and natural meaning of the words. Only if the wording is ambiguous will the courts look outside the written words of the contract to the context in which it was concluded. The courts also apply **the *contra proferentem* rule**, described below.

> **Key term: the *contra proferentem* rule**
>
> Any ambiguity or doubt in wording in a contract is to be interpreted in the way least favourable to the party seeking to rely on it to limit or exclude their liability.

### The *contra proferentem* rule

If the meaning of an exemption clause is ambiguous, the *contra proferentem* rule requires that the ambiguity is interpreted in the way that is least favourable to the party that seeks to rely on it.

You can see an example of how this works in practice in **Practice example 6.6**.

> **Practice example 6.6**
>
> Before Veronica goes on holiday with her five children, she takes out an insurance policy on her car. The insurance policy excludes liability for damage 'caused or arising whilst the car is conveying any load in excess of that for which it was constructed'. While Veronica is driving her car with her five children inside, she has an accident and the car is damaged. The insurance company refuses to pay Veronica on the grounds that the car was conveying a load in excess of that for which it was constructed (specifically, six people in a car designed for five people).
>
> Can the insurance company deny liability on that basis?
>
> The answer is no. This scenario is based on *Houghton v Trafalgar Insurance Co Ltd* [1954] 1 QB 247. The Court of Appeal commented that the reference to 'any load' in the exemption clause only covered cases where there was a specified weight that must not be exceeded, as in the case of lorries or vans. Further, the court considered the clause was ambiguous, so that it was not clear what it meant when applied to a private car. So a claim could be brought under the insurance policy.

### Exemption clauses and negligence

Special rules apply to clauses that seek to exclude liability for negligence. The rules are provided by statute and common law.

## Statutory control of exemption clauses in respect of death or personal injury resulting from negligence

Generally, statute renders unenforceable exemption clauses in respect of death or personal injury resulting from negligence. This is the position in both the B2B (Unfair Contract Terms Act (UCTA) 1977, s 2) and the B2C (Consumer Rights Act (CRA) 2015, s 65) regimes.

Exemption clauses in respect of negligence liability (other than in respect for death or personal injury) are subject to specific rules of construction that we will examine below.

## Common law rules that apply to attempts to exclude liability for negligence

Courts take a restrictive approach to interpreting exemption clauses in respect of claims for negligence as shown in **Table 6.1**.

Table 6.1: Common law rules that apply to attempts to exclude liability for negligence

| Common law rules that apply to attempts to exclude liability for negligence | |
|---|---|
| Does the exemption clause state that it exempts a person from liability in negligence? | If yes, the clause is effective. |
| If there is no express reference in the clause to negligence, is the wording in the clause wide enough to cover liability in negligence? | If yes, but the damage in question could also relate to another basis on which to claim, such as breach of contract, then the clause will exclude the contractual liability, but not liability for negligence. |

You will be forgiven for thinking that this approach sounds a bit complicated, but it should make perfect sense once you have worked through **Practice example 6.7**.

### Practice example 6.7

Caradog hires a bicycle and gets injured when the saddle tips and he falls off. Caradog reads his contract with the hire company, and sees that it contains an exemption clause that excludes the company's liability for any personal injuries, but it does not mention negligence. Caradog believes that the company is liable:
- in contract for breach of its contractual obligation to provide a bicycle that is fit for purpose, and
- in negligence for failing to ensure that the bicycle is safe.

## Contents of a contract 2: Exemption clauses and unfair terms

What is the effect on the exemption clause on Caradog's ability to claim against the hire company?

The exemption clause only excludes the hire company's liability in contract. The common law rule provides that if the wording in an exemption clause is wide enough to exclude liability in negligence *and* liability on another basis, but does not mention negligence specifically, the clause excludes the other head of damages, but not negligence. Caradog suffered damage due to breach of contract and negligence. Since the exemption clause does not specifically mention liability in negligence, it excludes liability in contract, but not negligence. This scenario is based on the case of *White v John Warwick & Co Ltd* [1953] 1 WLR 1285.

### Revision tip
The starting point when looking at claims in negligence is to understand whether the exemption clause is rendered unenforceable by statute. If it is not rendered unenforceable by statute, apply the common law test to determine whether the wording in the clause is effective to exclude other claims in negligence.

*Negligence liability other than for death or personal injury*
If you conclude that an exemption clause is effective to exclude liability in negligence (other than for death or personal injury), note that there remains a final hurdle.

In the B2B regime, an exemption clause for negligence is only enforceable if it is *reasonable* (s 2(2) of UCTA 1977). In the B2C regime, such an exemption is only enforceable if it is *fair* (s 62(4)). Guidance as to what is reasonable and fair is provided in **What is reasonable?, page 113** and **What is an unfair term?, page 114**.

## IS THE EXEMPTION CLAUSE OR UNFAIR TERM RENDERED INEFFECTIVE BY STATUTE?

We have looked at the regulation of negligence liability. In this section, we will look at the regulation of other types of liability in the B2B and B2C regimes.

### The statutory control of exemption clauses in the B2B regime
The key statutes are UCTA 1977 and the Sale of Goods Act (SGA) 1979.

## Liability for breach of contract

The terms implied by ss 13–15 of the SGA 1979 that you have seen in **Chapter 5** can be excluded from a contract, provided it is *reasonable* to do so (s 6 UCTA 1977).

## What is reasonable?

This test is set out at s 11 and Schedule 2 of the UCTA 1977 as reflected in **Table 6.2**. The starting point is that the term that purports to exclude liability must be fair and reasonable having regard to all the circumstances which were, or ought reasonably to have been, known to or in the contemplation of the parties when the contract was made.

*Table 6.2: Guidelines for the reasonableness test: relevant considerations*

| Guidelines for the reasonableness test: relevant considerations | |
| --- | --- |
| The bargaining power of the parties | Equal bargaining power suggests the clause is reasonable |
| Whether the customer received an inducement to agree to the term | An inducement supports the idea that the clause is reasonable |
| Whether the customer knew, or ought reasonably to have known, of the existence and extent of the term | This suggests that the clause is reasonable |
| If liability is restricted in the event that a term is not complied with, was it reasonable at the time of the contract to expect compliance with the term? | If it was not reasonable to comply with the clause, it suggests it was not reasonable |
| Whether the goods were manufactured, processed or adapted to the special order of the customer | This suggests that the clause is reasonable |

## The statutory control of unfair terms and exemption clauses in the B2C regime

The key statute is the CRA 2015. In addition to regulating exemption clauses, it regulates unfair terms. The CRA 2015 provides that certain included terms cannot be excluded. For example, a consumer is not bound if a trader excludes the terms deemed included by ss 9–16 CRA 2015 (see **Chapter 5**) and a trader cannot exclude the term by s 49 CRA 2015 that they will supply a service *with reasonable care and skill*. Section 62 CRA 2015 goes further still by providing that an unfair term in a contract or notice does not bind a consumer.

## What is an unfair term?

Section 62(4) of the CRA 2015 states that a term is unfair if, *contrary to the requirements of good faith*, it causes a significant imbalance in the parties' rights and obligations under a contract to the detriment of the consumer. You need to take into account the nature of the subject matter of the contract and all the circumstances existing when the term was agreed and to all other terms of the contract.

> **Revision tip**
>
> You should familiarise yourself with the numerous examples of terms that may be regarded as unfair in Part 1 of Schedule 2 of the CRA 2015.

Now test your understanding of when the courts will determine that a term is unfair in **Practice example 6.8**.

> **Practice example 6.8**
>
> Barry wanted to park in town and saw a car park with 20 signs outside. The signs were large, prominent and legible and stated 'Two hour maximum stay – Customer only car park – Failure to comply with the following will result in a parking charge of £85 – Parking limited to two hours (no return within one hour)'. Barry parked his car, went shopping and returned three hours later. The car park company issued a charge of £85 to Barry.
>
> Can Barry argue that he is not bound by the £85 charge because it is an unfair term?
>
> The answer is no. This scenario is based on the case of *ParkingEye Ltd v Beavis* [2015] UKSC 67. The Supreme Court held that although there was an imbalance in the bargaining powers of the parties, the term was not 'contrary to the requirements of good faith', which is a key element in the definition of an unfair term. Considering all of the circumstances of the scenario, the court held that the motorist was being given two hours free parking, and that the car park company had a legitimate interest in levying the £85 fine to anyone who overstayed to allow it to efficiently manage its parking spaces and generate income. Moreover, the risk of whether the motorist had to pay the fine depended entirely on whether the motorist chose to leave his car in the parking space for more than two hours. The court held that the term was reasonable from an objective standpoint.

> **Revision tip**
>
> You might have felt sorry for the motorist in the case referred to in **Practice example 6.8**. However, this example contains lots of useful factors that illustrate how courts consider the nature of the contract and the surrounding circumstances.

## ■ KEY POINT CHECKLIST

This chapter has covered the following key knowledge points. You can use these to structure your revision around, making sure to recall the key details for each point, as covered in this chapter.

- Generally, a person is bound by a document they sign, unless they sign it as a result of fraud or misrepresentation, *non est factum* applies, or the document signed does not have contractual effect.
- A term may be incorporated into a contractual document by reasonable notice. You must be able to apply the three tests (Timely, Reasonable and Contractual) to reach the correct answer.
- A term may also be incorporated by consistent course of dealing.
- A term may also be deemed to have been incorporated by common knowledge/industry practice. Remember that this test can only be relied upon where the parties are in exactly the same industry.
- Once it is clear that an unfair term or exemption clause has been incorporated, you must test the language to see whether it covers the relevant claim. Remember the effect of the *contra proferentem* rule on ambiguous wording.
- A party cannot exclude negligence liability that results from death or personal injury.
- Remember the tests of interpretation for exemption clauses where there is liability for negligence and on another ground. If the exemption clause covers liability in negligence, the final hurdle is that the clause must be reasonable (B2B) or fair (B2C) to be enforceable.
- You should also note in respect of the B2B regime that a trader can only exclude ss 13–15 SGA 1979 if it is reasonable.
- The position is stricter in respect of the B2C regime because terms deemed included by ss 9–16 CRA 2016 cannot be excluded. Further, a consumer is not bound by an unfair term.

## ■ KEY TERMS AND CONCEPTS

- unfair term (**page 103**)
- exemption clause (**page 103**)
- contra proferentem (**page 110**)

# Contents of a contract 2: Exemption clauses and unfair terms

## ■ SQE1-STYLE QUESTIONS

### QUESTION 1

A man runs a café and is visited by a company selling coffee machines. The man agrees to buy a coffee machine from the company for £1,000 and signs the company's standard form sales agreement without reading it. The company delivers the coffee machine to the man. After a week, the coffee machine breaks and the engineer who examines the machine states that it is not of satisfactory quality. The man contacts the company to claim a new coffee machine on the grounds of breach of the implied term to supply goods of satisfactory quality. The company refers the man to a clause in the sales agreement that excludes any implied term into the contract that goods supplied are of satisfactory quality.

**Which of the following statements best describes whether the man can claim against the company?**

A. The man has no grounds to claim against the company because of the general rule that a person is bound by a contract that he signs, regardless of whether or not he has read the contract.

B. The man has no grounds to claim against the company because of the absolute rule that a person is bound by a contract he signs, regardless of whether or not he has read the contract.

C. The man can claim against the company if he can show that it was not reasonable for the company to exclude an implied term that its goods are of satisfactory quality.

D. The man can claim against the company on the basis that he is not bound by a contract that he signed due to fraud/misrepresentation.

E. The man is not bound by the contract because he can rely on the defence that, through no fault of his own, he did not understand what he signed, and that there was a radical difference between what he signed and what he believed he was signing.

### QUESTION 2

A man takes his car to the carwash to be cleaned. The woman who runs the carwash asks the man to sign a document that includes a term that the carwash company is not liable for any damage to the car. The man asks the woman about the term and she responds that it only applies to damage caused by birds while the car is waiting to be cleaned. The man signs the document and leaves the car at the carwash. When the man returns to collect his car, he discovers that the paintwork has been scratched because the woman used a wire brush to clean the car.

**Which of the following statements best describes the basis on which the man can claim against the woman?**

A. The man cannot claim against the woman because a written statement in an agreement has greater legal weight than an oral statement, such as that made by the woman.
B. The man can only claim against the woman if he can show that the exemption clause is unfair.
C. The man can claim against the woman because the woman cannot rely on the exemption clause because the man signed the document on the basis of the woman's misrepresentation.
D. The man cannot claim against the woman because the exemption clause was incorporated into the contract on a timely basis, which is when the contract between the man and the woman was made.
E. The man cannot claim against the woman because the exemption clause is incorporated into the contract by the man's signature.

## QUESTION 3

In a telephone call, a trading company agrees to buy oil from an energy company. The parties agree basic terms, including the price. After the call, the trading company sends its standard terms and conditions to the energy company. The trading company has made five previous transactions with the energy company in the last year and each transaction had been concluded in the same way. Subsequently, a dispute arises between the parties and the trading company claims that the dispute is governed by its standard terms and conditions.

**Which of the following best reflects the legal position of the parties?**

A. The dispute cannot be governed by the trading company's standard terms and conditions because contract was made through the telephone call, and the trading company's terms and conditions came too late to be part of the contract.
B. In view of the previous consistent course of dealing between the parties, the trading company's standard terms and conditions have been incorporated into the transaction.

118  Contents of a contract 2: Exemption clauses and unfair terms

C. The trading company's standard terms and conditions will only have been incorporated into the transaction if the energy company signed them and returned them to the trading company.

D. The trading company's standard terms and conditions will not have been incorporated into the transaction because the agreement concluded over the telephone was an oral agreement on which written documents have no effect.

E. The trading company's standard terms and conditions will not have been incorporated because such a document is not one that a reasonable person would expect to have contractual effect.

## QUESTION 4

A library provides a service of sending books by post to customers to read. Customers return the books to the library by post after the allotted reading time of ten days. A man orders a book from the library and receives it with a delivery note from the library. The delivery note stated that the book had to be returned in ten days and that a daily fee of £20 would be charged for every day the book was retained beyond that. The entire delivery note was in small print without any words in bold or any boxes around wording. The man forgot about the book for 30 days, then he received a large invoice from the library.

**Which of the following best reflects the man's position in this case?**

A. The man is bound to pay the invoice because he received timely notice of the term about the daily fee.

B. The man is not bound to pay the invoice if he can show that the daily fee was particularly onerous and unusual and there is no evidence to show that it was explicitly brought to the man's attention.

C. The man is bound to pay the invoice because even if he can show that the daily fee is particularly onerous and unusual, the daily fee was written in the delivery note and the man should have taken responsibility for reading it.

D. The man is bound to pay the invoice because it was entirely his choice to keep the book for the loan period of ten days, or to take the risk of paying the daily fee if he chose to keep the book for longer.

E. The man is not bound by the term in the delivery note because he did not sign it.

## QUESTION 5

A woman hires a horse from a farm. At the farm's request, the woman signs an agreement that states that the farm will not be liable for any damage caused to a rider, including injury or death as a result of negligence. During the ride, the horse's saddle slips off and the woman falls into a ravine and injures herself. The evidence shows that the farm was negligent because the horse's saddle was not attached safely.

**Which of the following statements most accurately describes the legal position of the parties?**

A. Since the woman chose to sign the agreement, she is bound by it even if she did not read it.
B. The exemption clause is effective to protect the farm from liability if it is reasonable.
C. An exemption clause that excludes liability for death or personal injury is unenforceable so the woman can claim against the farm for negligence.
D. If the woman can also claim on the grounds of breach of contract, this will exclude her ability to claim on the grounds of negligence.
E. The exemption clause is ineffective to protect the farm from liability because it is unreasonable.

## ■ ANSWERS TO QUESTIONS

### Answers to 'What do you know already?' questions at the start of the chapter

1) The exceptions to the rule that a term is incorporated by signature are if the person signs the document as a result of fraud or misrepresentation, *non est factum* (it is not my deed), and if the document signed does not normally have contractual effect.
2) False. The contract will be concluded when the guest checks into the hotel. A notice that comes after this is too late to be incorporated.
3) The *contra proferentem* rule provides that if the meaning of a term is ambiguous, the ambiguity is interpreted in the way that is *least* favourable to the person who seeks to rely on it.

4) In the B2B context, a trader may exclude liability for negligence (other than as relates to death or personal injury) to the extent that it is reasonable.
5) True. An unfair term is not binding on a consumer.

## Answers to end-of-chapter SQE1-style questions

Question 1:
 The correct answer was C. This reflects the law in the business to business (B2B) context. Section 6 UCTA 1977 provides that a person can only restrict liability for breach of the implied term (s 14(2) SGA 1979) that goods supplied under a contract are of satisfactory quality if it satisfies the requirement of reasonableness. Option A is the correct description of the general rule about a person being bound by a contract they sign, regardless of whether they read it; but Option A ignores the operation of UCTA 1977 and the SGA 1979, described above. Option B is wrong for the same reason; in addition, the rule that a person is bound by a document they sign is not an absolute rule. Option D is incorrect as there is no evidence of fraud or misrepresentation in the scenario. Option E is incorrect because a person can only claim not to be bound by an action (*non est factum/* it is not my deed) if, through no fault of their own, they did not understand the document they signed. Since it was the man's fault that he did not read the contract, he cannot rely on this defence.

Question 2:
 The correct answer was C. The woman cannot rely on the exemption clause because the man signed it on the basis of her misrepresentation. Option B is incorrect because although it is true to say that a trader cannot enforce an unfair term against a consumer, there is not enough information available to determine whether the term is unfair. By contrast, the misrepresentation provides a clear basis for the man not to be bound by the exemption clause. Option A is incorrect. Although it is easier to prove the existence of a written term from an evidential point of view, it is not true to say that a written statement overrides an oral one. Option D is incorrect because although the term was incorporated on a timely basis, the misrepresentation means that the man is not bound by the exemption clause. Option E is incorrect due to the effect of the misinterpretation.

Question 3:
 The correct answer was B. Where parties transact on a regular basis on standard terms and conditions, they may be incorporated into

# Key cases, rules, statutes and instruments

the contract provided the course of dealing is consistent. Watch out for scenarios where the previous dealings between the parties is not 100% consistent. This lack of consistency is likely to undermine an argument for incorporation based on consistent course of dealing. Option A is incorrect because the rationale behind the consistent course of dealing basis of incorporation is that the parties are deemed to be aware of the terms because they were consistently included in their previous trades. Option C is incorrect for the same reason. Incorporation by consistent course of dealing is not dependent upon signature. Option D is not correct because there is nothing to prevent an agreement being concluded on the basis of both oral and written communications. Option E is incorrect because a company's standard terms and conditions is the type of document that would be expected to have legal effect.

Question 4:

The correct answer was B. Onerous or unusual terms must be *explicitly* brought to the attention of the other party by being included in bold print, or by being put in a box, for example. The explicit notice requirements for unusual or onerous terms mean that Options A, C and D are incorrect. Option E is incorrect because terms can be incorporated by reasonable notice, as well as by signature.

Question 5:

The correct answer was C. This is governed by the B2C regime, and s 65 CRA 2015 provides that an exemption clause that excludes death or personal injury is unenforceable. This means that Options A and B are incorrect. Note that in scenarios where a person attempts to exclude liability for negligence (other than for death or personal injury) in the B2C context, this is only enforceable if it is *fair*. The requirement for exemptions to be *reasonable* applies in the business to business (B2B) context, which is not applicable in this scenario. Option E is therefore incorrect. Option D is incorrect because of Option C, but note that if an exemption clause mentions negligence, it *will* be effective to exclude liability for negligence (other than for death/personal injury) and subject to the requirement to be fair (B2C) or reasonable (B2B).

## ■ KEY CASES, RULES, STATUTES AND INSTRUMENTS

The SQE1 Assessment Specification does not require you to know any case names, or statutory materials, for this topic.

# 7

# Misrepresentation

## ■ MAKE SURE YOU KNOW

For the SQE1 assessment, you are required to know the law relating to misrepresentation. This will allow you to determine whether the person has been induced to enter into a contract by a misrepresentation. In addition, you are required to know the different categories of misrepresentation and the remedies available to the party who has been induced to enter into the contract by the misrepresentation.

1. Tests to be satisfied to bring a claim for misrepresentation
2. Categories of misrepresentation

Misrepresentation

4. Beware: factors that can undermine a claim for misrepresentation
3. Remedies for misrepresentation

## ■ SQE ASSESSMENT ADVICE

As you work through this chapter, remember to pay particular attention in your revision to:
- The tests and conditions to be satisfied to bring a claim for misrepresentation.
- The different categories of misrepresentation.
- The remedies for the different types of misrepresentation.
- The factors that can undermine a claim for misrepresentation.

## ■ WHAT DO YOU KNOW ALREADY?

Have a go at these questions before reading this chapter. If you find some difficult or cannot remember the answers, make a note to look more closely at that area during your revision.

1) What are the three broad categories of misrepresentation?
   [The categories of misrepresentation and their remedies, page 133]
2) True or false? Words or conduct can amount to a misrepresentation.
   [Statement, page 126]
3) True or false? Provided a statement is true at the time it is made, the representor is not under a duty to correct the statement if it becomes untrue.
   [False due to a change in circumstances, page 125]
4) Which four conditions does a representee need to satisfy to prove that the statement induced them to enter into the contract?
   [The statement must induce the representee to enter into the contract, page 130]
5) What are the remedies for misrepresentation?
   [The categories of misrepresentation and their remedies, page 133]

## INTRODUCTION TO MISREPRESENTATION

Parties frequently exchange statements before they make the contract (see **Chapter 5**). Some of these statements are classified as representations. Some representations are classified as **misrepresentations**.

> **Key term: misrepresentation**
>
> A misrepresentation is an unambiguous, false statement of fact (or law) addressed to the representee that induces the representee to enter into the contract.

There are separate regimes for contracts in the business to business context (B2B) and the business to consumer (B2C) context. Section 50 of the Consumer Rights Act 2015 applies to service contracts in the B2C context. It treats as a term of the contract anything that is said or written to the consumer by a trader about the trader or the service if the consumer takes it into account when deciding whether to enter into the contract. Since terms are treated differently from misrepresentations, they will not be discussed in this section. Similarly, other contracts in the B2C regime are governed by the Digital Markets, Competition and Consumers Act 2024. This Act provides certain remedies specifically for consumers and they will not be discussed in this section.

**Figure 7.1** provides an outline of the key features of a misrepresentation.

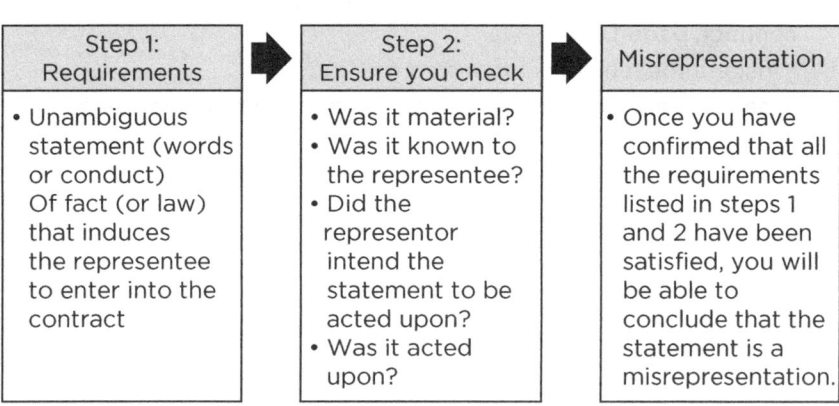

*Figure 7.1: Identifying a misrepresentation*

Now we shall unpick each of the elements to a misrepresentation.

## UNAMBIGUOUS

The first step in establishing whether a statement is capable of being a misrepresentation is that it must be unambiguous. The test is an objective one, looking at how a reasonable person would interpret the statement.

If a statement is ambiguous or unclear, it should be given the meaning that the representor intended or that the representor knew that the representee would understand. This means that a representee cannot claim that a true statement is a misrepresentation simply because they have interpreted it in an unreasonable way.

## FALSE

The next step is to establish that the statement in question was false, or incorrect, at the time it was made.

Check your understanding of this step in **Practice example 7.1**.

> **Practice example 7.1**
>
> Zeinab goes into Charlie's art gallery and admires a painting on the wall that was drawn the previous week by his baby daughter. Charlie tells Zeinab that the painting is by Pablo Picasso. Zeinab buys the painting.
>
> Was Charlie's statement that the painting was by Pablo Picasso false when it was made?
>
> **The answer is yes. This is because the painting was made by Charlie's baby daughter, rather than by Pablo Picasso.**

### False due to a change in circumstances

Watch out for statements that are correct at the time they are made, but subsequently become false, or incorrect, before the contract is concluded. For example, a person may tell a prospective buyer that their business generates an annual profit of £100,000, but by the time the prospective buyer actually buys the business, the annual profit could have changed. In such circumstances, the courts consider that the representor is under an obligation to correct the representation until the time when the sale is completed. If the person fails to correct this statement before the sale, it could be held to be a misrepresentation.

Now apply your knowledge in this area in **Practice example 7.2**.

### Practice example 7.2

Kwasi wants to sell his medical practice and talks to Matt who is interested in buying it. Kwasi tells Matt that the medical practice generates income of around £50,000 per annum. This statement is true at the time Kwasi makes it. But after Kwasi makes the statement, he loses interest in his practice and the income of the medical practice falls. By the time Matt buys Kwasi's business a few months after their discussions, the annual income of Kwasi's medical practice has fallen to £20,000 per annum.

Is Kwasi's statement to Matt that the medical practice generated £50,000 per annum a misrepresentation?

**The answer is yes. This example is based on the scenario in *With v O'Flanagan* [1936] Ch 575 CA. The court held that the representee was entitled to believe the statement about the income of the medical practice until he bought it. Clearly, the seller's statement was correct when he made it. But the statement *became* incorrect *before* the sale. The court held that the seller was under a duty to correct the statement that had become untrue before the sale took place. The seller's failure to correct the statement that had become incorrect meant that it was a misrepresentation.**

## STATEMENT

The requirement for a statement covers words communicated to the representee. But a misrepresentation can also be made by:
- a person's conduct or behaviour, or
- by a person's statement that fails to disclose all the relevant facts.

### Conduct

A statement can be conduct that conveys a false impression. **Practice example 7.3** provides a useful example of conduct conveying a false impression.

### Practice example 7.3

Elizabeth is planning to sell her flat, but she is worried about the fact that it will be difficult to sell as one of the walls shows signs of dry rot. So Elizabeth paints over the wall to hide the dry rot. Eryl, a prospective buyer, visits the flat and decides to buy it. After a few months, Eryl discovers that the flat has dry rot.

Does Eryl have a remedy against Elizabeth?

The answer is yes. This scenario is based on the case of *Gordon v Selico* (1986) 18 HLR 219. The court held that painting to hide the dry rot was a misrepresentation that there was no dry rot.

## Failure to disclose all the relevant facts

Generally, there is no rule of disclosure under English law. This means that where two parties are planning to enter into a contract, neither party is under an obligation to disclose to the other all relevant facts that they know. But note that this rule is subject to exceptions, including:
- change of circumstances (see **Practice example 7.2**), and
- not the whole truth.

### Not the whole truth

A statement that is misleading because it fails to disclose all the material facts can be a misrepresentation. Such statements might describe what appears to be factually true at the time they are made, but because they do not include all of the relevant facts, they communicate a false message to the representee. For example, imagine a client instructs a solicitor to act for them in the purchase of a land plot. When the client asks the solicitor to confirm if there are any restrictions on the land plot, the solicitor, *who has not read the legal documents*, responds that they are not aware of any restrictions. The solicitor's statement is a misrepresentation. Although it is technically true for the solicitor to say that they are not aware of any restrictions, their statement is misleading. This is because they have left out the important information that they are not aware of any restrictions because they have not read the relevant documents.

Now test your understanding of this area of law in **Practice example 7.4**.

## Practice example 7.4

Benazir decides to sell her property portfolio. Benazir's sales documentation refers to an office block as 'let to the Prudential Insurance Company for £800,000 per annum'. Eskander buys Benazir's property portfolio and is shocked to find that Benazir had been notified that the Prudential Insurance Company had given notice to end its rental of the office block before she prepared the sales documentation.

Has Benazir made a misrepresentation?

The answer is yes. This scenario is based on *Dimmock v Hallett* (1866–67) LR 2 Ch App 21. The court held that the seller's statement led the purchaser to believe that he was buying a property with a continuing tenancy. Whereas, in reality, the purchaser had to find new tenants soon after completing his purchase. It was this failure to present the full picture to the representee that amounted to a misrepresentation.

## Exam warning

Watch out for scenarios where one party to a contract knows more than the other, but fails to disclose the full story, or behaves in a way that does not disclose the full story.

## STATEMENTS OF FACT OR LAW

The general position is that a misrepresentation must be a statement of fact or law, and not of opinion, belief or intention.

### Statements of opinion or belief

Remember the general rule that a misrepresentation must be a statement of fact or law. This means that false statements of opinion or belief are not misrepresentations, provided the representor is not in a better position to know the facts than the representee.

Now apply your knowledge in **Practice example 7.5**.

## Practice example 7.5

Jacqui decides to sell a piece of agricultural land. She is in discussions with Shaun, a prospective buyer. Shaun is interested in buying the land to farm sheep on it so he asks Jacqui how many sheep the land could support. Shaun is aware that the land has never been used to farm sheep. Jacqui tells Shaun that if she worked the land, she thought it could support 2,000 sheep. Shaun buys the land, but then discovers that it cannot support 2,000 sheep.

Can Shaun claim against Jacqui for misrepresentation?

The answer is no. This scenario is based on *Bisset v Wilkinson* [1927] AC 177 PC (NZ). The court held that such a statement was not a misrepresentation. This was because the buyer was aware that the land had not been used as a sheep farm, so the representor was not in a better position to know the facts than the representee (the buyer). This meant that the representor's statement could only be a statement of opinion.

## *Statements of opinion or belief where the representor knows the facts*

There is an exception to the general rule that a statement of opinion is not a misrepresentation. This exception applies to a statement of opinion by a representor who is in a *better* position to know the facts than the representee. This is because such opinions imply that the representor knows the facts that justify their opinion.

Let us explore how this might arise by working through **Practice example 7.6.**

### Practice example 7.6

A hotel chain wishes to sell one of its hotels. In its sales documentation it describes a long-term tenant in the hotel as a 'most desirable tenant'. Hamid reads the sales documentation and buys the hotel. Hamid soon finds out that the tenant was behind with her rent when the sales documentation was written.

Can Hamid claim against the hotel chain for misrepresentation?

The answer is yes. This scenario is based on *Smith v Land & House Property Corporation* (1884) LR 28 Ch D 7 CA. The court held that in cases where the representor knows the facts best, their statement of opinion involves a material statement of fact.

## Statements of intention

As with statements of opinion, statements of intention do not generally amount to misrepresentations. But beware that if a person *fraudulently* claims to have an intention that they do not have, the law interprets this as a false statement of fact and therefore a misrepresentation.

Consider how this might arise in practice in **Practice example 7.7**.

> **Practice example 7.7**
>
> Ezinne offers shares in her company to the public, stating that the company intends to raise money to grow its business. In actual fact, Ezinne's business has liquidity problems and Ezinne intends to use the funds raised from the share sale to pay off existing liabilities.
>
> Is Ezinne's statement of intention a misrepresentation?
>
> The answer is yes. This is based on the case of *Edgington v Fitzmaurice* (1885) LR 29 Ch D 459 CA. In scenarios where a person states that they have an intention that in fact they do not have, the law treats such false statements of present intention as a misrepresentation.

> **Exam warning**
>
> Look carefully for words in statements that indicate the representor's *belief* or *intention*. These words lead you to the assumption that the statement is an opinion or belief, which, as a general rule, is not a misrepresentation. The next step is to test your assumption by checking whether the scenario indicates that the representor is in a better position to know the underlying facts than the representee or is falsely stating an intention that they do not have. The superior knowledge of the representor, or the false statement of intention, will displace the assumption that the statement of opinion or belief is not a misrepresentation.

## THE STATEMENT MUST INDUCE THE REPRESENTEE TO ENTER INTO THE CONTRACT

Once you have satisfied the first three steps (described previously), you must prove that the statement *induced* the representee to enter into the contract. To prove this, the representee must satisfy the four conditions below:
- the statement must be material,
- the representee must be aware of the statement,
- the representor must intend the representee to act on the statement, and
- the representee must act on the statement.

## The statement must be material
A statement is material if it would affect the judgment of a reasonable person in deciding whether or not to enter into the contract, or one that would induce them to enter into the contract without making such enquiries as they would otherwise make. For example, in a scenario in which a person is willing to sell a secret recipe to a person who is not a competitor, a statement from the purchaser that they are not a competitor is *material*.

> **Exam warning**
>
> It might sound like a daunting test for your assessments to have to consider whether the statement in question is material. But bear in mind that the scenario should help you. For example, in a scenario where a representee asks if the object being sold is in good condition, and the representor makes a statement that the object is in good condition, and then the representee proceeds to buy the object, then the statement will be material.

## The representee must be aware of the statement
A person needs to be aware of a misrepresentation before or at the time of contracting. In situations where a statement is made to the representee before the time of contracting, or a person inspects a damaged item that has been made to look perfect, it is easy to prove that the person was aware of the statement. But what about scenarios in which a person buys a damaged item that has been changed to look undamaged *without inspecting it*? If a person buys a damaged vase that has been made to look perfect *without inspecting it*, then the buyer cannot be aware of the representor's statement. This is an important point because it means that a person cannot rescind a contract on the grounds of misrepresentation if they discover the misrepresentation after they have concluded the contract.

## The representor must intend the representee to act on the statement
A person cannot bring a claim for misrepresentation unless they can show that the representor intended the person to act on the statement. For example, in a discussion between a seller of a car and a prospective buyer in a car showroom, a statement by the seller to the prospective buyer that the car is in good condition is not intended for a person who has just popped in from the street to use the toilet in the car showroom and hears the statement on their way back outside.

## Revision tip

It will help your revision to understand that the driver behind this condition is to narrow the number of persons who can bring a claim for misrepresentation. So, for example, if an SQE1 assessment question tells you that Party A makes a representation to Party B in respect of a sale, and that Party Y (who is hiding in a cupboard) overhears the statement by chance, acts on it and seeks to claim for misrepresentation, Party Y's claim will fail because Party A (being unaware of Party Y's presence) could not have intended Party Y to act on their statement. The law quite rightly limits the ability of persons who can bring a claim to those for whom the statement was intended.

## The representee must act on the statement in question

There must be a link between the statement and the action of the representee. The starting point is to ask whether the representee would have acted as they did if the statement had not been made. If it is clear that the representee would not have acted as they did, *but for* the statement, then the test is satisfied.

### Did the statement materially contribute to the act?

It is essential to note that even if the statement was not the sole reason for the representee's act, they may still be able to bring a claim for misrepresentation. To do this, the representee needs to prove that the statement made a material contribution to (or played a real and substantial part in) the representee's decision.

### Causation is presumed if the statement is fraudulent and material

If the misrepresentation is fraudulent and material, the burden of proof lies with the representor. So to avoid liability for misrepresentation, the representor must prove that the representee would have acted as they did *but for* the statement.

### What if the representee makes their own investigations?

In practice, parties often conduct their own due diligence before entering into a contract. If a representee makes investigations to verify the statement, this can undermine the argument that they acted on the statement. For example, in *Attwood v Small* 7 ER 684, a mine owner made false statements to a prospective buyer about the capabilities of a mine that he was selling. The prospective buyer hired agents to verify the mine owner's statements, and the agents confirmed that the mine owner's statements were correct. Subsequently, the buyer bought the mine, but later sought to rescind the contract when he discovered that the mine owner's statements were incorrect. The court refused to allow the buyer to rescind the contract. The court's logic was that the buyer did not rely on the seller's statement, but rather tested its accuracy by relying on his own agents. This rule does not apply if the representor is fraudulent.

> **Exam warning**
>
> Note that the representee's claim for misrepresentation will only be undermined if the representee relies *entirely* on their own due diligence/investigations. So if the representee relies partly on the statement, and partly on their own investigations, they will still be able to bring a claim for misrepresentation.

*What if the representee fails to test the accuracy of the statement?*

Where a person is offered the opportunity to test the accuracy of a statement, and fails to do so, they may still be able to claim misrepresentation. But be aware that the representee's damages could be reduced to reflect their contributory negligence.

## THE CATEGORIES OF MISREPRESENTATION AND THEIR REMEDIES

Once you determine that a statement is a misrepresentation, you need to identify its category of misrepresentation. This is important because the category of misrepresentation informs the damages that can be recovered.

> **Exam warning**
>
> In the SQE1 assessments, you need to pay careful attention to factors, including state of mind of the representor when a statement is made. For example, was the representor dishonest, or just careless? Focusing on factors such as these will help you to identify the correct type of misrepresentation, which is important because it tells you which remedies are available to the representee.

The remedy of **rescission** is available for all types of misrepresentation, unless it has been lost. For example, in a contract to sell a car, the remedy of rescission would require the car to be returned to the seller and the price of the car to be returned to the buyer.

### Key term: rescission

Setting the contract aside with the aim of putting the parties back in the position they were in before the contact was made.

### Revision tip

In some circumstances, rescission may not be available as a remedy. Make sure that you are aware of the key reasons that make rescission unavailable. Key reasons that make rescission unavailable are:
- Affirmation, for example, where the representee, being aware of the misrepresentation and right to rescind, through actions or words, communicates to the representor their intention to continue with the contract. Examples of affirmation include a person continuing to hold shares that were bought on the basis of a misrepresentation, or continuing to use a vehicle bought on the basis of a misrepresentation.
- Destruction of the subject matter, for example, where the representee has demolished buildings that they acquired on the basis of a misrepresentation.
- Third party rights, for example, where the goods acquired on the basis of a misrepresentation have passed under a contract to an innocent third party without notice.

The different types of misrepresentation are shown in **Figure 7.2**.

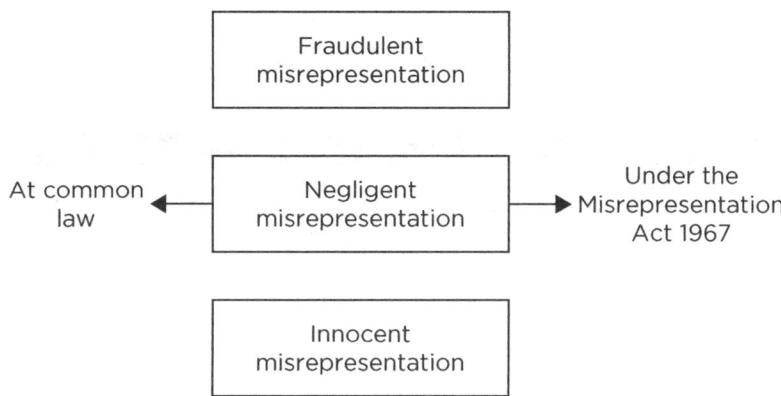

*Figure 7.2: The categories of misrepresentation*

We will consider each category of misrepresentation and its remedies in turn.

## Fraudulent misrepresentation
The representee must establish that the representor:
- knew that the statement was false,
- did not believe the statement was true, or
- was reckless, not caring whether the statement was true or false.

> **Exam warning**
> Be careful when determining the category of misrepresentation in any scenario. The key test in fraudulent misrepresentation is to show that the representor knew that their statement was not true. So if a representor believes their statement to be true, it will not be a fraudulent misrepresentation.

*Remedies for fraudulent misrepresentation*
You are required to know the two remedies that are available to a claimant who successfully proves fraudulent misrepresentation, namely:
- rescission, and
- damages.

Damages for fraudulent misrepresentation cover all direct loss that flows from the transaction that was induced by the statement, regardless of whether it was foreseeable. The aim of damages for fraudulent misrepresentation is to put the representee in the position they would have been in if the contract had not been made. So if a person buys a vase on the basis of a fraudulent misrepresentation that it is Ming dynasty, whereas in reality, it is from IKEA, the representee can recover damages to reflect the difference between the amount they paid and the value of the vase they acquired.

## Negligent misrepresentation
There are two categories of negligent misrepresentation, but in both cases, the representor is honest and believes their statement to be true. The misrepresentation arises because the representor has not exercised reasonable care and skill in making the statement. In other words, the representor has been careless.

It is important to know that there are two different grounds on which to bring claims for negligent misrepresentation:
- at common law in tort, and
- under statute by the Misrepresentation Act 1967.

### Negligent misrepresentation at common law

To bring a claim for negligent misrepresentation at common law, the representee must prove that there is a special relationship between the representor and the representee. This special relationship gives rise to a duty of care owed by the representor to the representee. This is important because it allows a representee to claim against a person who is not party to a contract with the representee, provided the representee can prove that the representor owed them a duty of care *and* that they breached the duty of care.

### Remedies for negligent misrepresentation at common law

You are required to know the two remedies that are available to a claimant who successfully proves negligent misrepresentation, namely:
- rescission, and
- damages.

Damages for negligent misrepresentation at common law are more limited than damages for fraudulent misrepresentation. Damages for negligent misrepresentation cover all direct loss that flows from the transaction that was induced by the statement, *provided it was reasonably foreseeable*. The aim of damages for negligent misrepresentation is to put the representee in the position they would have been in if the contract had not been made.

### Negligent misrepresentation under the Misrepresentation Act 1967

A key distinction between a claim for negligent misrepresentation under the Misrepresentation Act 1967 and at common law is that the claim under statute does not require a special relationship and duty of care. Once the statement is shown to be false, the representor must prove that they had reasonable grounds to make the statement and that they believed that the statement was true up to the time the contract was concluded.

### Remedies for negligent misrepresentation under the Misrepresentation Act 1967

You are required to know the two remedies that are available to a claimant who successfully proves negligent misrepresentation, namely:
- rescission, and
- damages.

Damages under the Misrepresentation Act 1967 for misrepresentation cover all direct loss that flows from the transaction that was induced by the statement. The aim of damages for negligent misrepresentation is to put the representee in the position they would have been in if the contract had not been made.

## Innocent misrepresentation

A representee may be able to claim for a misrepresentation for a statement that was not made fraudulently or negligently. This is an important ground because a representor can be liable for a statement that they had reasonable grounds to make. In other words, a representor can be liable for a statement where they have not been careless.

### Remedies for innocent misrepresentation

You are required to know the remedies that are available to a claimant who successfully proves innocent misrepresentation, namely:
- rescission.
- There is no automatic right for damages, but the court *may* exercise its discretion under s 2(2) of the Misrepresentation Act 1967 to award damages *instead of* rescission. The court will exercise this discretion if it considers it to be equitable having regard to the circumstances as a whole. In contrast to the other types of damages referred to previously, the representee of an innocent misrepresentation can only have one remedy.

| Revision tip |
|---|
| Remember that the different types of misrepresentation start with the most serious (fraudulent misrepresentation). The remedies for the representee reflect this scale of seriousness, with the most limited remedy available for an innocent misrepresentation. |

Now work through **Practice example 7.8** to check your understanding of the circumstances in which a court will exercise its discretion to award damages in lieu of rescission as a remedy for innocent misrepresentation.

| Practice example 7.8 |
|---|
| Roberta runs a building company and buys land to develop from a county council. After Roberta bought the land for £5 million, the property market deteriorated and the value of the land reduced to £2 million. Roberta's company discovered a sewer running through the land. The council had not disclosed this sewer before the sale and had told her that there were no encumbrances on the land. The sewer on the land can be removed at a cost of £18,000. |

Would a court allow Roberta's company to rescind the contract to purchase the land on the grounds of misrepresentation?

The answer is no. This scenario is based on *William Sindall plc v Cambridgeshire County Council* [1994] 1 WLR 1016. The court exercised its discretion on the basis of factors including:
- the cost of £18,000 to deal with the sewer, which it viewed as of minor importance,
- the loss that could be caused to the buyer if the contract were not rescinded, and
- the loss that would be caused to the county council by rescission.

This decision should remind you that rescission is a very strong remedy that may be considered disproportionate when compared to the effect of the misrepresentation. In such cases, if the courts are entitled to award damages in place of rescission, they are likely to do so.

## ■ KEY POINT CHECKLIST

This chapter has covered the following key knowledge points. You can use these to structure your revision around, making sure to recall the key details for each point, as covered in this chapter.
- Misrepresentation is an unambiguous, false statement of fact (or law) addressed to the representee that induces the representee to enter into the contract.
- Remember that the statement must be a false statement. Note that a statement that is true when it is made can become a misrepresentation if it becomes false before the contract is concluded.
- A statement can be conveyed by words or conduct.
- Remember that if the representor fails to tell the whole story, this may amount to a misrepresentation.
- The general rule is that a statement of opinion or intention cannot be a misrepresentation, but note the exceptions.
- Remember that the misrepresentation must induce the representee to form the contract. Note that four tests must be satisfied to prove inducement.
- It is essential to know the different categories of misrepresentation and what must be shown to prove each category.
- It is essential to know the different remedies for each category of misrepresentation.

- Remember to be aware of the factors that undermine a claim for misrepresentation, including actions by the representee that will prevent them from claiming a remedy for misrepresentation. For example, if a representee fully relies on their own investigations.

## ■ KEY TERMS AND CONCEPTS
- misrepresentation (**page 124**)
- rescission (**page 134**)

## ■ SQE1-STYLE QUESTIONS

### QUESTION 1

A company decides to sponsor a pop group's world tour in August. In March of the same year, the pop group, with all five group members, participate in promotional activities for a company's product in respect of a forthcoming tour. All five members of the pop group know that the fifth member of the group is not planning to participate in the tour but they say nothing. In June, the company discovers that the fifth member of the group will not be on the tour, and as a result the company decides not to pay the sponsorship fee and wishes to rescind the contract.

Can the company rescind the contract for misrepresentation?

A. No, because conduct can never amount to misrepresentation.

B. No, because damages is the primary remedy for misrepresentation and rescission is only at the discretion of the court if damages would be an inadequate remedy.

C. No, because by participating in the promotional activities, the company has affirmed the contract.

D. Yes, because the pop group's conduct amounted to a misrepresentation.

E. Yes, because this is a clear case of fraudulent misrepresentation.

### QUESTION 2

A woman runs an art gallery. A man who is an art dealer enters the art gallery and admires a painting. The woman tells the man that the painting is by a famous artist because the woman wants to sell the painting for a very high price. In fact, the painting was created by the woman's baby daughter. The man takes a photograph of the painting and asks an art expert to confirm whether it is by the famous artist. The expert confirms that, in his view, the painting is by the famous artist. The man buys the painting and later finds out the truth.

**Can the man rescind the contract?**

A. No, because making his own investigations will undermine the man's argument that he relied on the representation.
B. Yes, because the woman was dishonest and so the man's investigations do not undermine his ability to claim.
C. No, because this was an innocent misrepresentation so the court only has the power to award damages.
D. Yes, provided the man can show that he relied to some degree on the woman's statement about the famous artist.
E. No, but the man is entitled to claim damages.

## QUESTION 3

A shopkeeper wants to sell an antique gun. As the barrel of the gun is damaged, the shopkeeper sprays it with paint to make it look as if it is not damaged. The man then shuts the gun in a wooden case. A woman, who represents a clay pigeon shooting company, arrives at the shop and informs the man that she is looking for a gun. The man gives the woman a list of available guns. The woman is in a hurry, so she points to a wooden case from across the room and says she will take that one. When the woman subsequently opens the case she discovers the defect.

**Can the woman rescind the contract on the grounds of misrepresentation?**

A. Yes, because painting the barrel of the gun to look as if it is not damaged is a clear misrepresentation.
B. No, because the shopkeeper did not say anything about the condition of the gun and silence cannot amount to a misrepresentation.
C. No, because by taking the gun away from the shop, the woman has affirmed the contract.
D. No, because the woman had not inspected the gun before she bought it.

E. Yes, because the intention of the shopkeeper was fraudulent, which means that the woman can rescind the contract.

## QUESTION 4

A landowner sells a plot of land to a developer for £3 million. Prior to the sale, the landowner had told the developer that there was nothing on the land that would hinder development of the land. After the developer bought the land, it found that there was a colony of newts on the land that would cost £2,000 to rehome. The developer understands that the statement about nothing hindering development was an innocent misrepresentation.

Can the developer rescind the contract?

A. Yes, because rescission is always available as a remedy for innocent misrepresentation.
B. No, because rescission is not available as a remedy for innocent misrepresentation.
C. No, because the court is likely to exercise its discretion to award damages instead of rescission.
D. Yes, provided the statement satisfies the tests for an innocent misrepresentation.
E. No, because restitution is impossible.

## QUESTION 5

A transport company bought a lorry after being told that it was in good condition. When the transport company drove the lorry, it discovered that it had serious faults. The transport company highlighted these faults to the seller, who agreed to pay half the cost of repairs. When the transport company used the lorry for the second time, it broke down.

Can the transport company rescind the contract for misrepresentation about the condition of the lorry?

A. No, because the subject matter of the representation has been destroyed.
B. No, because the lapse of time between buying the lorry and bringing the claim means that the transport company has lost its ability to claim a remedy.

C. Yes, because the transport company did not expressly state that it affirmed the contract.
D. No, because using the lorry for a second time amounts to affirmation.
E. Yes, because the statement that the lorry was in good condition was a clear misrepresentation.

# ■ ANSWERS TO QUESTIONS

## Answers to 'What do you know already?' questions at the start of the chapter

1) The three broad categories of misrepresentation are fraudulent, negligent and innocent misrepresentation. Make sure that you note that there are two different types of negligent misrepresentation: at common law, and under the Misrepresentation Act 1967.
2) True.
3) False. A representor is under a duty to correct a statement that has become false until the time the contract is concluded.
4) A representee needs to satisfy the four following conditions (MAIA):
   - the statement must be *material*,
   - the representee was *aware* of the statement,
   - the representer must *intend* the representee to act on the statement, and
   - the representee must *act* on the statement.
5) The remedy of rescission is available for all categories of misrepresentation, unless it is lost through affirmation or the destruction of the subject matter. Damages is also available in addition to rescission for fraudulent misrepresentation and both types of negligent misrepresentation. Damages is available *as an alternative* to rescission for non-fraudulent misrepresentation.

## Answers to end-of-chapter SQE1-style questions

Question 1:
The correct answer was D. This is because taking part in the promotional activities amounts to a misrepresentation that the pop group did not know (and did not have reasonable grounds to believe) that a member of the group would not participate in the tour. This means that Option A is incorrect. Option B is also incorrect because

rescission is a remedy for all types of misrepresentation. But note that the discretion is wrongly described in Option B. It is only in respect of non-fraudulent misrepresentation that the court has the discretion to award damages instead of rescission. Option C is incorrect because affirmation can only take place after the representee has discovered the truth, which is not the case in this scenario. Option E is incorrect because the remedy of rescission is available for all types of misrepresentation, not only fraudulent misrepresentation.

Question 2:
The correct answer was B. A representee's investigations do not impact their ability to claim if the misrepresentation was fraudulent, as it was in this scenario. This means that Option A is incorrect. Option C is incorrect because the scenario highlights the woman's dishonesty so this is a case of fraudulent misrepresentation, not innocent misrepresentation. Option D is incorrect because a representee's investigations do not impact a representee's ability to claim a remedy in the case of fraudulent misrepresentation, as in this scenario. Option E is incorrect. The general position is that rescission is available as a remedy once a misrepresentation is established. It is only in the case of innocent misrepresentation that the court has the discretion to award damages instead of rescission. This is not relevant to the present scenario, which concerns fraudulent misrepresentation.

Question 3:
The correct answer was D. Remember that a key test to satisfy in showing that that statement induced the contract is that the representee was aware of the misrepresentation. In this scenario, the representee was not aware of the misrepresentation as she had not inspected the gun before buying it. This lack of awareness means that Option A is incorrect. Option B is incorrect because although the general rule about silence not amounting to a misrepresentation is correctly stated, the action of the shopkeeper in this scenario would amount to a misrepresentation by conduct and would lead to an action for misrepresentation *if* the representee had been aware of it when she bought the gun. Option C is incorrect because affirmation can only take place when the representee knows the truth and the woman did not know the truth when she took the gun away from the shop. Option E is incorrect because although the intention of the shopkeeper was fraudulent, the action did not induce the contract so does not give the representee a remedy.

Question 4:
The correct answer was C. In cases of innocent misrepresentation, the court has the discretion to award damages instead of rescission.

# Misrepresentation

This discretion can be exercised where rescission seems to be a disproportionately severe remedy and where damages would be an adequate remedy. Considering the purchase price of £3 million and the cost of remedying the problem by rehoming the newts, it is very likely that the court would exercise its discretion to award damages. This means that Option A and Option D are incorrect. Option B is incorrect because rescission is available but can be replaced with damages at the discretion of the court, as noted above. Option E is incorrect because although restitution would appear to be disproportionate in this case, it is not impossible.

Question 5:

The correct answer was D. The transport company would be held to be entitled to test out the vehicle after buying it to check whether the statement about it being in good condition was true or false. But after the first repair, the law treats a second journey as affirmation that is made when the representee knows that the representation about the vehicle being in good condition is false. This means that Option E is incorrect. Option A is not correct as the vehicle still exists. Option B is incorrect because we are not aware of the lapse of time between the statement being made and the second test drive. Further, although the law previously held that lapse of time would undermine a claim for rescission, the position now appears to be that rescission is available, provided the claim is brought within a reasonable time. Option C is incorrect as actions can amount to affirmation, such as taking the car for a second drive. No words are necessary.

## ■ KEY CASES, RULES, STATUTES AND INSTRUMENTS

The SQE1 Assessment Specification does not require you to know any case names, or statutory materials, for this topic.

# Mistake, duress, undue influence and illegality

## ■ MAKE SURE YOU KNOW

For the SQE1 assessment, you are required to know the various factors that undermine the enforceability of an agreement. In addition to the factors of misrepresentation (see **Chapter 7**) and unfair contract terms (see **Chapter 6**), you are required to know the law relating to mistake, duress, undue influence and illegality.

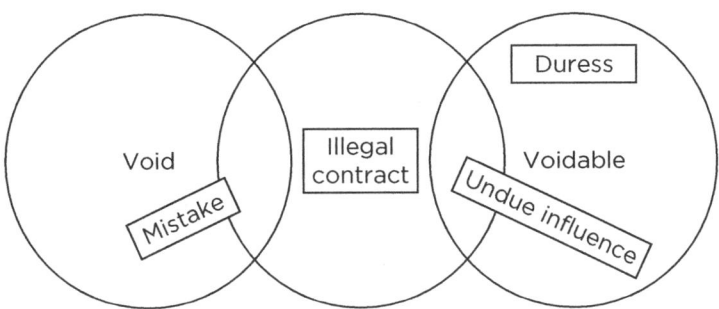

146    Mistake, duress, undue influence and illegality

## ■ SQE ASSESSMENT ADVICE

As you work through this chapter, remember to pay particular attention in your revision to:
- The impact of face to face dealings on claims for unilateral mistake.
- The effect of mistake on goods sold under a contract.
- The different types of evidence that support a claim for duress.
- Actual undue influence and the different grounds on which undue influence is *presumed*.
- The different legal consequences that result from a contract being illegal at common law and under statute.

## ■ WHAT DO YOU KNOW ALREADY?

Have a go at these questions before reading this chapter. If you find some difficult or cannot remember the answers, make a note to look more closely at that area during your revision.

1) True or false? Mutual mistake, which describes a situation where both parties to a contract have made a fundamental mistake in respect of a term of the contract, renders the contract void.
   **[Introduction to mistake, page 147]**
2) In face to face interactions, if one party believes the person with whom they are dealing to be someone else as a result of the other party's behaviour, does this render the contract void or voidable?
   **[Mistake as to identity in face to face scenarios, page 150]**
3) What is duress?
   **[Duress, page 152]**
4) In which two scenarios is presumed undue influence found?
   **[Presumed undue influence, page 156]**
5) True or false? An agreement in restraint of trade is *prima facie* voidable.
   **[Agreements in restraint of trade, page 159]**

## INTRODUCTION TO MISTAKE

In some scenarios where parties believe that they have reached an agreement, it may turn out that one or both of the parties has made a fundamental mistake in respect of the agreement (sometimes referred to as agreement mistake). The law regards such agreements (contracts) as void.

There are two main categories of agreement mistake:
- Where both parties have made a fundamental mistake in respect of a contract term, this is described as **mutual mistake**.
- Where only one party to the agreement has made a fundamental mistake in respect of a contract term, this is described as unilateral mistake (see **Unilateral mistake, page 149**).

## MUTUAL MISTAKE

There is no agreement when parties to a contract both make a fundamental mistake as to what they have agreed. So there is no agreement because both parties to the contract are at cross purposes. For example, in *Scriven Bros and Co. v Hindley* [1913] 3 KB 564 KBD, a buyer bid for a product at auction believing it was hemp. In fact, the product was tow, which was a cheaper product than hemp. When the buyer discovered that he had bid for tow, he refused to pay. The court found that the buyer mistakenly believed he was bidding for hemp, and the auctioneer understood that he was selling tow but that the buyer was mistaken about the value of the tow. This mutual mistake meant that there was no actual agreement between the parties, so the contract was void.

### Key term: mutual mistake
The scenario in which both parties to a contract have made a fundamental mistake in respect of a contract term.

Check your knowledge of how mutual mistake might arise by working through **Practice example 8.1**.

### Practice example 8.1
Heather agrees to buy socks from Jacqui to be delivered by a tanker called Scorpios, sailing from Greece. Heather believes that the socks will be delivered on a tanker called Scorpios sailing from Greece in October. Jacqui believes that the socks will be delivered on a tanker called Scorpios sailing from Greece in December. In this scenario,

there are two different tankers, both called Scorpios, due to sail from Greece in October, and December, respectively.

Can Heather refuse to accept and pay for the socks that Jacqui ships to her in December?

**The answer is yes.** This example is based on the scenario in *Raffles v Wichelhaus and Another* 159 ER 375. The court concluded that the contract was ambiguous because one party understood that the contract referred to the October ship, and the other party understood that it referred to the December ship. Based on the evidence presented, the court held that it was impossible to determine to which ship the contract referred. This mutual mistake meant that there was no agreement between the parties so the contract was void.

## The impact of one party being at fault for the mistake

It is important to note that in *Raffles v Wichelhaus* neither party was at fault for the mistake. This is because there were two different ships that answered the description of the ship referred to in the contract. So a reasonable person could not objectively determine which of the two ships each party had in mind.

In a scenario where the court determines that the buyer is to blame for the mistake, and did *not* have reasonable grounds to justify the mistake, the court will not declare the contract to be void. For example, in *Tamplin v James* (1880) LR 15 Ch D 215, the buyer accepted an offer to buy an inn in the mistaken belief that gardens were included in the sale. The buyer believed that the gardens were included in the sale because they had always been used by the inn. But if the buyer had looked at the sales particulars for the inn, he would have seen that the gardens were not included in the sale. The court refused to declare that the agreement to buy the inn was void for mistake on the grounds that there was no ambiguity in the sales particulars and the buyer was responsible for his mistake because he failed to check the sales particulars. The court held that the buyer was bound by the agreement.

### Exam warning

Watch out for scenarios where a mistake is made due to fault of the party who is mistaken. In **Practice example 8.1**, and the case on which it is based, neither party was at fault. But in a scenario where one of the parties is mistaken because they have been careless or reckless, (for example, *Tamplin v James*), rather than because of ambiguity or misrepresentation, the party at fault will be bound by the agreement.

## UNILATERAL MISTAKE

It is important to understand the difference between mutual mistake and **unilateral mistake**. In scenarios involving mutual mistake, *both* parties to the contract are fundamentally mistaken as to a term of the contract. By contrast, in scenarios involving unilateral mistake, only one of the parties is fundamentally mistaken as to a term of the contract, and the other party knows (or should know) that the first party is mistaken. For example, imagine that Elena is in charge of selling Christmas geese and mistakenly offers to sell a whole goose to Ayatullah for £10, rather than at £10 per kilogram (which, on the evidence presented, is the usual market practice). If Elena subsequently discovers her mistake, she may be able to convince the court to declare that her agreement with Ayatullah is void *if* she can prove that Ayatullah was aware that it was usual market practice to sell Christmas geese at a price per kilogram, rather than per goose, and that Ayatullah was aware (or should have been aware) that Elena was mistaken.

> **Key term: unilateral mistake**
>
> The scenario in which one party to a contract is fundamentally mistaken as to a term of the contract, and the other party to the contract is aware, or should be aware, of the mistake.

Unilateral mistake renders a contract void. To rely on unilateral mistake to make a contract void, the mistaken party must provide evidence to satisfy the three following conditions:
- the other party was aware, or should have been aware of the first party's mistake at the time the contract was made (for example, in the scenario with Elena and Ayatullah above, Elena would need to show that Ayatullah was aware, or ought to have been aware, that Elena was mistaken),
- the mistake was in respect of a term that induced the first party to enter into the contract, not a collateral matter – for example, in the case of *Smith v Hughes* (1871) LR 6 QB 597, a buyer who contracted to buy oats, and received oats, was not able to rely on unilateral mistake to make his contract void when he received new oats even though he had wanted old oats. The matter of the oats being old or new was not

a term of the contract, it was a collateral matter (it was not mentioned in the contract), and
- the mistaken party was not at fault (for example, if the mistaken party is careless or negligent in reaching their mistaken conclusion, they cannot rely on unilateral mistake).

> **Exam warning**
>
> When analysing scenarios be careful to check that *all three conditions* are satisfied.

In the next section, we shall examine the circumstances in which the court will hold a contract to be void on the grounds of **mistake as to identity**.

## Mistake as to identity

A key area of unilateral mistake is mistake as to identity. Mistake as to identity describes the situation in which one party (A) enters into a contract believing the other party to be X, when in fact the other party is Y. A's mistake often results from Y (sometimes referred to as the **rogue**) fraudulently misrepresenting themselves to be another person in order to persuade the other party to contract with them. Since an essential requirement for the operation of the doctrine of mistake is that the mistake must relate to a term of the contract, you need to understand the presumptions that the law applies to these scenarios.

> **Key term: mistake as to identity**
>
> A category of unilateral mistake where one party makes a mistake as to the identity of the other party.

> **Key term: rogue**
>
> In the context of mistake as to identity, the party to a contract who misrepresents their identity by pretending to be someone else.

### Mistake as to identity in face to face scenarios

The first presumption that we will examine applies where parties make contracts face to face. English law applies a presumption that the mistaken party intends to deal with the person physically present, regardless of their identity. So unless the seller can rebut this presumption by providing evidence to prove that their decision to sell the goods to the other party was made on the basis of the other party's identity (for example, I will sell to Party A, and no-one else), they will not be able to claim that the identity of the other party to the contract was a term of the contract. This in turn means that they cannot satisfy an essential requirement to rely on the doctrine of mistake, although they may be able to rely on fraudulent misrepresentation, which renders the contract voidable (see **Chapter 7**).

If the person is mistaken in respect of a collateral matter (for example, whether the buyer was creditworthy, so that the seller would allow the buyer to leave the shop with the goods in return for a cheque or a promise to pay), the mistaken party cannot rely on the doctrine of mistake. In such cases, the seller might only be able to bring a claim for fraudulent misrepresentation (considered in **Chapter 7**).

Now test your understanding of this subject in **Practice example 8.2**.

> **Practice example 8.2**
>
> Sharon goes into a jewellery shop and asks Clive, the shop assistant, to show her a ring and some pearls. Sharon selects the ring and pearls, telling Clive that she would like to buy them and that she likes them so much that she must take them home immediately. When Sharon takes out her chequebook to pay, Clive tells Sharon that he cannot accept a cheque, only cash. But Sharon tells Clive that she is Sophie, Countess of Wessex, and she provides her address as Bagshot Park, near Bagshot. Clive checks the address online and is able to confirm that Sophie, Countess of Wessex, lives at Bagshot Park. So Clive accepts Sharon's cheque and allows her to depart with the ring and some pearls. Unfortunately for Clive, the cheque is a forgery and worthless.
>
> Is Clive able to claim that his contract to sell the ring and pearls was void for mistake as to identity?
>
> **The answer is no. This scenario is based on *Phillips v Brooks* [1919] 2 KB 243 KBD. The court held that the shopkeeper intended to contract with the person physically in front of him in the shop. The court held that the name and address of the customer were collateral matters relating to creditworthiness because the question of identity was discussed only after the shopkeeper had taken the decision to sell to the person physically present. So the shopkeeper could not claim that he made a mistake as to a term of the contract.**

> **Exam warning**
>
> In scenarios where you determine that the contract is not void for mistake, but voidable for misrepresentation, check carefully the timeline of events. Are the goods sold by the innocent party still with the rogue, in which case the innocent party can rescind the contract and reclaim the goods. Or has the rogue sold the goods to an innocent third party, who will have acquired title?

*Mistake as to identity in communications at a distance*

Where parties make contracts at a distance the courts generally take the opposite approach, compared to contracts concluded face to face. This means that if a rogue writes to an innocent party, pretending to be another person, and the innocent party enters into a contract with the rogue, the courts consider that the identity of the other party is a term of the contract, which means that the innocent party can claim that the contract is void for mistake as to identity.

Now put your knowledge to the test and attempt **Practice example 8.3**.

> **Practice example 8.3**
>
> A rogue sets up an office at Knightsbridge under the name Herrods. A well-known company called Harrods operates next door. The rogue orders goods from a seller of silk in a letter that is made to look as if it comes from Harrods. The seller believes that the order has been made by Harrods and posts the silk to the rogue, who immediately sells it to Mrs Smith of Fulham. When the seller does not receive payment for the silk, he discovers the truth.
>
> Is the contract between the rogue and the seller void for unilateral mistake?
>
> **The answer is yes. This scenario is based on similar facts to the case of *Cundy v Lindsay* (1877–78) LR 3 App Cas 459. The House of Lords held that evidence showed that the claimants only ever intended to deal with the well-known brand and that this identity was key to the seller's decision to send the goods on credit. This meant that the identity was a term of the contract, which allowed the contract to be held void for unilateral mistake.**

## DURESS

A contract is voidable at common law if it is proven to be made under **duress**. The right to rescind of the innocent party must be exercised promptly.

Duress is illegitimate pressure by actions, or threats of action, to make a person agree to do something. It includes:
- physical violence or threats,
- forcing a party to pay money for the release of goods wrongfully held, or to prevent goods being wrongfully held, and
- economic duress, being illegitimate pressure that threatens the economic interests of a party, and is a significant factor in making that party enter into a contract.

| Key term: duress |
| --- |
| Illegitimate pressure by actions or threats of action that makes a person agree to something. |

Test your understanding of duress in **Practice example 8.4**.

| Practice example 8.4 |
| --- |
| Nadia's company agreed to put up exhibition stands for Mustafa's business. One week before the exhibition was due to start, Nadia's company told Mustafa that it would not complete the work on the exhibition stands unless Mustafa paid Nadia £4,500. Mustafa had already agreed with his clients that they could use the exhibition stands that Nadia was due to put up, so he would have faced large claims from his clients if the stands were not ready. So Mustafa paid Nadia the £4,500 to avoid facing claims from his clients. The following week Nadia sends Mustafa a final invoice for the work. |
| Does Mustafa have grounds to argue that his agreement to pay the additional £4,500 is voidable due to duress? |
| **The answer is yes. Provided Mustafa promptly protests the final invoice on the basis that his agreement to pay the £4,500 was made under duress, he will not be bound by his payment of £4,500. The consequences of a refusal of Mustafa to pay Nadia the amount she demanded would have been serious and this left him no option but to agree to pay £4,500.** This scenario is based on the case of *B&S Contracts & Design Ltd v Victor Green Publications Ltd* [1984] ICR 419. It is an example of economic duress because the cancellation of the contract would have caused such serious damage to the economic interests of the party organising the exhibition stands for his clients that he had no choice but to pay. |

> **Revision tip**
>
> Remember that the doctrine of duress can apply to the formation of a contract or an amendment to a contract (see **Chapter 2**).

## UNDUE INFLUENCE

**Undue influence** is an equitable doctrine that allows a person to rescind a contract to which they are party if they can show that they were influenced or pressured into making a decision by another person so that they did not act of their own free will.

> **Key term: undue influence**
>
> Wrongful influence or pressure by one person over another person so that such person does not act of their own free will.

Subject to certain exceptions, a contract is voidable at common law if it is proven to be made under undue influence. Undue influence includes:
- actual undue influence, and
- presumed undue influence.

Once proven in relation to a contract, the doctrine of undue influence allows the party that was subjected to undue influence to rescind the contract. The innocent party must exercise their remedy promptly. If the court believes that the person has taken too long to bring a claim, it may determine that the innocent party has affirmed the contract.

### Actual undue influence

Actual undue influence describes a scenario in which one party proves that they were subject to undue influence at the time they entered into an agreement. In other words, a party must prove that they did not decide to enter into an agreement of their own free will. We can see an example of this illegitimate pressure in the case of *Williams v Bayley* [1866] LR 1 HL 200 HL. In this case, bankers notified a father that his son had forged documents and they were entitled to prosecute his son. The bankers told the father that they would not prosecute his son if the father settled his son's debts. So the father mortgaged his property to settle his son's debts. The House of Lords held that the father had been subject to undue influence, which meant that he was entitled to rescind the mortgage.

Now work through **Practice example 8.5** to test your understanding.

### Practice example 8.5

Faye and Anjoum are a married couple and jointly own their matrimonial home. Anjoum wants to take out a loan secured on the home and invest the loan proceeds in stocks and shares. Faye does not want to do this, but Anjoum pressures Faye for a substantial period of time until she agrees to take out the loan and grant security over their home.

Has Faye been subject to actual undue pressure?

The answer is yes. This scenario is based on the case of *CIBC Mortgages plc v Pitt* [1994] 1 AC 200. The evidence of pressure exerted on the husband by the wife sustained the argument of actual undue influence.

## The effect of third party undue influence

In scenarios where the undue influence is exercised by a third party (for example, a husband who pressures a wife to enter into a contract as surety for his business with a bank), the ability of the innocent party to exercise its remedy in respect of the contract with the bank depends upon establishing one of the following factors:
- that the party exerting the undue influence acted as agent of the contractual party, or
- that the contractual party has notice (explained below) of the undue influence.

Only if the innocent party can establish one of the factors above can they exercise their right to rescind the contract.

### Exam warning

In scenarios on undue third party influence, make a note to check whether either of the relevant factors is satisfied for the innocent party to be able to exercise its remedy to rescind.

### *Actual notice and constructive notice*

Make sure that you understand that *notice* of undue influence includes *actual* notice and *constructive* notice.

A party has *actual notice* of undue influence if it *knows* that one of the parties to the contract has been subjected to undue influence. *Constructive notice* describes a scenario in which the party *ought to have known* of the undue influence. The law in this area is focused on scenarios where a husband and wife create security for a creditor (typically a bank) over their home. In such scenarios, the existence of constructive notice for a creditor is determined by using two steps:

Step 1: a creditor is put on inquiry if it knows of the relationship between the two parties signing (for example, the husband and wife (or other cohabitee)), and the transaction is not obviously to the financial advantage of the wife (or other cohabitee).

Step 2: once a creditor has been put on inquiry, it has constructive notice of the undue influence over one of the parties to the agreement, unless it takes *reasonable steps* to ensure that the other party is making the agreement of her own free will and with full knowledge of the facts.

## *What are reasonable steps?*
Reasonable steps are:
- the creditor insisting on a private meeting with the wife alone and a representative of the creditor in which the wife is warned of her liability under the agreement in question, warned of the risks and urged to take independent advice,
- obtaining confirmation from a solicitor, acting for the wife, that he has advised the wife appropriately, and
- ensuring that the wife has understood, in a meaningful way, the practical implications of the proposed transaction.

## Presumed undue influence
In certain relationships, the law *presumes* that one of the parties is under the undue influence of the other. The two classes of relationships in which the law presumes undue influence are as follows:
- in relationships that the law views as relationships of trust and confidence (class 2A), or
- in relationships where one party has, as a matter of fact, placed trust and confidence in another person (class 2B).

## Presumed undue influence and the evidential burden
Presumed undue influence is important because it creates a rebuttable presumption that the weaker party in the relationship entered into a transaction as a result of the undue influence of the other. This is important because it requires the person who wants to rely on the relevant agreement to prove that the other person agreed to the

transaction of their own free will. For example, the presumption may be rebutted where there is evidence that the weaker party received competent independent financial advice.

## Presumed undue influence: relationships of trust and confidence (class 2A)

Examples of the *established* class of relationships where undue influence is presumed include those between parent and child, solicitor and client, religious leader and disciple, and doctor and patient.

> **Revision tip**
>
> Make sure that you check your knowledge of those relationships that the law places in class 2A. It is important to remember that marital relationships (or those between parent and adult child) *do not* fall within class 2A.

> **Exam warning**
>
> Read the scenario carefully to confirm that both parties in the relationship have entered into the transaction. If only one party has entered into the transaction, the presumption will not apply.

## Presumed undue influence: relationships of trust and confidence (class 2B)

The second class of relationships where undue influence is presumed is, in contrast to class 2A, not fixed. Instead, a relationship will be included in this class if the person alleging that they were under undue influence proves the existence of a relationship of trust and confidence. Once the relationship is established, the other party must rebut the presumption of undue influence. An example of such a relationship might include that between a customer and a bank manager *if it is proven* that the relationship of trust and confidence exists as a matter of fact. **Practice example 8.6** provides an example of such a case.

> **Practice example 8.6**
>
> Arkhip is an elderly farmer who has banked with Barley Bank for many years. Kathleen is Arkhip's bank manager and visits Arkhip with Arkhip's son to tell him that his company can only continue to run if Arkhip allows Barley Bank to take additional security over his house. Arkhip agrees to grant additional security over his house. Subsequently, the business fails and Barley Bank seeks possession of Arkhip's house.

Can Arkhip rescind his agreement with Barley Bank on the grounds of presumed undue influence?

The answer is yes. This scenario is based on the case of *Lloyds Bank Ltd v Bundy* [1975] QB 326. During the trial, the evidence showed that the farmer had always trusted his bank, and in this case, he just did what the bank manager told him to do. The farmer did not take independent advice. The court held that the bank's knowledge that the farmer trusted it completely, and the evidence that the father trusted the bank, proved the farmer's relationship with the bank was one of trust and confidence and this raised the presumption of undue influence. This placed the burden upon the bank manager to rebut the presumption of undue influence by showing that the old farmer had obtained independent financial advice. Since the farmer had not obtained independent financial advice, the bank manager was not able to provide evidence to rebut the presumption.

## ILLEGALITY

If a contract is shown to be illegal, the court may refuse to enforce it. The effect of the illegality can make the contract void or voidable.

For the purposes of the SQE1 assessment, you are required to understand the grounds on which a court may hold a contact to be unenforceable:
- under statute, or
- at common law.

### Illegal under statute

Certain statutes specify that certain acts are illegal. Some statutes specify the effect of acts they declared to be illegal. For example, s 197(1) of the Companies Act 2006 provides that a loan by a company to a director needs to be approved by the members of the company. So if a company makes a loan to a director without approval of the members, the loan is *voidable*, so the company may choose to rescind the loan agreement (s 213(2) Companies Act 2006).

### Illegal at common law

Courts may refuse to enforce contracts that conflict with the common law. Key areas include:
- agreements that are contrary to public policy, and
- agreements in restraint of trade.

## Agreements that conflict with public policy

Common examples of contracts that are unenforceable on public policy grounds are found in agreements that the court views as harmful to the integrity of the English legal system. For example, courts will refuse to enforce an agreement to bribe a person to give false evidence or to carry out another dishonest activity.

The court considers the following range of factors in determining whether the activity is harmful to the integrity of the legal system:
- What is the underlying aim of the prohibition of the activity in question (for example, why has the bribe been paid)?
- Are there any other relevant public policies?
- Would refusal to enforce the contract be proportionate?

## Agreements in restraint of trade

As a general rule, agreements that limit a party's freedom to trade are *prima facie* void. Examples of such agreements might include limiting a person's trade activities to a geographical area, or limiting a person's rights to work for a competitor.

> **Key term:** *prima facie*
> At first sight, based on the first impression.

As an exception to the general rule, agreements in restraint of trade *are enforceable* if the person seeking to enforce the contract can satisfy the court that the restriction is reasonable and not contrary to the public interest. For example, the courts view restrictions on employees disclosing secrets to a competitor as reasonable, but they do not usually uphold restrictions that prevent an employee from working for a competitor. The courts consider the circumstances in existence at the time the contract was made.

Check your understanding of what the court considers to be reasonable in **Practice example 8.7**.

> **Practice example 8.7**
>
> Elaine is a 17-year-old football star. She enters into a contract with Devsports, giving Devsports exclusive control over her image rights for eight years at a flat commission rate of 20%. Elaine signs the contract without receiving independent financial advice.

Is the contract between Elaine and Devsports unenforceable by Devsports on the grounds of restraint of trade?

The answer is yes. This scenario is based on *Proactive Sports Management Ltd v Rooney* [2011] EWCA Civ 1444. The court considered that the contract imposed very substantial restrictions upon the footballer's freedom to exploit his earning capacity over a very long period of time (eight years). The court also took other factors into account, including the fact that the footballer was 17 when the contract was made, the footballer and his parents were unsophisticated in legal and commercial matters, and the footballer did not take independent legal advice. The party seeking to enforce the contract failed to show that the restrictions were reasonable.

## ■ KEY POINT CHECKLIST

This chapter has covered the following key knowledge points. You can use these to structure your revision around, making sure to recall the key details for each point, as covered in this chapter.

- When both parties to a contract are fundamentally mistaken as to a term of the contract, this is described as mutual mistake and it renders a contract void.
- When only one of the parties to a contract is fundamentally mistaken as to a term of the contract, this is described as unilateral mistake. Often the mistake results from the other contract party pretending to be someone else. It is essential that you remember the presumption that in face to face dealings the innocent person intends to deal with the person physically present, regardless of their identity. Unless the presumption is rebutted, it prevents the innocent party from providing that the identity was a term of the contract, so it cannot rely on mistake as to identity to make a contract void. The opposite is true in respect of contracts concluded at a distance.
- Make sure that you understand the different meanings of void and voidable. A voidable contract is valid until it is rescinded. This means that a person can acquire title under a voidable contract before it is rescinded. By contrast, a void contract has no legal effect, so title never passes under it.
- Watch out for scenarios in which one person pressures another to make them enter into a contract (or threatens to do so). This is likely to be duress, which makes the contract voidable.
- Look out for scenarios in which a person does not act of their own free will as a result of undue influence, as this renders the contract

voidable. Undue influence might be demonstrated in the scenario, or it might result from a presumption because of the class of relationship (for example, parent and child).
- It is essential that you know that the courts generally refuse to enforce illegal contracts. Under common law, key examples of illegal contracts involve bribery and corruption. Watch out for contracts that restrict a person's ability to trade or run their business. The courts will not enforce such contracts, unless they are *reasonable*. Certain actions are rendered unenforceable by statute.

## ■ KEY TERMS AND CONCEPTS
- mutual mistake (**page 147**)
- unilateral mistake (**page 149**)
- mistake as to identity (**page 150**)
- rogue (**page 150**)
- duress (**page 153**)
- undue influence (**page 154**)
- *prima facie* (**page 159**)

## ■ SQE1-STYLE QUESTIONS

### QUESTION 1

A man sees a notice advertising the sale of a restaurant that he knows. The man knows that the restaurant has beautiful gardens and he assumes that the gardens are included in the sale. The man does not read the particulars of sale or the sale agreement that clearly states that the gardens are excluded from the sale. When the man has completed the purchase of the restaurant, he is upset to see that the gardens were not included in the sale agreement.

**Which of the following statements most accurately reflects the legal position?**

A. The sale agreement is void because of the man's mistake.

B. The sale agreement is enforceable because it was the man's fault that he has made a mistake.

C. The sale agreement is enforceable, but the court will order specific performance to require the gardens to be included in the sale to satisfy the man's reasonable expectations.

**162** Mistake, duress, undue influence and illegality

D. The sale agreement is voidable due to fraudulent misrepresentation.
E. The sale agreement is voidable because the notice advertising the sale should have made it very clear that the gardens were excluded from the sale.

## QUESTION 2

A woman telephoned a car showroom and told the dealer that she was interested in buying a car. The woman did not give her real name to the dealer, but instead gave the name of a colleague, whose driving licence she had stolen. After the telephone call, the woman emailed the dealer a copy of her colleague's driving licence to confirm her fake identity. Subsequently, the dealer agreed to sell the woman a car in exchange for a cheque for £22,000. The woman then sold the car to a third party. The dealer's bank was unable to clear the cheque as it was a worthless forgery.

Which of the following statements best describes the legal position in this case?

A. The agreement between the woman and the dealer is void for mistake.
B. The dealer cannot reclaim the car from an innocent third party.
C. The agreement between the woman and the dealer is void for fraudulent misrepresentation.
D. The agreement between the woman and the dealer is voidable for fraudulent misrepresentation.
E. The agreement between the woman and the dealer is voidable and the dealer should rescind the agreement immediately to prevent title from passing to the third party.

## QUESTION 3

A company is the only supplier of essential car parts to a carmaker. At a time when the carmaker has a very limited amount of car parts in stock, the company threatens to stop supplying the essential car parts *unless* the carmaker agrees to a significant price increase for the essential parts. The carmaker agrees to pay the company more because the failure to receive the essential car parts from the company would cause severe financial losses to the carmaker's business.

Which of the following statements most accurately reflects the legal position of the parties?

A. The carmaker is bound to pay the company the increased price for the car parts because both parties were operating in the business to business (B2B) context.
B. The carmaker is only bound to pay the company a reasonable amount for the car parts.
C. The carmaker is bound to pay the company the increased price for the car parts.
D. The carmaker's agreement to pay an increased price for the car parts is voidable.
E. The carmaker's agreement to pay an increased price for the car parts is void.

## QUESTION 4

A man is in a religious sect and has taken a vow of poverty and promised unquestioning obedience to the leader of the religious sect. During the time the man is in the sect, he gives £7,000 to the leader. Subsequently, the man escapes from the sect and five years later the man decides to claim the money that he gave to the leader.

Which of the following is true?

A. The man can reclaim the money on the grounds of actual undue influence.
B. The man can reclaim the money on the grounds of presumed undue influence.
C. The man cannot reclaim the money on the grounds of presumed undue influence because he has not exercised his remedy promptly.
D. The man cannot reclaim the money because presumed undue influence does not apply to such relationships.
E. The man cannot reclaim the money because undue influence does not apply to gifts.

## QUESTION 5

A man works for a small tailor's business in a suburb of London. In his contract with the tailor, the man agrees that if he leaves his current job, he will not enter into similar employment within 25 miles of London for three years.

**Is the man bound by the term of his contract?**

A. Yes, a business owner such as a tailor is entitled to protect his business.
B. Yes, provided the man agreed to the term without duress or undue influence.
C. No, because the term is not reasonable.
D. No, because such a contract is illegal as a restraint of trade.
E. Yes, if the man freely agreed to the term.

## ■ ANSWERS TO QUESTIONS

### Answers to 'What do you know already?' questions at the start of the chapter

1) True. Mutual mistake as to agreement makes a contract void.
2) Voidable. The explanation is that it is almost always the behaviour of the other party that makes the first party believe them to be someone else. The law treats such behaviour as fraudulent misrepresentation. The effect of fraudulent misrepresentation makes a contract voidable. In face to face scenarios, English law presumes that the first party intends to deal with the person physically present, and that the question of identity is a collateral matter, unless the facts of the scenario indicate the contrary.
3) Duress is illegitimate pressure by actions, or threats of action, that makes a person agree to do something.
4) Presumed undue influence is found in two classes of relationship. The first is relationships that the law views as relationships of trust and confidence (class 2A). An example of this is a parent and child relationship. The second is relationships where one party has, as a matter of fact, placed trust and confidence in another person (class 2B).
5) False. An agreement in restraint of trade is *prima facie* void. This means that the person seeking to enforce the contract must prove that the restriction is reasonable and not contrary to public interest if they are to convince the court to allow them to enforce it.

## Answers to end-of-chapter SQE1-style questions

Question 1:
The correct answer was B. This reflects the requirement that a mistaken party must satisfy three conditions, including that they were not at fault. In this scenario, the mistake was the person's own fault because he assumed that the gardens were included, but did not bother to read the sale particulars or the sales agreement. Option A is therefore incorrect. Option C is incorrect because there are no grounds to support a claim for specific performance (see **Chapter 10**). Option D is incorrect as there is no evidence in the scenario to support a claim for fraudulent misrepresentation as we are told that the sales particulars and sales agreement clearly stated that the gardens were excluded from the sale. Option E is incorrect as there is no requirement for an advertisement that is not an offer to contain all the relevant details.

Question 2:
The correct answer was A. This is because where parties transact in writing at a distance, the presumption is that the innocent party intends to deal with the person whose identity is presented. This means that the agreement will be void for mistake. This means that Option B is incorrect because the contract is void for mistake and title does not pass under a void contract. This also means that Option C is incorrect as it incorrectly states the law: fraudulent misrepresentation does not render a contract void, it renders it voidable. The present scenario is a clear case of mistake, which renders the contract void. Option D is incorrect because although it is correct to state that fraudulent misrepresentation renders a contract voidable, this scenario is a case of mistake, not fraudulent misrepresentation. Option E is incorrect because the contract is void for mistake. In addition, in the event that the contract were voidable, title would have already passed to a third party, so any attempt to rescind the contract after title has passed in this way is of no effect.

Question 3:
The correct answer was D. This is because when you consider the severe financial consequences for the carmaker of refusing to pay the increased price, this puts the carmaker under illegitimate pressure that gives it no option but to agree to the increased price. This illegitimate pressure amounts to duress, which makes the contract voidable. This means that Options C and E are incorrect. Option A is incorrect because duress can provide a remedy in the business to business (B2B) context. Option B is incorrect

because the remedy for the innocent party is that the contract is voidable. There is no requirement to subject the costs in question to reasonableness.

Question 4:
The correct answer was C. The religious leader/disciple relationship is a clear example of the established class 2A relationships to which presumed undue influence applies. However, delays in bringing a claim are likely to be held by the court as affirmation of a scenario. In this case, the man took five years to bring a claim and this is too long. This means that Option B is incorrect. Option A is incorrect as there is no evidence in the scenario of actual undue influence over the man by the leader. Option D is incorrect as presumed undue influence *does* apply to this class of relationship. Option E is incorrect as undue influence *does* apply to gifts.

Question 5:
The correct answer was C. This is because the restriction is much greater than is reasonably required for a small tailor's business in a suburb of London. This means that Options A, B and E are incorrect. Option D is incorrect because not all restraint of trade agreements are unenforceable.

## ■ KEY CASES, RULES, STATUTES AND INSTRUMENTS

The SQE1 Assessment Specification does not require you to know any case names, or statutory materials, for this topic.

# 9

# The discharge of contracts

## ■ MAKE SURE YOU KNOW

A contract is discharged when the obligations in the contract have been brought to an end. For the SQE1 assessment, you are required to know the different ways in which contracts are discharged. You are also required to know the effect of discharge on the parties to the contract.

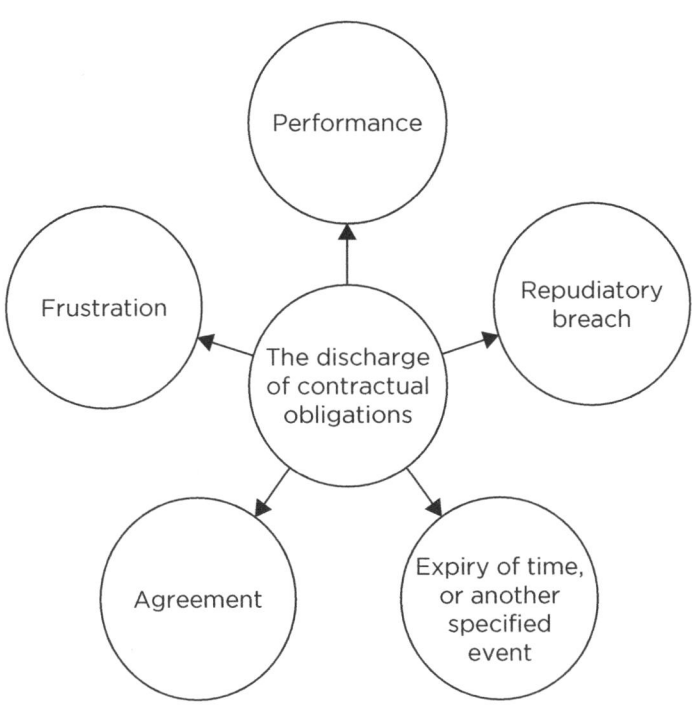

## ■ SQE ASSESSMENT ADVICE

As you work through this chapter, remember to pay particular attention in your revision to the different ways in which contracts are discharged, namely:
- performance
- repudiatory breach
- expiry of time, or another specified event
- agreement
- frustration.

## ■ WHAT DO YOU KNOW ALREADY?

Have a go at these questions before reading this chapter. If you find some difficult or cannot remember the answers, make a note to look more closely at that area during your revision.

1) What is the difference between a strict contractual obligation and a qualified contractual obligation?

   **[Performance, page 169]**

2) What is a repudiatory breach?

   **[Repudiatory breach, page 169]**

3) What is the doctrine of substantial performance?

   **[The entire obligations rule, page 175]**

4) True or false? Frustration allows a party to a contract to choose whether to discharge the future performance of the contract or to affirm a contract.

   **[Frustration, page 179]**

5) Which of the following factors does not discharge a contract for frustration?

   a) illegality
   b) impossibility
   c) loss of the main purpose
   d) impracticability

   **[Frustration, page 179]**

# PERFORMANCE

The first way in which a contract may be discharged is where the parties have performed their obligations under it.

There are two broad categories of contractual obligations:
- strict contractual obligations, and
- qualified contractual obligations.

### Strict contractual obligations

A strict contractual obligation must be performed *exactly* as it is described. For example, if party A agrees to deliver 1 kilogram of apples to party B *before* 2 PM in London on a particular day, if party A delivers the apples to party B *after* 2 PM in London on the particular day, they will not have discharged their contractual obligation. This means that party A will be in breach of contract. The remedies for breach of contract are considered in **Chapter 10**.

### Qualified contractual obligations

Some contractual obligations are *qualified*. The scenario in which party A agrees to use *reasonable endeavours* to deliver 1 kilogram of apples to party B at 2 PM in London on a particular day is an example of a qualified obligation. This means that provided party A uses reasonable endeavours to deliver the apples to party B at 2 PM in London on the particular day, they will not be in breach of the qualified obligation if they fail to deliver the apples at 2 PM. This is because party A will have performed their obligation to use reasonable endeavours to deliver the apples.

# REPUDIATORY BREACH

A failure by a party to perform their obligations under a contract is a breach. In some circumstances, a contract will *expressly* set out what remedy is available to the non-breaching party and such provisions are usually enforceable. However, if the contract does not *expressly* set out the remedy for breach, the non-breaching party must check the common law (and statute, if applicable) to determine what effect the breach has on the contract.

It is important to understand that although every breach of contract will allow the non-breaching party a remedy against the breaching party in damages, only a **repudiatory breach** will allow the non-breaching party to elect to discharge the contract.

## Key term: repudiatory breach

A breach of a major term of a contract that goes to the root of the contract and deprives the non-breaching party of substantially the whole benefit of the contract. It gives the non-breaching party the right to choose whether to discharge the contract (which will release both parties from their outstanding obligations under the contract), or to affirm it (which means that both parties continue to be bound by their remaining contractual obligations).

## Revision tip

Make sure that you understand that a repudiatory breach does not automatically discharge a contract. It gives the non-breaching party the *choice* to either discharge the contract, which releases both parties from their outstanding obligations, or to affirm the contract, which requires both parties to continue to perform their obligations under it.

## Anticipatory repudiatory breach

In some scenarios, one party to a contract tells the other party that they will not perform their *future* obligations under the contract. An example of this would be where John has hired Tracey in March to start lecturing in June. But on 1 April, John tells Tracey that he no longer wants her to lecture in June. This is a clear example of a breach of John's obligation to hire Tracey to lecture. The breach is repudiatory because it goes to the root of the contract and deprives Tracey of the whole benefit of the contract. However, because neither John's nor Tracey's obligations were due at the time John tells Tracey that she is no longer needed, the breach is called *anticipatory*. Where the anticipatory breach goes to the root of the contract, it is called an **anticipatory repudiatory breach**. It gives the non-breaching party the same rights as a repudiatory breach.

## Key term: anticipatory repudiatory breach

A communication from one party under a contract to another that the first party will not perform future obligations that go to the root of the contract and deprives the non-breaching party of substantially the whole benefit of the contract.

Since the non-breaching party's remedy for an anticipatory repudiatory breach is the same as for a repudiatory breach, the non-breaching party can:

- discharge the contract, releasing both parties from all future obligations under the contract, or
- affirm the contract, requiring both parties to perform their remaining obligations under the contract.

In the scenario above, after John tells Tracey that he no longer wants her to lecture in June, Tracey can choose to discharge the contract. Tracey can claim damages from 1 April, although she is under an obligation to mitigate her loss (for example, by looking for another lecturing job). If Tracey affirms the contract with John, then the contract will remain in force so that Tracey will be obliged to lecture in June and John will be obliged to pay her for it.

## HOW TO DETERMINE WHETHER A BREACH IS REPUDIATORY

When you determine whether a breach is *repudiatory*, there are three categories of contract provisions to consider:
- condition – a major term, the breach of which is *repudiatory*
- warranty – a minor term, the breach of which is *not repudiatory*
- innominate term – a provision that is not clearly intended to be a condition or warranty. The breach of an innominate term only allows the non-breaching party to repudiate the contract if its effect goes to the root of the contract.

Let us start our exploration of contract terms whose breach would be repudiatory by considering the common law.

### Common law guidance to determine whether a breach is repudiatory

The starting point is to consider the intention of the parties to the contract. So if a contractual provision is called a *condition*, the courts generally treat it as a condition so that its breach is a repudiatory breach. In addition, if a contract provides that time is of the essence in respect of a provision to perform an action, the breach of such provision will generally be held to be repudiatory. But the court will not treat a breach as repudiatory unless it believes that the parties intended the breach to allow the non-breaching party to discharge the agreement.

Let us explore how this might arise by working through **Practice example 9.1**.

## Practice example 9.1

Merkel Manufacturing (Merkel) agrees with a distributor, Bougies, that Bougies will have the exclusive right to sell Merkel's goods in the United Kingdom for four and a half years. One provision in the agreement, described as a *condition*, provides that one of two named sales representatives will visit six car manufacturers each week to promote and sell Merkel's goods (amounting to 1,400 visits during the duration of the contract). Bougies' representatives fail to make one of the visits.

Can Merkel treat the contract as discharged on the grounds of a repudiatory breach of the condition?

The answer is no. This scenario is based on the case of *L. Schuler AG v Wickman Machine Tools Sales Ltd* [1974] AC 235. The House of Lords held that the manufacturing company could not terminate the contract on the grounds that the sales company's breach of the provision was a condition. The House of Lords did not believe that it was the intention of the parties that the sales company's failure to make just one visit out of 1,400 would allow the other party to terminate the agreement.

### Statutory guidance to determine whether a breach is repudiatory

Statute provides that certain provisions in contracts are conditions. It provides guidance in the:
- business to business (B2B) context; and
- the business to consumer (B2C) context.

#### Statutory guidance in the B2B context

The Sale of Goods Act (SGA) 1979 implies certain terms into contracts for the sale of goods as *conditions*:
- goods will match their description (s 13(1) of the SGA 1979),
- goods sold in the course of a business are of satisfactory quality (s 14(2) of the SGA 1979), and
- where goods are sold by sample the bulk will correspond with the sample in quality (s 15(2) of the SGA 1979).

This is important because it tells us that these implied terms are *conditions* so that the breach of such terms is a *repudiatory breach*.

However, note that there is an exception to the general rule under s 15A of the SGA 1979, which provides that if the breach of the relevant condition is so slight that it would be unreasonable for the buyer to reject the goods, the relevant condition will be treated as a warranty.

### Exam warning

Unfortunately, there is no judicial guidance on how s 15A SGA 1979 is interpreted in practice, so you will need to watch out in scenarios when you are told that the breach of these implied terms is very slight, and the buyer uses the goods supplied for the purpose that they originally intended. In such circumstances, it is likely that s 15A SGA 1979 will apply so that it will be unreasonable for the buyer to treat the breach as a repudiatory breach.

## Statutory guidance in the B2C context

The B2C context is governed by the Consumer Rights Act (CRA) 2015. Sections 19 to 24 of the CRA 2015 set out the various remedies available to consumers for breach, including the short-term right to reject, the partial right to reject, the right to repair or replacement, the right to a price reduction, or a refund in the case of a contract relating to digital content. There are limited circumstances in which a party may treat a contract as at an end, including if the parties state that an express term is a condition. The SQE1 Assessment Specification has not stated that candidates need to be aware of consumer remedies and they will not be discussed in this section.

## Warranties

Warranties are contractual provisions whose breach does not undermine the overall purpose of the contract. So a breach of warranty is not a *repudiatory breach*, and the contract remains in force after the breach, but gives the non-breaching party a remedy in damages.

Consider how this might arise in practice in **Practice example 9.2**.

### Practice example 9.2

Mr Rossini is an opera singer who agrees with Mr Smith to perform Italian opera in Mr Smith's theatre, and also in halls and private houses in the United Kingdom between 30 March and 13 July for £10,000 per month *pro rata*. In the agreement, Mr Rossini also agrees not to perform opera within 50 miles of London from 1 January until 30 March, unless agreed with Mr Smith. In addition, Mr Rossini agrees to arrive six days in advance of 30 March to participate in rehearsals. Due to illness, Mr Rossini only manages to arrive three days before 30 March.

Can Mr Smith discharge Mr Rossini of his obligations under the contract on the grounds of repudiatory breach?

The answer is no. This scenario is based on *Bettini v Gye* (1876) QBD 183. The court considered that the requirement for the singer to be in London six days before 30 March was not a condition. In reaching this conclusion the court took into consideration the relative importance of *all* the terms in the agreement, including the singer's agreement not to sing within 50 miles of London from 1 January of the same year. The court also considered the requirement that the singer would not only sing at the theatre (where it admitted that his presence for the rehearsals was vital), but in addition, the singer was to sing in halls and private houses over a relatively long period of time, and also that, despite arriving only three days in advance of 30 March, the singer was able to perform his other obligations under the contract.

## Innominate terms

In some scenarios, it is not clear whether a particular provision is a condition or a warranty – these provisions are known as innominate (unclassified) terms. This lack of clarity may be due to the fact that the contract does not label a particular provision as a condition or a warranty. In such cases, the courts decide whether the provision is a condition or a warranty by considering the effect of the breach *at the time it occurs*. As a general approach, if an innominate term is breached, the courts only classify it as a condition if the breach *deprives the non-breaching party of substantially all the benefit of the contract*.

Test your understanding of the courts' approach in **Practice example 9.3**.

### Practice example 9.3

Fodder & Co. agreed to sell animal food to Holland & Co. for £100,000. The contract provided that the animal food must be shipped in good condition. The market price for animal food dropped after the contract was concluded, but before the cargo was delivered. On delivery, Holland & Co. found that some of the cargo was damaged. Holland & Co. treated the delivery of partially damaged animal food as a breach of the obligation to deliver animal food in good condition, and that this was a breach of condition, which allowed it to repudiate the contract. Fodder & Co. disagreed, but because Holland & Co. refused to take delivery of the animal food, Fodder & Co. sold it to a third party for £30,000. The third party then sold the animal food to Holland & Co., which used the entire cargo to make animal food.

Was Holland & Co. entitled to treat Fodder & Co.'s breach of the provision to deliver in 'good condition' as a breach of a condition that allowed it to reject the entire cargo?

The answer is no. This scenario is based on *Cehave NV v Bremer Handelsgesellschaft MBH* [1976] QB 44. The court held that the provision that the cargo be made 'in good condition' was not a condition. It was an innominate term. The court concluded that because the buyer used the entire cargo for its original purpose (after it bought it from the third party), the breach did not go to the root of the contract or deprive the buyer of substantially the whole benefit of the contract. This meant that although the buyer was entitled to a remedy in damages because some of the cargo was not in good condition, it was not entitled to treat the breach as a repudiatory breach of condition.

### Exam warning

One of the reasons why the courts will intervene on the remedy for a breached innominate term is to avoid the non-breaching party from discharging a contract due to the breach of a provision of minor importance to the contract as a whole. So watch out in scenarios for attempts by a non-breaching party to discharge a contract in the case of a breach of an innominate term. In such scenarios, unless the provision specifically states that the breach of the provision allows the non-breaching party to repudiate the contract, the courts will apply the innominate term analysis. This analysis means that unless the breach goes to the root of the contract, or deprives the non-breaching party of substantially the whole benefit of the contract, the breach will not be a repudiatory breach.

## The entire obligations rule

Some agreements are drafted so that party A must perform *all* of their obligations under a contract *before* party B is required to pay party A. Such agreements are called entire obligations agreements. For example, where a contract provides that party A will be paid £1,000 if he travels to Jamaica to deliver a letter to party B, party A will not be able to claim any part of the £1,000 (for example, on a *quantum meruit* basis) if he fails to deliver the letter, even if he has spent time and money in attempting to do so.

> **Key term: *quantum meruit***
> A remedy that allows a party to claim a reasonable amount for the benefit conferred to the other party under a contract.

## Mitigating the effect of the entire obligations rule
In practice, there are three ways in which the entire obligations rule can be mitigated:
- severable contracts,
- the *acceptance* of the performance by the other party, and
- the doctrine of substantial performance.

### Severable contracts
Contracts can be drafted to provide for work to be performed in stages, requiring the other party to make payments in instalments after the completion of each stage of performance.

### The acceptance of the performance by the other party
If the non-breaching party chooses to accept the performance of the party in breach, the party in breach can claim for the benefit of the work they have carried out on a *quantum meruit* basis. A *quantum meruit* claim can only be made if the non-breaching party can *choose* whether or not to accept performance.

Now work through **Practice example 9.4** to check your understanding of when the court will allow a claim for *quantum meruit*.

> **Practice example 9.4**
>
> Bertie agrees to build two houses on Elizabeth's land. The contract provides that Elizabeth will pay Bertie the full amount of the contract (£565) after he has completed building the two houses. Unfortunately for Bertie, he runs out of money halfway through the project, when the value of the work he has completed is £333. Bertie abandons the half-completed houses and leaves materials on Elizabeth's land. Elizabeth completes building the houses herself with the materials that Bertie had left on the land.
>
> Can Bertie recover payment for the work he has done, and for the materials that he left on the land?
>
> **Bertie cannot recover payment for the work he has done, but he can recover payment for the materials left on the land. This**

scenario is based on *Sumpter v Hedges* [1898] 1 QB 673 CA. The court's decision was driven by the fact that the contract was an entire obligations agreement where the other party's payment obligation only arose on the builder's completion of the two houses. Further, the other party had no choice but to accept the builder's performance of the half-completed houses. By contrast, the other party was free to choose whether to complete the building using the materials left by the builder on the land, or any other materials. On the grounds that the other party *chose* to use the materials left by the builder, the court allowed the builder to recover the value of the materials left on the land.

### Exam warning
Check carefully in scenarios that relate to entire obligations whether the non-breaching party can choose to accept any part of the performance. If the non-breaching party is free to choose, and does choose to accept any part of the performance, they will be liable to pay the other party on a *quantum meruit* basis for that part of the work that they have chosen to accept.

## The doctrine of substantial performance
The doctrine of **substantial performance** provides an important mechanism in respect of entire obligations agreements.

### Key term: substantial performance
The doctrine that allows a party to recover a substantial part of their fee if they have substantially completed their performance, albeit with defects, under an entire obligations agreement.

Now apply your knowledge in **Practice example 9.5**.

### Practice example 9.5
Louisa is an interior designer who agrees to decorate and furnish Charlie's home for a lump sum payable on completion of £750. Louisa completes her work on Charlie's home, but Charlie refuses to pay the amount owed to Louisa on the grounds that part of Louisa's work was defective. Specifically, Charlie argues that Louisa's work is defective in respect of a wardrobe and a bookcase. The evidence shows that it would cost £55 to fix the defects in the wardrobe and the bookcase.

Can Louisa force Charlie to pay her under the doctrine of substantial performance?

The answer is yes. Louisa can force Charlie to pay her the full amount under the contract, less the amount required to fix the defects. This scenario is based on *Hoenig v Isaacs* [1952] 2 All ER 176. The court held that not every breach of an entire obligations agreement allows the non-breaching party to discharge the contract. Discharge is only permitted for breaches that go to the root of the contract, for example, where work is abandoned when it is only half finished. This means that where the work has been completed, *albeit with some minor defects*, the non-breaching party must pay the price agreed under the contract, minus a deduction to fix the defects.

### Revision tip

Look carefully at the case law on this topic. The doctrine of substantial performance only applies in respect of minor defects. The case law provides clear examples of scenarios in which the courts have held that the amount (or value) of the work performed is not enough for the doctrine of substantial performance to apply.

## EXPIRY OF TIME OR OTHER SPECIFIC EVENT

A contract may provide that it will end after a certain period of time, or when a specified event happens. For example, an energy supplier may wish to limit an obligation to supply energy at a given price until the energy regulator next reviews its pricing to suppliers. This will allow them to supply energy to a customer at a given price for as long as they are aware of what the supply price is. Provided these are correctly drafted, the expiry of the time frame or the occurrence of the specified event will bring the contract to an end.

## AGREEMENT

Another way in which parties are discharged of their obligations under a contract is through their agreement. The parties simply need to agree to release each other from any outstanding obligations.

# FRUSTRATION

Frustration is an English law doctrine that automatically discharges both parties from their future obligations under a contract. Frustration takes effect as a result of events that make the future performance of a contract:
- impossible,
- illegal, or
- where the main purpose of both parties of the contract is lost.

> **Key term: frustration**
> A doctrine that automatically discharges both parties from their future obligations under a contract.

## The legal effect of frustration

It is essential to understand that frustration *automatically* discharges both parties from their outstanding obligations under a contract. This contrasts with the effect of a repudiatory breach, which gives the non-breaching party the *choice* to discharge the contract, or to affirm it.

If the parties to a contract have already performed some obligations under the contract, the position is regulated by the Law Reform (Frustrated Contracts) Act 1943. We will explore how this works in practice below (see **The effect of frustration on financial obligations, page 183**).

## Identifying frustration

In your SQE1 assessments, you need to look out for scenarios in which the performance of the contract following a specific event is fundamentally different from what was contemplated by the parties when the agreement was concluded. Make sure that you understand that the doctrine does not apply if the contract has become more difficult, expensive or inconvenient to perform. Parties are expected to provide for such eventualities in their contracts through clauses that allow them to increase their costs if, for example, materials or labour become more expensive.

Check your understanding of how this works in practice in **Practice example 9.6**.

# The discharge of contracts

> ### Practice example 9.6
>
> Jones Contractors agrees with a council to build 78 houses for a given amount within eight months. The work takes 22 months and costs Jones Contractors more than they had planned; this was due to a shortage of materials and a shortage of labour.
>
> Does Jones Contractors have grounds to claim that the contract is frustrated?
>
> The answer is no. This scenario is based on the case of *Davis Contractors v Fareham UDC* [1956] AC 696. The House of Lords held that the contractor had accepted the risk of the cost being more or less than he expected. The delay was not caused by a new or unforeseeable factor or event. So although the contractor's job became more difficult, it had not become a job that was different from what was contemplated in the original contract. So the contract was not frustrated.

In addition, the courts will not allow a claim for frustration where the event in question is self-induced, or results from the fault of one of the parties (see **Frustration and fault, page 182**).

## Frustration when performance is impossible

The impossibility of performing a contractual obligation *may* be a ground on which a contract is held to be frustrated. Note the importance of the word *may*, which means that in some cases a contract that has become impossible to perform will not be held to be frustrated. We will explore these cases in the following sections.

### Frustration due to impossibility when the subject matter is destroyed

A contract may be held to be frustrated when its subject matter is destroyed and this makes the contract impossible to perform. For example, in *Taylor v Caldwell* (1863) 122 ER 309, the destruction of a concert hall by fire was held to frustrate a contract in which concerts were to be held in the concert hall. Neither party to the contract was to blame for the fire. The court's logic was that the parties had contracted on the basis that the existence of the concert hall was essential to the performance of the contract.

## Frustration due to impossibility where a person is ill or dies

Many contracts can be fulfilled by any one of a number of individuals so that if one individual in a team is ill or dies, the contract is not frustrated. But if a contract is specific to a particular person, the illness or death of such person can serve as a ground to discharge the contract for frustration. The classic example is provided in the case of *Robinson v Davison* (1870-71) LR 6 Ex 269 where the contract provided for a specific woman to play the piano at a concert given by the other party on a specific day. The woman was unable to perform on the day in question due to illness. The court held that the contract was frustrated.

## Frustration due to impossibility where the agreed means of performance becomes unavailable

In scenarios where the parties have agreed that the contract will be performed by a specific means (for example, delivery on a named boat), the unavailability of such means will be held to frustrate the contract.

Note that in scenarios where the means of performance is only *temporarily* unavailable, you will need to consider all of the information in the scenario, including the duration of the unavailability. If the temporary delay is so long that the purpose for which the means of performance (for example, a ship) was originally hired has become very different, then the contract is likely to be frustrated. For example, if a ship hired to collect a commodity is unavailable for eight months.

> **Revision tip**
>
> Make sure that you distinguish between scenarios in which the means of performance that has become unavailable is a *term* of the contract, and scenarios in which the parties *envisage* that contract will be performed in a specific way (for example, by following a particular route), but they have not *expressly agreed* this route in the contract. This distinction is critically important because if the route (or other means of performance) is not an agreed term of the contract (but is simply envisaged by the parties) the fact that the route (or means of performance) is no longer available will not frustrate the contract.

## Frustration when performance is illegal

If, after a contract has been concluded, the law changes in such a way that renders the future performance of the contract illegal, this can frustrate the contract if the new law would have made performance of the contract illegal at the time the contract was made.

## Frustration when the main purpose of both parties to the contract is lost

A further way in which a contract is frustrated is where the *main purpose* of both parties to the contract is lost. So although it may be possible for both parties to perform the contract, a dramatic change in the surrounding circumstances means that the *entire basis* on which the contract was concluded has been lost. For example, in *Krell v Henry* [1903] 2 KB 740 CA, a contract to hire rooms on a specific date at a higher than usual price on Pall Mall to watch the coronation procession of King Edward VII was held to be frustrated when the coronation procession was postponed. Although the contract could still be performed because the rooms could still be used for a social gathering, the purpose of hiring the rooms in that location at such a high price with the main purpose of watching the coronation had been lost.

## Frustration and fault

A key element in any claim for frustration is that it should *not* result from the act or choice of the party that seeks to rely on it.

You can practice your understanding of how this works in practice in **Practice example 9.7**.

> ### Practice example 9.7
>
> Morritson Drilling agreed with Tarzan Shipping that Tarzan Shipping would transport Morritson's shipping rig either on its ship *Greystoke 1*, or on its other ship, *Greystoke 2*. Tarzan Shipping intends to use *Greystoke 2*, but this is not mentioned or recorded in the contract. Since Tarzan Shipping intends to use *Greystoke 2*, it agrees to hire out *Greystoke 1* to a third party. Due to unforeseen circumstances, *Greystoke 2* sinks and cannot be used. *Greystoke 1* is not available because it is being used by a third party.
>
> Can Tarzan Shipping claim that the contract is frustrated?
>
> The answer is no. This scenario is based on *J. Lauritzen A/S v Wijsmuller BV, The Super Servant Two* [1990] 1 Lloyd's Rep 1. The Court of Appeal highlighted the point that an essential requirement

for frustration is that the event must significantly change the nature of the outstanding contractual obligations from what the parties could reasonably have contemplated at the time the contract was made. In this scenario, the contract provided an alternative to the ship that had sunk. The fact that the alternative ship was no longer available was the fault of the shipping company that had hired it to a third party.

## The effect of frustration on financial obligations

We have already seen that frustration automatically discharges both parties from all future obligations under the contract. In this section, we will explore the effect of frustration where a party to the contract has already paid money, or incurred expenses under the contract. We will also set out the effect of frustration on future obligations to pay under a contract. The position is governed generally by the Law Reform (Frustrated Contracts) Act (LRFCA) 1943, or under the common law, where the Act does not apply. Scenarios where the LRFCA 1943 does not apply include those where the parties have included provisions to deal with the consequences of frustration. In such cases, the contractual provisions will apply. The LRFCA 1943 does not apply to certain types of insurance contract, but this topic will not be discussed in this book.

### The effect of frustration on claims for money

If the LRFCA 1943 applies:
- money paid under the contract is recoverable by the party that paid it, and
- money due to be paid no longer needs to be paid.

But note carefully that if the party to whom money was paid under a contract has incurred expenses under the contract before it is frustrated, the court may, having regard to all of the circumstances, allow such person to retain an amount of money received under the contract (or recover an amount that was payable before the contract was discharged). So if a person has incurred expenses in excess of the amount they have received under the contract and the other party was not obliged to pay any further amounts before the contract was discharged, they cannot recover the excess.

Similarly, if one party has received a valuable benefit from the other party before the contract is frustrated, the court may allow the party that has conferred the benefit to recover from the other party an amount to reflect that benefit. The court takes into account all the circumstances of the case, and, in particular, any expenses recovered and the events that led to the frustration in the first place.

## ■ KEY POINT CHECKLIST

This chapter has covered the following key knowledge points. You can use these to structure your revision around, making sure to recall the key details for each point, as covered in this chapter.
- A contract can be discharged by performance. Make sure that you understand the difference between strict contractual obligations and qualified contractual obligations.
- Remember the tests used to determine whether a breach is repudiatory. You need to apply these tests to contracts that do not already specify the effect of a particular breach. Does the breach go to the root of the contract and deprive the non-breaching party of substantially the whole benefit of the contract? Is there statutory guidance?
- A repudiatory breach gives the non-breaching party the choice to affirm or discharge the contract.
- Make sure that you understand the entire obligations rule and the exceptions to the rule that allow the breaching party to recover amounts under the contract.
- It is essential to know the circumstances that give rise to frustration. In addition, you must also know that frustration automatically discharges both parties to a contract.

## ■ KEY TERMS AND CONCEPTS

- repudiatory breach (**page 170**)
- anticipatory repudiatory breach (**page 170**)
- *quantum meruit* (**page 176**)
- substantial performance (**page 177**)
- frustration (**page 179**)

## ■ SQE1-STYLE QUESTIONS

### QUESTION 1

A developer and an investor enter into an agreement pursuant to which the developer will build four blocks of flats by a given date. The agreement provided that the developer would lease the flats to the investor on a 999-year lease. The developer runs behind schedule, and completes the building of two of the blocks over a year late at a time when it is still working on the other two blocks in order to complete them.

**Which of the following most accurately reflects the legal position in this case?**

A. The investor can discharge the contract on the grounds of the developer's repudiatory breach.

B. The investor cannot repudiate the contract with the developer, but is entitled to claim damages.

C. If the investor repudiates the contract, the developer can elect to affirm the contract, which will oblige both parties to continue to perform their obligations under the contract.

D. The contract is discharged by frustration.

E. The investor can discharge the contract on the grounds of the developer's anticipatory repudiatory breach.

## QUESTION 2

A man agrees to build a garage for a woman for a lump sum of £10,000. The man runs out of money half-way through building the garage and abandons the half-built garage. The man estimates that the value of the building he has completed is £5,900. The man also leaves wood and other building materials on the woman's land. The woman uses the materials that the man has left on the land to finish building the garage.

**Which of the following statements most accurately describes the legal position in this case?**

A. The man can claim £5,900 from the woman.

B. The man can claim £5,900 from the woman plus the value of the materials left on the woman's land.

C. The man cannot claim anything from the woman as this is an entire obligations agreement.

D. The man cannot claim anything from the woman and is liable to compensate the woman for her work in finishing the garage.

E. The man can claim the value of the materials that he left on the woman's land.

## QUESTION 3

A plumber agreed with a man that she would install a central heating system for him. The contract provided that the plumber would be paid £3,000 in a lump sum once the work was completed. There were numerous defects in the work so that the system did not heat adequately, and it gave off fumes. The cost to fix the work was £930.

Which of the following statements best represents the legal position in the case?

A. The contract has been frustrated.
B. The plumber is not entitled to claim any payment for the work done.
C. The plumber is entitled to the £3,000.
D. Provided the plumber used reasonable endeavours, she will have satisfied her obligation under the contract.
E. The plumber is entitled to claim the £3,000, minus the amount required to fix the work of £930.

## QUESTION 4

A contractor agrees to deliver building materials to a developer over a period of five years. At some stage during the five-year period, the contractor's existing supplier decides to stop supplying the contractor. As a result, the contractor can no longer deliver the building materials to the developer.

Which of the following statements most accurately reflects the approach of the court in this case?

A. The court will recognise the contract as frustrated for illegality.
B. The court will not recognise the contract as frustrated.
C. The court will recognise the contract as frustrated for impossibility.
D. The court will recognise the contract as frustrated due to the loss of the main purpose.
E. The court will recognise the contract as frustrated because it has become impracticable.

## QUESTION 5

A shipping company agrees with a dealer to transport a cargo from one country to another. Both parties assumed that the cargo would be shipped through the most direct route between the two countries, but this was not mentioned in the contract. After the contract was concluded but before the cargo was delivered, the most direct route was unavailable, having been closed. There was an alternative route available but it would cost the shipping company twice as much, and take twice as long to ship the goods via the alternative route.

**Which of the following statements best reflects the legal position of the shipping company in the case?**

A. The shipping company can affirm or discharge the contract.

B. The shipping company is automatically discharged from its obligations under the contract.

C. The shipping company is bound to perform its obligations under the contract.

D. The shipping company is bound to perform its obligations under the contract but can obtain damages from the dealer.

E. There is an implied term in the contract that the cargo will be shipped by the most direct route and because this is no longer an option, this is an anticipatory breach.

# ■ ANSWERS TO QUESTIONS

## Answers to 'What do you know already?' questions at the start of the chapter

1) A strict contractual obligation must be performed *exactly* as it is described. This means that if a party agrees to deliver apples at 2 PM, any failure to do this will be a breach. By contrast, a qualified contractual liability is subject to a qualification, for example, that a party will use reasonable endeavours to deliver apples by 2 PM. This means that so long as a party uses reasonable endeavours to deliver apples by 2 PM, they will not be in breach of their obligation, even if they fail to deliver the apples by 2 PM.

2) A repudiatory breach is a breach of a major term of a contract that goes to the root of the contract and gives the non-breaching party the right to choose whether to discharge the contract or to affirm it.

3) The doctrine of substantial performance applies in respect of entire obligations agreements. The doctrine provides for the party in breach to recover a substantial part of the agreed fee if they can show that they have substantially completed their performance under the contract, albeit with some defects.

188   The discharge of contracts

4) False. Frustration automatically discharges a contract so that the parties are automatically released of their future obligations under the contract.
5) The correct answer was (d). Impracticability. The doctrine of frustration is narrowly applied so does not relieve a party of their obligations under a contract simply because the contract has become impracticable or more onerous.

## Answers to end-of-chapter SQE1-style questions

Question 1:
   The correct answer was B. In assessing whether a breach is repudiatory in scenarios such as these, you need to consider whether the breach deprives the non-breaching party of substantially the whole benefit of the contract. Pay attention to the time frames in the scenario. The leases for the investor were for 999 years, and the delays were very short in comparison. Since the developer was working on the two remaining blocks at the time of the investor's possible discharge for repudiatory breach, it is not possible to say that the breach at that point had deprived the investor of substantially the whole benefit of the contract. The factual delay at the time of the investor's possible repudiation could be sufficiently compensated in damages. This means that Options A and C are incorrect. In addition, in relation to Option C you should note that it is only the non-breaching party that can elect to affirm the contract (in this case, the investor). Option D is incorrect as the contract was still capable of being performed. Option E is incorrect because the breach in question was not anticipatory.

Question 2:
   The correct answer was E. This is due to an exception to the entire obligations agreement rule that applies where the non-breaching party has a choice of whether or not to accept the other party's performance. In this case, the woman is not liable to pay the man for the work on the garage as it is not movable. By contrast, the materials that the man has left on the land are movable and this gave the woman the choice whether to use these materials or not. On the basis that the woman has chosen to accept the materials, the court will allow the builder to recover the value of the materials. This means that Options A, B, C and D are incorrect.

Question 3:
   The correct answer was B. This is because the agreement is an entire obligations agreement since it provides for a lump sum payment on

the completion of the work. The work has not been completed so the plumber is not entitled to anything. This means that Option C is incorrect. Option E is incorrect because the nature of the defects in the work and the cost of remedying them are too great for the doctrine of substantial performance to apply. Option A is incorrect because there is no indication of any of the grounds that invoke the doctrine of frustration. Option D is incorrect because the scenario does not provide for the plumber to use reasonable endeavours. Rather the plumber is under a strict contractual obligation and has failed to perform her obligation in accordance with the contract.

Question 4:
The correct answer was B. In scenarios such as these, the court's position is that it is the responsibility of the party who agrees to supply to make arrangements to deal with the risk that their supply fails. The contractor could have done this by adding a provision in the contract to provide that his obligation to deliver was dependent upon being able to obtain the relevant building materials without undue difficulty. Since the contractor has made an unqualified promise, he takes the risk that his contemplated source of supply will fail. This means that Option C is incorrect. This also means that Option E is incorrect because the impracticality does not cause frustration. Option A is incorrect as there is nothing in the scenario to suggest that the performance of the contract has become illegal. Option D is incorrect because the main purpose of the contract has not changed.

Question 5:
The correct answer was C. Although the contract has become more difficult and expensive for the shipping company to perform, these factors do not trigger the doctrine of frustration. This means that Option B is incorrect as it sets out the effect of frustration on the contract. Option D is incorrect as there is no basis in the scenario on which the dealer is liable to the shipping company in damages. Option A is incorrect because the choice to affirm or discharge arises in the case of a repudiatory breach and there is no evidence in this scenario to support an argument for repudiatory breach. Option E is incorrect because although the parties assumed that the route would be via the most direct route, such assumption does not give rise to an implied term.

## ■ KEY CASES, RULES, STATUTES AND INSTRUMENTS

The SQE1 Assessment Specification does not require you to know any case names, or statutory materials, for this topic.

# 10

# Remedies

## ■ MAKE SURE YOU KNOW

This chapter will cover the remedies for breach of contract. The primary remedy for breach of contract is damages. However, there are a number of other remedies that you need to understand for the SQE1 assessments. This chapter explains those remedies and outlines the scenarios in which the court may exercise its discretion to award the equitable remedies.

**Remedies for breach of contract**

| At law | Under the contract | At equity |
|---|---|---|
| • Damages | • Debt claim (an action for an agreed amount) | • Specific performance |
| • Repudiation (if the breach is repudiatory, see **Chapter 9 Repudiatory breach, page 169**) | • Liquidated damages (if provided for in the contract)<br>• A claim under a guarantee or indemnity (if provided) | • Injunction<br>• Restitution (unjust enrichment) |

## ■ SQE ASSESSMENT ADVICE

As you work through this chapter, remember to pay particular attention in your revision to:
- The different ways in which damages are calculated to compensate the injured party.
- The limitations on the recoverability of damages including causation and remoteness.
- Other factors that limit the injured party's ability to claim damages.
- The circumstances in which an injured party can claim an agreed amount (such as a debt) under a contract.
- The circumstances in which a court will grant the equitable remedies of specific performance, injunction and restitution (unjust enrichment).

## ■ WHAT DO YOU KNOW ALREADY?

Have a go at these questions before reading this chapter. If you find some difficult or cannot remember the answers, make a note to look more closely at that area during your revision.

1) What is the primary remedy for breach of contract under English law?
   **[Introduction to remedies, page 192]**
2) True or false? The purpose of English law damages is to punish the party in breach.
   **[The aim of damages for breach of contract, page 192]**
3) Which one of the following is not a limitation on the injured party's ability to claim damages for loss under English law?
   a) remoteness
   b) causation
   c) contributory negligence
   d) indemnity
   **[Factors that limit a person's ability to claim damages, page 196]**
4) True or false? As a general rule, an injured party cannot claim for distress, frustration, anxiety, displeasure, vexation, tension or aggravation under English law.
   **[Damages for non-financial loss, page 198]**
5) What steps must the injured party take to mitigate their loss?
   a) onerous
   b) reasonable
   c) exceptional
   **[Mitigation, page 198]**

## INTRODUCTION TO REMEDIES

In **Chapter 9** we explored certain actions and events that discharge the future obligations of both parties under a contract (either as a result of the injured party *choosing* to do this in the case of repudiatory breach, or *automatically* in the case of frustration).

In this chapter, we will focus on the remedies that are available to the injured party for breach of contract. For the SQE1 assessment you are required to know the law relating to:
- damages (and the principles of causation and remoteness)
- action for an agreed amount (such as a debt)
- liquidated damages and penalties
- guarantees and indemnities
- specific performance
- injunction
- restitution (to prevent unjust enrichment).

Let us start our exploration of this topic by looking at the remedy of damages.

## DAMAGES

**Damages** are the primary remedy under English law for breach of contract.

> **Key term: damages**
> Financial compensation for breach of contract.

### The aim of damages for breach of contract

The aim of damages for breach of contract is to put the injured party in the same position as if the contract had been performed. As a general rule, damages for breach of contract are *not* aimed at punishing the party in breach, but aim to compensate the injured party for their loss.

If the injured party does not incur a loss as the result of the breach, they can only claim **nominal damages**.

> **Key term: nominal damages**
> A small amount of money (for example, a few pounds as a token gesture) awarded as damages to an injured party who has not suffered any loss due to a breach of contract.

## The time for calculating damages

As a general rule, damages are calculated at the time that the breach takes place. For example, if a buyer fails to accept and pay for goods that they have ordered, the seller's damages are calculated at the time when the goods ought to have been accepted. So if there is a liquid market (in which the goods in question are readily available), the damages will be calculated as the difference between the price that the buyer promised to pay, and the price that the seller is able to achieve by selling the goods to another person. There is an exception to the rule that allows the court to calculate damages on another date, if necessary, to avoid injustice. For example, if the seller is dealing with an unusual product for which there is no ready market, the seller will be allowed to take reasonable time to find a buyer; if a buyer cannot be found, the damages will be calculated as the price that was agreed with the breaching party, and the value of the produce when the seller was obliged to keep it (on account of not being able to find an alternative buyer).

## CALCULATING DAMAGES FOR BREACH OF CONTRACT

Damages for breach of contract are calculated in different ways:
- loss of expectation
- wasted expenditure.

### Loss of expectation

**Loss of expectation** refers to a way of calculating damages by measuring the benefit that the injured party *expected* to make from the contract.

> **Key term: loss of expectation**
> The measure of calculating damages to put the injured party in the position that they would have been in if the contract had been performed.

There are three different ways of calculating damages through the loss of expectation method.

#### *Loss of expectation: loss of profit*

Damages calculated on the loss of profit basis aim to compensate the injured party for the profit that they lost as a result of the breach.

A classic example of loss of profit is where party A agrees to buy apples from party B. If party A intended to sell the apples to a third party at a profit, party B's failure to deliver the apples to party A will prevent party A from making a profit by selling the apples to a third party. In such scenarios, party A's claim for damages is the amount of profit that it has lost through not having apples to sell to the third party.

## Loss of expectation: difference in value

In some scenarios, the injured party may receive something that is less valuable than was described in the contract. For example, the injured party may receive a house with cracks in the new plasterwork. In such scenarios, if the injured party can still use the house (or other product as the case may be), then damages may be calculated to *compensate* them for the difference between what they paid for and what they received. So if the evidence shows that the house was actually worth £450,000, rather than the £460,000 that the injured party paid for it, their damages will be £10,000.

## Loss of expectation: cost of cure

Alternatively, a court may award damages to cure the breach of contract. For example, if you buy a new oven that should heat above 200 degrees Celsius, but it does not, you may wish to keep the oven and claim an amount of damages to repair the oven so that it meets its specifications. Once you receive the cost of cure, you will be in the position you would have been if the contract had been performed as originally agreed.

A key point to note is that the courts will only award the cost of cure when it is a reasonable option. So if the cost of cure is out of all proportion with the benefit that the injured party will receive, the court will not allow it.

Test your understanding of the court's approach to claims for cost of cure damages in **Practice example 10.1**.

### Practice example 10.1

Mr Smith hires a contractor to build a swimming pool with a maximum depth of seven feet and six inches for £17,797. The contractor builds the swimming pool with a maximum depth of six feet and nine inches. This contractor is in breach of contract so Mr Smith can claim damages. However, the evidence shows that there is no difference in *value* between the pool with the depth described in the contract and the pool that the contractor built. This means that Mr Smith cannot claim against the contractor on the basis of difference in value. In addition, the evidence shows that Mr Smith is able to use the pool as he planned to. The only way to give the pool the depth specified in the contract is to demolish it and then rebuild it at the cost of £21,560.

Can Mr Smith claim against the contractor on the cost of cure basis?

The answer is no. This scenario is based on the case of *Ruxley Electronics & Construction Ltd v Forsyth* [1996] AC 344. The House of Lords held that the cost of cure was only available as a remedy if it was reasonable. Based on the facts of the case, the House of Lords considered the cost of cure (spending £21,560 on a new swimming pool) would be 'wholly disproportionate' to any benefit that the injured party would gain. Since the evidence showed that there was no difference in value between what the injured party contracted for, and what he received, no cost of cure would be awarded.

### Revision tip
Remember that the different measures of damages described above are alternatives. So the injured party will only be entitled to *one* of the above measures to put them in the same position as if the contract had been correctly performed.

## Wasted expenditure

In some scenarios, it might not be possible to determine what a person's profit under a contract would have been if the breach had not occurred. For example, if an actor breaches their contract by pulling out of a film when it is being made, it may not be possible for the injured party (for example, the producer) to claim for loss of profit because it is uncertain how much profit the film will generate. In such scenarios, the only way to compensate the injured person for their loss is to award damages to cover their wasted expenditure, which is the expense incurred in performing (and preparing to perform) their obligations under a contract.

### Exam warning
Note that there is a limitation on a party's ability to claim damages for wasted expenditure. A party cannot claim damages for wasted expenditure where they have entered into a bad bargain. For example, if a tenant agrees that all of the materials he uses to fit out a shop outlet will become the property of the landlord, if the landlord evicts the tenant before the end of the lease, the tenant will not be able to claim any damages for his costs of fitting out the shop outlet

on the grounds of wasted expenditure because it would put him in a better position than he would otherwise have been. The explanation for this is that the tenant had already agreed with the landlord that the materials he used to fit out the shop outlet would become the property of the landlord.

## FACTORS THAT LIMIT A PERSON'S ABILITY TO CLAIM DAMAGES

The following factors limit a person's ability to claim damages:
- causation
- contributory negligence
- remoteness
- mitigation.

### Causation

The injured party's loss must be caused by the breach of contract. So if the injured party would have suffered the loss regardless of the breach of contract, they will not be able to claim damages for their loss. Note that if the injured party performs an act (often referred to as an intervening act) that breaks the chain of **causation**, they will not be able to claim damages for the breach. For example, in *Lambert v Lewis* [1982] AC 225, a farmer's claim against the supplier of a defective towing hitch was denied because the farmer repeatedly used the hitch knowing that it was defective.

> **Key term: causation**
>
> The requirement that damages for breach of contract will only be awarded to compensate loss that is *caused* by the breach.

### Contributory negligence

The injured party's claim may be *reduced* on the grounds of **contributory negligence**. In contract law, contributory negligence can only reduce the injured party's right to damages if the other party breached:
- a qualified obligation (for example, a duty to exercise reasonable care and skill), *and*
- a duty of care in tort.

> **Procedural link: elements of a claim in tort law**
>
> Tort law is concerned with imposing civil liability for breach of obligations imposed by law. The most common tort is the tort of

negligence. For the SQE1 you need to understand this area of law. You should refer to the *Revise SQE: Tort Law* book for a detailed overview of this subject.

> **Key term: contributory negligence**
> A defence that reduces the measure of damages to the injured party to reflect the injured party's contribution through negligence to the loss incurred.

## Remoteness

Damages cannot be recovered for a loss that is too remote. As a general rule, the principle of **remoteness** means that a loss can be recovered if, at the time the contract was made, it was in the reasonable contemplation of the parties as the probable result of its breach. In other words, when the parties entered the contract, could they have predicted that the loss in question would have resulted from a breach of the contract?

> **Key term: remoteness**
> The principle that determines the extent to which damages that result from a breach are recoverable.

Now work through **Practice example 10.2** to check your understanding of how the courts apply the remoteness test.

> **Practice example 10.2**
> Victoria runs a laundry and agrees with a contractor to buy a new boiler to be delivered on 5 June. In breach of contract, the contractor delivers the boiler five months late. As a result, Victoria cannot heat water to wash clothes and loses income from the day to day business of washing clothes, and cannot accept a lucrative contract with the Government.
>
> Can Victoria recover damages for her losses from her day to day business and the Government contract?
>
> **Victoria can only recover damages for her day to day losses. This scenario is based on the facts of *Victoria Laundry (Windsor) Ltd v Newman Industries Ltd* [1949] 2 KB 528. Since the contractor did not know about the lucrative contracts, the loss relating to them was not in the contractor's reasonable contemplation and was too remote to be recovered.**

## Mitigation

The injured party must take *reasonable steps* to **mitigate** their loss. This is because a party cannot recover damages for a loss that they could have avoided by taking reasonable steps.

> **Key term: mitigate**
> The taking of reasonable steps to minimise a loss, and the avoidance of taking unreasonable steps that increase a loss.

### Mitigation leading to increased loss
Provided the injured party takes *reasonable steps* to mitigate their loss, they will be able to recover their loss *even if* the reasonable steps increase the loss. For example, imagine that a soft drink producer discovers that his drinks are contaminated due to a contaminated ingredient from one of his suppliers that poses a negligible health risk to the public. The producer has a number of options available to it, including notifying the public of the contamination, or recalling and destroying all of the contaminated drinks. Although the mitigating act of withdrawing and destroying the drinks will increase the producer's loss, he will be able to recover its loss from the supplier as damages for breach of contract if he can show that his steps were reasonable (for example, to protect his reputation).

## DAMAGES FOR NON-FINANCIAL LOSS

As a general rule, a person cannot recover damages to compensate them for mental distress, or loss of enjoyment. However, there are exceptions to the general rule, which we will now explore.

### Damages for mental distress
As an exception to the general rule, a person can recover damages for mental distress where it results from physical inconvenience. For example, a person who suffers distress and discomfort after buying a property with serious defects, based on a negligent survey that stated the property was sound, is able to claim damages for vexation and inconvenience.

### Damages for loss of enjoyment
Another exception to the general rule applies where a major purpose of the contract is to bring pleasure, relaxation, peace of mind, or freedom

from molestation. For example, a holidaymaker is able to claim damages in the amount they paid for their holiday, and an additional amount for their loss of enjoyment on the holiday, if the holiday company does not provide the facilities and the entertainment that it promised.

### Damages for loss of reputation

The last exception to the general rule is that a person is able to recover damages from a previous employer for the loss they incur if the previous employer's reputation makes it impossible for them to find a job. For example, if an employer becomes known for acting in a corrupt way, its former employee might also be perceived as corrupt. In such a scenario, the employee can claim damages for the financial loss that results from them not being able to find a job.

> **Exam warning**
>
> As a matter of policy, awards of damages for distress are only made to individuals. The courts never award damages for distress for the breach of commercial contracts.

## ACTION FOR AN AGREED AMOUNT (DEBT CLAIM)

If one party to a contract fails to pay the other, the injured party (Party A) may claim against the other party (Party B) for the amount that Party A is owed under the contract. A claim for an agreed amount is distinct from a claim in damages as it is not a claim for compensation for loss, but simply a claim for what the injured party is owed under the contract. For example, consider a scenario in which a person (Party A) agrees to sell apples to another person (Party B) for £500. If Party A delivers the apples to Party B, but Party B fails to pay the consideration of £500, Party A's remedy will be to sue Party B for the amount Party A is owed under the contract.

> **Key term: action for an agreed amount**
>
> A claim by a party who has performed their obligations under the contract for the amount owing to them under the contract.

## LIQUIDATED DAMAGES AND PENALTIES

As an alternative to common law damages, parties may decide when negotiating a contract to specify what each party's liability will be in the case of a breach of contract. Clauses that provide for the payment of a fixed amount on a breach of contract are called liquidated damages clauses. For example, if party A fails to deliver supplies to party B next Tuesday, it will be liable to pay party B liquidated damages of £1,000. Liquidated damages clauses are enforceable unless they are deemed to be a penalty (discussed below).

### Liquidated damages clause or penalty?

When considering whether a liquidated damages clause is a penalty, the starting point is whether the clause is a genuine pre-estimate of the injured party's loss. If it is, the liquidated damages clause will be enforceable.

If it is not a genuine pre-estimate of loss, then you need to consider whether the clause imposes a detriment on the contract breaker that is out of all proportion with the injured party's interest in the contract being performed. The case of *ParkingEye Ltd v Beavis* [2015] UKSC 67 discussed in **Chapter 6** (see **Practice example 6.8**) provides an example of an injured party's legitimate interest. Although ParkingEye Ltd did not suffer any loss as a result of Mr Beavis overstaying the two hour limit, the court held that it was justified in charging Mr Beavis £85. The charge deterred people from parking for too long and ParkingEye Ltd had the legitimate interest in deterring people from parking for too long as it managed the parking spaces for the shops nearby, their customers and the general public.

## GUARANTEES AND INDEMNITIES

A contract may also provide for the injured party to have a remedy under a guarantee or an indemnity. The terms are often used interchangeably in practice, but they have distinct legal meanings.

### Guarantee

A **guarantee** is a promise by one person to be responsible if another person breaches their obligation. A guarantee of debt must be in writing to be enforceable.

> **Key term: guarantee**
>
> A guarantee is a promise by one person to be responsible if another person breaches their obligation.

For example, imagine a scenario in which Big Bank lends money to Jonny, and Mary guarantees in writing that Jonny will repay the money. Jonny is primarily liable (this is also referred to as a primary obligation) for the money borrowed. But if Jonny breaches his primary obligation to repay the money to Big Bank, the obligation under Mary's guarantee (this is a secondary obligation because it only arises when Jonny breaches his primary obligation) arises, which means that:
- Mary is responsible for ensuring that Jonny repays his debt, and
- Big Bank has a claim against Mary if Jonny fails to repay his debt.

Big Bank has a remedy against Mary because her secondary obligation arises if Jonny fails to repay his debt.

### Indemnity

An **indemnity** is a primary obligation from a person (often referred to as the surety) to pay the debt of another. The importance of the surety being under a primary obligation, rather than a secondary one as in the case of a guarantee, stems from the creditor's option of suing the surety for the debt, rather than having to first sue the debtor, which is the case for guarantees. In contrast to guarantees, there is no requirement that an indemnity be in writing, although in practice it usually is.

> **Key term: indemnity**
>
> An indemnity is a primary obligation from one person to pay the debt of another.

> **Exam warning**
>
> It is very important to note that the secondary nature of the guarantor's obligation means that if the agreement that contains the primary obligation with the debtor is held to be unenforceable, or is otherwise set aside, then the guarantee will also be unenforceable, or otherwise set aside. The opposite is true in the case of an indemnity on the basis that it is a primary obligation and the surety will remain liable even if the agreement with the debtor is set aside.

## EQUITABLE REMEDIES: SPECIFIC PERFORMANCE, INJUNCTIONS AND RESTITUTION

The courts have the discretion to make awards for specific performance and injunctions. As a general rule, the courts exercise their discretion to award equitable remedies when damages would not compensate the injured party for their loss.

## Specific performance
The first equitable remedy we will consider is **specific performance**.

> **Key term: specific performance**
> Specific performance is an equitable remedy to make the party in breach perform its obligations under the contract.

The courts most often exercise their discretion to make an order for specific performance in respect of items that are unique, such as an agreement to deliver the original manuscript of William Shakespeare's Othello. Specific performance is also available as a remedy in contracts to acquire land or a house, because the law considers all land to be unique. As a general rule, the courts do not make orders for specific performance when the goods or services that the party in breach has failed to deliver are readily available from another source.

## Injunction
The second equitable remedy we will consider is the **injunction**.

> **Key term: injunction**
> An injunction is a court order to stop a person from doing something.

A court will make an order for an injunction where damages will not compensate the injured party. For example, in *Sky Petroleum Ltd v VIP Petroleum Ltd* [1974] 1 WLR 576, the court ordered an injunction to stop an oil company from cutting off petrol supplies to the owner of petrol stations during a nationwide petrol shortage. Since petrol was not available from any other sources, damages would not have put the owner of the petrol stations in the position he would have been in if the petrol had been delivered pursuant to the contract. This is because the owner would not have been able to buy petrol from any other sources and keep its petrol stations open.

## Restitution (to prevent unjust enrichment)
In some circumstances, a contract may be terminated before one or both parties have fully performed their obligations under it. Restitution,

based on the principle of unjust enrichment, provides a remedy for a party who has provided a service or made a payment under a contract to recover money paid under such contract, or to recover an amount reflecting the benefit that accrued to the other party under the contract. An example of this was described in **Chapter 9, Practice example 9.4**. In this example, the party in breach was allowed to claim the value of the building materials he had left on the site. A key aim of restitution is to unwind the unfair advantage obtained by one party (in the example, free building materials) at the expense of the other party. Another example might be of one party (Party A) paying another person (Party B) £5,000 for 500 sets of ear pods, but only receiving 250 sets of ear pods. Restitution would provide for Party A to receive half the money back (£2,500) as it would be unfair for Party B to retain the full amount having only delivered half of the promised goods.

> **Key term: restitution**
>
> Restitution is an equitable remedy that returns the unfair benefit received by one party in favour of the person who provided the benefit.

> **Key term: unjust enrichment**
>
> Unjust enrichment is the basis on which a claim is made to restore to an innocent party the gains that another party has obtained from them.

## ■ KEY POINT CHECKLIST

This chapter has covered the following key knowledge points. You can use these to structure your revision around, making sure to recall the key details for each point, as covered in this chapter.

- Damages are the primary remedy for breach of contract. Damages for breach of contract are generally calculated accordingly to loss of expectation and/or wasted expenditure.
- The following factors limit a person's ability to claim damages:
  - causation
  - contributory negligence
  - remoteness
  - mitigation.
- Damages for non-financial loss might be available as an exception to the general rule.

- Liquidated damages clauses are contractually agreed damages. Where a liquidated damages clause is seen as punishing the breaching party, rather than compensating the injured party for its loss, it is likely to be considered to be a penalty, which renders the clause unenforceable.
- A contract may also provide the injured party with a remedy under a guarantee or an indemnity.
- In some circumstances, damages may not compensate the injured party for their loss. In such cases, the courts *may* exercise their discretion to award the equitable remedies of specific performance, injunction or restitution.

## ■ KEY TERMS AND CONCEPTS

- damages (**page 192**)
- nominal damages (**page 192**)
- loss of expectation (**page 193**)
- causation (**page 196**)
- contributory negligence (**page 197**)
- remoteness (**page 197**)
- mitigate (**page 198**)
- action for an agreed amount (**page 199**)
- guarantee (**page 200**)
- indemnity (**page 201**)
- specific performance (**page 202**)
- injunction (**page 202**)
- restitution (**page 203**)
- unjust enrichment (**page 203**)

## ■ SQE1-STYLE QUESTIONS

### QUESTION 1

A contractor agrees to build a house for a woman. In breach of contract, the contractor's work on the house's foundations is slightly defective. Specifically, the defect in the foundations causes some of the plasterwork in the house to crack slightly. However, the evidence shows that the cracks are only minor and cosmetic, and that there is no significant damage to the house, and the woman can use the house to live in, which was her intention when she commissioned the builder to build the house.

In a claim for breach of contract, which of the following measures of damages is the court most likely to award?

A. Nominal damages.
B. Difference in value.
C. Mental distress.
D. Cost of cure.
E. Loss of profit.

## QUESTION 2

A production company enters into a contract with an actor to make a film. The production company spends money on designs, props and consultants in preparation for the film. In breach of contract, the actor pulls out of the film six days before filming is due to start. The production company cannot find a replacement and abandons the film project.

In a claim for breach of contract, which of the following measures of damages is the court most likely to award?

A. Nominal damages.
B. Liquidated damages.
C. Mental distress.
D. Loss of profit.
E. Wasted expenditure.

## QUESTION 3

A woman books a package holiday that is described as 'an idyllic tranquil beach resort in a green paradise with a wide range of water sports available and equipment to hire. There will be delicious French food on offer. Every evening, local people will perform traditional French folk songs to entertain the numerous guests at the resort'.

The woman books a week-long stay at the resort. When the woman arrives at the resort, she finds that the resort is set on an artificial beach that is 20 miles from the sea, and there is just sand and rock, but no greenery. The only water activity offered is an inflatable paddling pool. The woman is the only guest and the menu every night is curry and chips. There is only one evening of entertainment, when the barman plays a CD with French techno music. The woman is distressed, but stays in the resort for the week anyway.

**Which of the following statements best represents the woman's legal position?**

A. The woman cannot claim damages because English law does not award damages for disappointment.
B. The woman cannot claim damages because she stayed at the resort and used its facilities.
C. The woman can claim damages for the cost of the holiday.
D. The woman can claim damages for the cost of the holiday and an additional amount to compensate her for her loss of enjoyment.
E. The woman can claim damages to compensate her for her loss of enjoyment, but not for the cost of the holiday because she stayed at the resort for a week and used its facilities.

## QUESTION 4

A company commissions a baker to bake 100 pies for its office party for an agreed total price of £1,000. On the day of the office party, the company decides to cancel the office party and to cancel its order for the pies. But when the company tells the baker that it no longer wants to buy the pies, the baker has already baked the pies. The baker's shop was open, but the baker decided to donate the pies to a homeless charity, and to focus on selling his usual range of bread from his shop. When the baker claims damages of £1,000 from the company as compensation for loss, the company refuses to pay and argues that the damages should be lower.

**Which of the following statements best represents the company's legal position?**

A. The company is not correct because although the baker is under a duty to take reasonable steps to minimise his loss, it is not reasonable to expect the baker to sell pies in addition to bread.
B. The company is correct because the baker is under a duty to take reasonable steps to minimise his loss and could have done so by selling the pies in his shop.
C. The company is not correct because it must pay the baker damages to put the baker in the position it would have been in if the contract had been performed.

D. The company is not correct because, as it was the company that breached the contract, it is legally bound to compensate the injured party for any loss that results from its breach.

E. The company is correct because the aim of damages is to put the injured party in the position it would have been in if the contract had never been made. As a result, the baker can only claim for the cost of his ingredients.

## QUESTION 5

A bank grants a loan to a bakery. The bakery's parent company agrees orally to act as surety and indemnify the bakery's debt to the bank. Subsequently, the loan agreement between the bank and the bakery is held to be unenforceable.

**Which of the following statements best describes the bank's legal position?**

A. The bank cannot claim repayment of the debt from the bakery's parent company because the indemnity was oral, and it must be in writing to be enforceable.

B. The bank cannot claim repayment of the debt from the bakery's parent company because the loan agreement to which the indemnity relates is unenforceable.

C. The bank can claim repayment of the debt from the bakery's parent company because the indemnity remains in force despite the loan agreement being unenforceable.

D. The bank can claim repayment of the debt from the bakery's parent company because indemnities do not need to be in writing.

E. The bank can claim repayment of the debt from the bakery's parent company only after trying to recover the debt from the bakery.

## ■ ANSWERS TO QUESTIONS

### Answers to 'What do you know already?' questions at the start of the chapter

1) The primary remedy for breach of contract is damages.
2) False. The purpose of English law damages is to *compensate* the injured party for their loss.

3) The correct answer was (d). Indemnity. An indemnity is a separate primary obligation often used in addition to a debt obligation. It gives the injured party the choice to sue the debtor or the surety, so it is not a limitation on the injured party's ability to claim damages for loss under English law. In fact, the opposite is true.
4) True. As a general rule, the injured party cannot claim for distress, frustration, anxiety, displeasure, vexation, tension or aggravation under English law. But there are exceptions to the rule (see **Damages for non-financial loss, page 198**).
5) The correct answer was (b). The injured party must take reasonable steps to mitigate their loss.

## Answers to end-of-chapter SQE1-style questions

Question 1:
The correct answer was B. The aim of damages under English law is to compensate the injured party for their loss. Since the house can still be used for the intended purpose, the most likely measure of damages is the difference in value between what was contracted for and what was received. Option C is incorrect because as a general rule, damages for mental distress are not recoverable under English law. They can be recovered as an exception to the general rule where the whole object of the contract is to provide pleasure, relaxation and peace of mind, but there is no evidence in the scenario of this. Option D is incorrect because the house can still be used as intended, so the damages to cure the defect by changing the foundations appears to be wholly disproportionate to the disadvantage of having some cracks in the plasterwork. Option E is incorrect because there is no evidence in the scenario that the woman intended to make a profit on the house; we are told that she intended to live in the house. Option A is incorrect because nominal damages are awarded where the injured party has not suffered any loss despite a breach of contract. In this case, the woman has suffered the loss of receiving a house with cracks in the plaster.

Question 2:
The correct answer was E. The measure of profit that will be generated by a film is likely to be too uncertain to serve as a measure for damages. In such scenarios, the only certain way of determining what the injured party has lost due to the breach is to look at the expenses it has incurred preparing for the contract and to award it damages in this amount to compensate it for its loss. This lack of

certainty as to the measure of lost profit means that Option D is incorrect. Option A is incorrect because nominal damages are only awarded if the injured party has not suffered any loss. Option B is incorrect because liquidated damages are awarded on the basis of a liquidated damages clause and the scenario does not refer to one. Option C is incorrect because this exceptional ground for the award of damages does not apply to companies.

Question 3:
The correct answer was D. This means that Options C and E are incorrect. Option A is incorrect because although the general rule under English law is that damages are not awarded for distress, there is an exception in the case of a holiday where the major object of the contract is to provide relaxation and enjoyment. Option B is incorrect. The fact that the woman stayed at the resort for the anticipated time does not undermine her ability to claim.

Question 4:
The correct answer was B. The injured party is under a duty to mitigate their loss by taking reasonable steps. Based on the information in the scenario, it seems reasonable for a baker to sell pies in his shop. This means that Option A is not correct. Option C is not correct because although it correctly states the aim of damages for breach of contract, it leaves out the requirement for the injured party to take reasonable steps to mitigate their loss. Option D is not correct for the same reason as in Option C. In addition, be wary of such a broad description of a party's obligation to compensate the injured party because it leaves out the important limitations on the ability to claim damages, namely causation and remoteness. Option E is not correct because the aim of damages for breach of contract is to put the injured party in the position they would have been in if the contract had been performed, rather than, as stated, as if the contract had never been made.

Question 5:
The correct answer was C. This is because an indemnity is a separate primary obligation from the bakery's obligation to repay the bank. As such, the parent company's indemnity remains in force, despite the related loan agreement being unenforceable. Option D is incorrect because although it is correct that indemnities do not need to be in writing, the description of the legal position is incomplete because it does not refer to the indemnity as a primary obligation of the bakery's parent company. Option A is incorrect because an indemnity does not need to be in writing (the writing requirement applies to a guarantee). Option B is incorrect because the indemnity

is a separate primary obligation that remains in force even if the underlying loan agreement is unenforceable. Option E is incorrect as there is no requirement for the bank to try to recover its money from the bakery before it seeks repayment from the bakery's parent company. This is because the indemnity is a separate and primary obligation.

## ■ KEY CASES, RULES, STATUTES AND INSTRUMENTS

The SQE1 Assessment Specification does not require you to know any case names, or statutory materials, for this topic.

# Index

acceptance viii, 1-5, 6-8, 10-16, 19-25, 26, 45, 176; 'battle of the forms' 'last shot' rule 13; communication methods 2, 11, 13-19, 20-2, 24, 25, 152, 160, 162, 165; by conduct 11, 16, 17, 19, 25, 53, 57; definition 1-2, 10-16, 19; email acceptance 15; forms of acceptance for bilateral offers 13-16, 19, 20-1, 24; forms of acceptance for unilateral offers 13, 16, 17, 19, 22-3, 24, 25; instantaneous media acceptance method 14-15, 20-1, 24; knowledge/awareness-of-the-offer requirements 3-4, 13, 20, 24, 149-50; mirror image rule 2, 10-11, 19, 23; postal acceptance rule 14-17, 19, 21-2, 25; receipt rule 13-16, 19; requests for flexibility in payment terms 12, 19, 24; silence rule 13-14; termination of an offer 1-2, 11, 16-19; website acceptance 15, see also counter-offers; offer; offeree
action for an agreed amount 199
adequate/sufficient rule of consideration 27, 28-30, 39-40, 43
advertisements 5-8, 50-2, 57, 59-60, 63, 85-6, 100
affirmation, misrepresentation 134, 142, 143-4; presumed undue influence 166; repudiatory breach of contract 170-1, 179, 184, 187, 188

agency 65, 69-70, 75, 81, 155
agreement mistake *see* mistake
agreement to discharge contract 167-8, 178
amended contracts, consideration 27, 32-44
anticipatory repudiatory breach of contract 170-1, 184
arbitrators, certainty 52-4, 57
asbestos 74
assignments, third-party-rights structures 65, 68-9, 75
auction sales, example of invitations to treat 6
auctions 'without reserve' unilateral offers 8
awareness of representees, misrepresentation 130-4, 141-4

'battle of the forms' 'last shot' rule 13
bilateral offers 2, 9-10, 13-16, 17, 19, 20-1, 23, 24; revocation of bilateral offers 17, 19, 22, 25
'binding in honour only' statement, rebuttable presumption 50
breach of contract 89, 96, 99, 111-13, 167-8, 169-79, 184, 190-210; common law 169-70, 171-5, 199; conditions/warranties/innominate-terms 171-5; definition 167-8, 169-79, 184; entire obligations rule 168, 175-8, 184,

187, 188–9; statutory provisions 169–70, 172–3, 184, see also remedies; repudiatory
'business efficacy' test, implied terms 91–2, 95
business to business regime (B2B regime) 84, 92–3, 95, 100, 101–2, 108, 111–13, 115, 120–1, 124, 165–6, 172–3
business to consumer regime (B2C regime) 92–4, 95, 100, 101–2, 111–15, 121, 124, 172–3

capacity 45–6, 54–8, 61–2, 63, see also corporate/company; intoxication; mental incapacity; minors
car parks 114–15, 200
cases see separate Table of cases
causation, damages-limiting-factor 132, 191–2, 196, 203–4, 209
certainty 45–6, 48, 50, 52–4, 57, 61–2
collateral issues 4, 65, 70–1, 75, 78, 80, 81, 149–51, 164
comfort letters, intention to create legal relations 50–2, 57
common knowledge/industry practice 101, 103, 109, 115
common law see individual topics; separate Table of cases
communication methods 2, 5, 7, 9–19, 20–2, 24, 25, 152, 160, 162, 165
conditions (major terms) 171–2, 174–5
by conduct 11, 16, 17, 19, 25, 53, 57, 123–30, 138, 143–4
consideration ix, 3, 26–44, 45, 65, 81; amended contracts 27, 32–44; definition 3, 26–31, 38–9, 42–4; exchange aspect 27–33, 38, 42–3; existing contractual/legal duties 27, 31–6, 39; past-consideration rule 27, 30–1, 38–9, 40, 43; paying-less contract amendments 27, 35–40, 41–2, 44; paying-more contract amendments 27, 32–6, 39, 40–1, 44; practical benefit of paying more 33–4, 39, 40–1, 44; previous-request device 31, 38; promissory estoppel 26, 27, 36–40, 42, 43–4; sufficient/adequate rule 27, 28–30, 39–40, 43; third parties 32, 39, 44
contents of a contract 83–100, 101–21
contra proferentem 102, 110, 115, 119
contracts of convenience 65, 73–4, 78–9, 80, 81–2
contributory negligence 191, 196–7, 203–4
corporate/company capacity 54, 56–7
cost-of-cure damages, remedies 194–5, 208
counter-offers 2, 11–12, 17, 18–19, 21, 23–5
courts, interpretation 83–5, 94–6, 99–100, 101–21, see also individual topics; separate Table of cases
COVID-19 36, 37
creditworthiness, mistake 151–2
custom, implied terms 83–4, 90, 92, 95

damages, calculation methods 192–6, 203–4, 209–10; cost-of-cure damages 194–5, 208; definition 190–200, 203–4, 207–8; limiting factors 191, 195, 196–8, 203–4, 206, 209; loss-of-expectation calculation method 193–6, 203–4, 208; non-financial loss 198–9, 203, 206, 207, 209; time calculations 193; wasted-expenditure calculation method 193, 203, 205, 208, see also remedies

death/personal-injury/illness 102, 111–15, 119, 120–1, 181
deeds 26, 38
destruction, of offer 2; of the subject matter 134, 142, 180–1
discharge of contracts 167–89, see also agreement; breach; expiry; frustration; performance; repudiatory breach
disclosure issues, misrepresentation 126–8, 137
display-of-goods example of invitations to treat 6
due-diligence effects, misrepresentation 132–3
duress 34, 37, 44, 145–6, 152–4, 160–2, 164, 165–6
duty of skill and care 135–6, 196–7, 198

email acceptance 15
enjoyment-loss damages, remedies 198–9, 206, 209
entire agreement clauses 88, 98–100
entire obligations rule 168, 175–8, 184, 187, 188–9
equitable remedies 190–2, 201–4, see also injunctions; restitution; specific performance; remedies
exchange aspect of consideration 27–33, 38, 42–3
exemption clauses 101–4, 107–15, 119, 120–1
existing contractual/legal duties, consideration 27, 31–6, 39
expiry-of-time/another-specified-event discharge 167–8, 178
express terms 83–5, 90, 92, 95

face-to-face dealings, mistake 146, 150–2, 160, 164

fairness in the B2C regime 112–15, 121
family and friends, rebuttable presumption, intention to create legal relations 48–9, 57, 58–9, 62, 156–7
family holidays, contracts of convenience 73–4, 81
fax acceptance 14–15
financial obligations, frustration 183–4
forms of acceptance 13–16, 17, 19, 20–1, 22–3, 24, 25
four corners interpretation approach 94, 99–100
fraud 89, 104, 115, 119, 129–30, 132–7, 139–40, 142–3, 150–2, 164–5, see also misrepresentation
free-holiday-insurance, unilateral advertisement 7–8, 51–2, 59–60, 63
frustration 167–8, 179–84, 188, 189, 192
further-information requests on offers 2

gifts, undue influence 166
guarantees 51, 56, 68, 190–2, 200–1, 204, 209

identity mistake 150–2, 160, 162, 164, 165
illegal contracts 145–6, 158–61, 164, 166, 181–2; public-policy conflicts 158–9, 161; restraint of trade 146, 158, 159–60, 161, 164, 166, see also void; voidable
immoral contracts see illegal contracts
implied terms 65, 80, 83–4, 88, 90–4, 95, 97–8, 100, 111–13, 116, 120, 124, 172–3; B2B regime 84, 92–3, 95, 100, 112–13, 116, 120, 124, 172–3; B2C regime 92–4, 95, 100, 111–12, 113–15, 124, 172, 173; 'business efficacy' test 91–2, 95; custom 83–4, 90, 92, 95; definition 83–4, 90–4, 95, 172–3; 'necessary incident' test 90; 'officious

bystander' test 91-2, 95; statutory provisions 83-4, 90, 92-4, 95, 97, 100, 111-13, 116, 120-1, 124, 172-3
'importance attached' test for terms/ representations 87-8
incomplete terms, certainty 52, 53-4, 57
indemnities (sureties) 190-2, 201, 204, 207, 209
injunctions 73, 75, 190-2, 201-4
innocent misrepresentation category 134, 137-8, 141, 142, 143-4
innominate (unclassified) terms 171, 174-5
instantaneous media acceptance method 14-15, 20-1, 24
intention to create legal relations ix, 3, 7, 26, 45-52, 57-8, 61-3, 86; advertisements 5-8, 50-2, 57, 59-60, 63; comfort letters 50-2, 57; commercial context 45-7, 50-2, 57, 59-63; document names 50-2, 57, 59-60, 63; divorcing/separating couples 48-9, 58, 62; social and domestic context 45-8, 57, 58-9, 61-2
interpretation (construing) of contract terms 83-5, 94-6, 99-100, 101-21
intoxication, capacity issues 54, 55, 56
invitation to treat 1-3, 4-7, 8-9, 19, 23

knowledge/awareness-of-the-offer requirements 3-4, 13, 20, 24, 149-50

land law, specific performance 202
lapse-of-time termination of an offer 18-19
leases 67, 68, 94-5, 98, 100
legal consequences of pre-contractual statements 88-9

legally binding contracts 1, 3-10, 12-16, 19, 23-39, 43-7, 52, 57-8, 81, 104, 119-20; morally binding contract 47; signatures 104, 119-20, *see also* acceptance; consideration; intention; offer
limitation clauses, agency 69-70
limited liability partnerships 57
liquidated damages 190-2, 199-200, 204
loan guarantees 51, 56
loss-of-expectation damages calculation method 193-6, 203-4, 209
lost-animal-reward unilateral advertisement 7, 10, 20, 24, 30

material statements, misrepresentation 124, 127, 129, 130-2, 142
mental distress damages 198, 208, 209
mental incapacity 54-6
minors 46, 54, 55-8, 61-2, 63
mirror image rule, offer and acceptance 2, 10-11, 19, 23
misrepresentation 89, 104, 115, 116-17, 120, 122-44, 145, 149-52; acts of the representees 132-4, 142-4; affirmation by the representee 134, 142, 143-4; awareness of representees 130-4, 141-4; categories 122-4, 133-8, 142-4, 150-2; changing circumstances 123, 125-6, 127, 138; common law 134, 135-7; by conduct 123-30, 138, 143-4; damages 89, 133-4, 135, 136-8, 139-44; definition 122-39, 142-4; destruction of the subject matter 134, 142; disclosure issues 126-8, 137; due-diligence effects 132-3; inducing-the-representee conditions 122-3,

Index  215

124, 130-3, 136-7, 138, 143; innocent misrepresentation category 134, 137-8, 141, 142, 143-4; inspections 131, 133, 143; material statements 124, 127, 129, 130-2, 142; negligent misrepresentation category 134, 135-7, 142; not-the-whole-truth disclosure issues 127-8, 138; opinion/belief/intention distinctions 128-32, 138; remedies 89, 122-4, 127, 131-44, 152; rescission remedy 131-9, 140-4, 152; rogue fraudulent misrepresentation 150-2, 161, 164, 165; signatures 104, 115, 116-17, 119, 120; third parties 134; unambiguous false statements of fact/law 124-30, 138; undermining factors 122-3, 125, 132-3, 139, 144, *see also* fraud; representations
mistake 3-4, 52, 145-6, 147-52, 160-1, 164-5
mitigation damages-limitation-factor 191, 196, 198, 203-4, 206, 208, 209
morally binding agreements, legally binding contrct47
mutual mistake 146, 147-9, 160-1, 164 *see also* mistake

necessaries, capacity 55, 56, 57, 63
'necessary incident' test, implied terms 90
negligence 101-2, 111-15, 119-21, 134-7, 142, 191, 196-7, 198, 203-4
new-offer termination of an existing offer 18-19
nominal damages 192-3, 203-4
*non est factum* (it is not my deed) 104-5, 115, 119, 120
non-financial loss, damages 198-9, 203, 206, 208, 209

not-the-whole-truth disclosure issues 127-8, 138
notice, undue influence 155-6

objective test 1, 3, 7, 19, 47-9, 54, 86-7, 91-5, 114, 125, 148
offer viii, 1-25, 26, 45, 51-2, 81; communication methods 2, 5, 7, 9-10, 17-18, 152, 160, 162, 165; counter-offers 2, 11-12, 17, 18-19, 21, 23-5; definition 1-10, 19, 23, 24-5; destruction of offer 2; further-information requests 2; identifying an offer 6, 7-10; mirror image rule 2, 10-11, 19, 23, *see also* acceptance; bilateral; invitation to treat; termination; unilateral
offeree 2, 3-4, 7, 10-19, 24-5, *see also* acceptance
offeror 2, 3-4, 7, 13-19, 24-5 *see also* acceptance
office hours, instantaneous media acceptance method 15
'officious bystander' test, implied terms 91-2, 95
onerous/unusual terms, unfair terms 107, 118, 121
opinion/belief/intention distinctions, misrepresentation 128-32, 138
oral/verbal statements 83, 85, 96, 99, 120-1, 124, 126-30, 206, 209

parol evidence rule 84, 88, 96, 98-100
past-consideration rule 27, 30-1, 38-9, 40, 43 *see also* consideration
paying-less contract amendments 27, 35-40, 41-2, 44
paying-more contract amendments 27, 33-6, 39, 40-1, 44

penalties (punishments) *see also* liquidated damages
peppercorn rents 28–9
performance 167–8, 169, 176–7, 179–84, 187
postal acceptance rule 14–17, 19, 21–2, 25
practical benefit of paying more, consideration 33–4, 39, 40–1, 44
pre-contractual statements 83–100, 124
prenuptial agreements 49, 58, 62
presumed undue influence 156–8, 161, 164, 166
previous-request device, consideration 31, 38
*prima facie* (at first sight) 159, 161, 164
primary obligations, guarantees and indemnities 201, 209
privity of contract xvii, 64–82; CRTPA 1999 rights 65, 67–8, 72, 75, 80–2; definition 64–6, 75–6, 80–2; St Martins Property exception xvii, 73, 74–5, 82; structures that give third-party rights 65, 68–72, 75, 78, 81, *see also* third parties
promisee/promisor 28–9, 39
promises 9–10, 19, 23, 26–44, 83–5, 95, 99–100
promissory estoppel 26, 27, 36–40, 42, 43–4
public-policy conflicts, illegal contracts 158–9, 161
puff 83–9, 95–6

qualified contractual obligations, definition 168, 169, 184, 189
*quantum meruit* 175–7, 184

'reasonably fit for any particular purpose' implied term 93, 97, 100, 111–12

rebuttable presumption, intention to create legal relations, 'binding in honour only' statement 50; commercial context 45–7, 50–2, 57, 59–63; definition 45–6, 47–52, 57–8, 61–3, 156–8; divorcing/separating couples 48–9, 58, 62; document names 50–2, 57, 59–60, 63; family and friends 48–9, 57, 58–9, 62, 156–7; presumed undue influence 156–8, 161, 166; reliance on the agreement 48, 49, 57; social and domestic context 45–6, 47–9, 57, 58–9, 61–2; 'subject to contract' statement 50, 60–1, 63; wording used 50, 57, 60–1, 63
receipt rule, acceptance 13–16, 19
'red hand rule' 107
reliance on the agreement 48, 49, 57
remedies 72–82, 89, 96, 99, 122–4, 127, 133–46, 152, 165, 190–210; breach of contract 169–78, 184, 185, 188, 190–210; equitable remedies 190–2, 201–3; fraudulent misrepresentation 135, 136, 137, 143, 164; misrepresentation 89, 122–4, 127, 131–44, 152; negligence 136–7, *see also* damages; guarantees; indemnities; injunctions; rescission; restitution; specific performance; termination; voidable contracts
remoteness damages-limitation-factor 191–2, 196, 197, 203–4, 209
representations 83–9, 95–6, 99, 124–44; definition 83–9, 95–6, 99; legal consequences of pre-contractual statements 88–9
representee/representor 85–9, 96
repudiatory breach of contract, affirmation option 170–1, 179, 184, 187, 188, 190–2; common law 171–2;

Index 217

definition 167-8, 169-75, 179, 184, 187, 188, 190; statutory provisions 172-3, see also breach of contract; remedies
reputation-loss due to previous employers, damages 199
requests for flexibility in payment terms 12, 19, 24
rescission remedy 89, 99, 131-9, 140-4, 152-8, see also voidable contracts
restaurant meals for parties, contracts of convenience 73-4, 78-9, 81-2
restitution 202-3
restraint of trade 146, 158, 159-60, 161, 164, 166
revocation 17-18, 19, 22-3, 25
rewards 7, 10, 13, 20, 24, 30, 52
rogue, fraudulent misrepresentation 150-2, 161, 164, 165

St Martins Property exception xvii, 73, 74-5, 82
'satisfactory quality' implied term 93, 116, 120, 172
secondary obligations, guarantees and indemnities 201
service contracts 124
severable contracts 176
signatures 101-2, 103-5, 115, 116-17, 119, 120
silence rule, acceptance 13-14
'special knowledge' test for terms/ representations 87, 96-7, 99-100
specific performance 73, 75, 165, 190-2, 201-4
statutes see separate Table of statutes
strict contractual obligations 168, 169, 184, 187
'subject to contract' statement 50, 60-1, 63

subjective test 1, 3-4
substantial performance 168, 176, 177-8, 184, 187
sufficient/adequate rule of consideration 27, 28-30, 39-40, 43

taxi-hiring for groups, contracts of convenience 73-4, 81
telephone acceptance 14-15, 20-1, 24
telex acceptance 14-15
tender, unilateral offers 8
tender-requests (quotes and bids) example of invitations to treat 6
termination of an offer 1-2, 11, 16-19, 21, 22, 24, 25; lapse-of-time termination of an offer 18-19; new-offer termination of an existing offer 18-19; revocation of bilateral offers 17, 19, 22, 25; revocation of unilateral offers 17-18, 19, 22-3, 25
terms 4, 48, 53-4, 83-9, 95, 96-103, 115, 120, 171-5; common law 84, 86-9, 95, 96-7, 99-100, 110-15; conditions/ warranties/innominate-terms 171-5; damages 89, 96, 99, 171, 173-4, 185, 188; definition 83-9, 95, 99-100, 101-3, 115, 120, 171-5; entire agreement clauses 88, 98-100; incomplete terms 53-4; legal consequences of pre-contractual statements 88-9; parol evidence rule 84, 88, 96, 98-100; statutory provisions 83-4, 88, 92-4, 95, 101, 110-16, 120-1, 124, 135-7, 172-3, see also express; implied; mistake; promises; representations; unfair
third parties xvii, 17, 22-5, 32, 39, 44, 52-4, 57, 64-82, 155-6, 200-1; arbitrators 52-4, 57; consideration 32, 39, 44; CRTPA 1999 rights 65, 67-8,

72, 75, 80–2; definition 64–5, 66–72, 75–6, 80–2; existing contractual/legal duties and consideration 32, 39, 44; misrepresentation 134; remedies 72–5, 78–82; revocation of bilateral offers 17, 22, 25; St Martins Property exception xvii, 73, 74–5, 82; statutory exceptions 64, 66, 67–82; structures that give third-party rights 65, 68–72, 75, 78, 81, *see also* privity of contract

time calculations, damages 193

timely/reasonable notice, unfair terms 101–8, 115, 118, 119, 121

timesheets/invoices/receipts 105, 107–8

tort duty of care 196–7, 198

train tickets 105, 107

trust-and-confidence relationships 156–8, 164, 166

trusts 72–3, 75, 82

unambiguous false statements of fact/law, misrepresentation 124–30, 138

uncertainty 46, 50, 52–4, 57, 61–2

undue influence 145–6, 154–8, 160–1, 164, 166, *see also* voidable contracts

unfair terms 101–21, 145, 199–200; common knowledge/industry practice 101, 103, 109, 115; consistent course of dealing 101, 103, 108–9, 115, 117, 120–1; definition 101–9, 114, 115, 120–1; enforcement issues 101, 103, 111–15, 121; incorporation 101–9, 115, 117–21; negligence 101–2, 111–15, 119, 120–1; signatures 101–2, 103–5, 115, 116–17, 119, 120; statutory provisions 101–2, 103, 110–16, 120–1; timely/reasonable notice 101–2, 103, 105–8, 115, 118, 119, 121; wording used 101–3, 109–10, 115, 119

unilateral mistake 146, 147, 149–52, 160–1, 164, 165

unilateral offers 2, 6–10, 13, 16–19, 20, 22–3, 24, 25, 81; revocation 17–18, 19, 22–3, 25

unjust enrichment 202–3

vague agreements 52–4, 57

valuers 53–4

vending-machine offers 8

void contracts 30, 52, 55, 57–8, 61, 145–52, 160–1, 164–6, *see also* certainty; illegal; mistake

voidable contracts, definition 54–6, 57–8, 61, 62, 63, 145–6, 152–4, 160–1, 164–6, *see also* duress; illegal; remedies; rescission remedy; undue influence

warranties (minor terms) 171, 173–4

wasted-expenditure damages calculation method 193, 203, 205, 209

websites 6, 15

wills 49

wine-lists, example of invitations to treat 5

wording used 50, 57, 60–1, 63, 95–6, 100, 101–3, 109–10, 115, 119

written statements 83–8, 94, 98–100, 120–1, 124, 126–30, 201, 209